For the Nation

For the Nation

Jesus, the Restoration of Israel and Articulating
a Christian Ethic of Territorial Governance

Nicholas R. Brown

Foreword by
Joel Willitts

☙PICKWICK *Publications* • Eugene, Oregon

FOR THE NATION
Jesus, the Restoration of Israel, and Articulating a Christian Ethic of Territorial Governance

Copyright © 2016 Nicholas R. Brown. All rights reserved. Except for brief quotations in critical publications or reviews, no part of this book may be reproduced in any manner without prior written permission from the publisher. Write: Permissions, Wipf and Stock Publishers, 199 W. 8th Ave., Suite 3, Eugene, OR 97401.

Pickwick Publications
An Imprint of Wipf and Stock Publishers
199 W. 8th Ave., Suite 3
Eugene, OR 97401

www.wipfandstock.com

PAPERBACK ISBN: 978-1-4982-7903-1
HARDCOVER ISBN: 978-1-4982-7905-5
EBOOK ISBN: 978-1-4982-7904-8

Cataloguing-in-Publication data:

Names: Brown, Nicholas R.

Title: For the nation : Jesus, the restoration of Israel, and articulating a Christian ethic of territorial governance / Nicholas R. Brown.

Description: Eugene, OR: Pickwick Publications, 2016 | Includes bibliographical references and index.

Identifiers: ISBN 978-1-4982-7903-1 (paperback) | ISBN 978-1-4982-7905-5 (hardcover) | ISBN 978-1-4982-7904-8 (ebook)

Subjects: LSCH: Jesus Christ—Historicity | Israel (Christian theology)—Biblical teaching | Jews—Restoration—History of doctrines

Classification: BS2655.J4 B6 2016 (print) | BS2655.J4 (ebook)

Manufactured in the U.S.A.   09/22/16

To my father, Charles Anthony Brown, and my mentor, Dr. Glen Harold Stassen—two men who, by their lives and their love, have taught and continue to teach me what it means to be grounded.

Somewhere is better than anywhere.
—FLANNERY O'CONNOR

Contents

Foreword by Joel Willitts | xi

Introduction | 1
    I. Origins of the Project | 1
    II. Prolegomena and Questions | 3
    III. Thesis | 5

1. W(h)ither the Land? The De-territorialization of Jesus and the Kingdom of God in New Testament Scholarship | 8
    1.1 Introduction | 8
    1.2 Scholarly Incongruities and Puzzling Conundrums | 9
    1.3 Texts for Examination | 14
    1.4 W. D. Davies: *The Gospel and the Land: Early Christianity and Jewish Territorial Doctrine* | 14
    1.5 Marcus Borg: *Conflict, Holiness and Politics in the Teachings of Jesus* | 31
    1.6 N.T. Wright: *Jesus and the Victory of God* | 46
    1.7 Conclusion | 50

2. From a Territorial State into State of Ethical Praxis: Discerning the Roots and Structure of the Kingdom's De-territorialization in Christian Ethics | 53

   2.1 Introduction | 53

   2.2 From a Territorial State to a Non-territorial Religious Ethic: A Historical and Theological Etiology of the Kingdom's De-territorialization | 57

   2.3 The Ethical De-territorialization of the Kingdom in Three Acts: Praxification, Ecclesiofication, and Typofication | 65

      2.3.1 Praxification: The Kingdom of God as a Place-less Ethical Performance | 65

      2.3.2 Ecclesiofication: The Kingdom as a "Churchified" Spatial Reality | 69

      2.3.3 Typofication: Israel's Land as a Provisional Paradigm for Holy Space | 72

   2.4 The Politics of Jesus: Nonviolent Enemy Love | 83

   2.5 A Peaceable and Non-territorial Reign | 87

   2.6 Conclusion | 90

3. The Ground(s) on Which We Stand: De-territorializing the Kingdom of God in the Christian Imagination and Its Implications for Contemporary Theology and Ethics | 92

   3.1 Introduction | 92

   3.2 On Hollowed Ground: The Ambivalent Territoriality of St. Justin Martyr's and St. Irenaeus's Interpretations of the Kingdom of God | 94

      3.2.1 *Chiliasm* and Gnosticism in St. Justin Martyr's and St. Irenaeus's Theology | 95

      3.2.2 St. Justin Martyr's and St. Irenaeus' Interpretations of the Kingdom | 100

   3.3 Theological Implications of a De-territorialized Kingdom | 109

    3.3.1 Covenantal | 109

    3.3.2 Supersessionist | 111

  3.4 Ethical Implications of a De-territorialized Kingdom | 114

  3.5 Conclusion | 120

4. A Restoration of Land and a Restoration of Justice Governance: Restoration Eschatologies in Prophetic Texts and Late Second Temple Literature | 121

  4.1 Introduction | 121

  4.2 נַחֲלָה: Jeremiah's Theological and Ethical Symbiosis between Yahweh, Israel and the Land | 122

    4.2.1 Jeremiah 29–34: A Return to the Land and a Return to Justice | 125

  4.3 Israel's Restoration in Isa 56–61: A Landed, Particular Universalism | 132

  4.4 Israel's Restoration in Late Second Temple Jewish Literature | 143

    4.4.1 The Book of *Jubilees* | 143

    4.4.2 *Psalms of Solomon* | 147

  4.5 Conclusion | 150

5. Jesus and the Kingdom: A Restoration of the Land and a Restoration of Just Governance for Israel and the Nations | 152

  5.1 Introduction | 152

  5.2 Matthew 5:5—Jesus' Beatitude of Blessing the Meek | 154

  5.3 The Lord's Prayer in Matt 6:9–13 || Luke 11:1–4 and Jesus' Appropriation of Isaiah's Jubilee in Luke 4:16–20 | 165

  5.4 Jesus' Proclamation of the Jubilee in Luke 4:16–21 | 178

  5.5 The *Palingenesia*/Kingdom in Matt 19:27–30 || Luke 22:24–30 | 182

5.6 Toward Articulating a Christian Ethic of Territorial Governance: A Proposed Normative Framework | 191

    5.6.1 Walzer's Reiteration—a Normative Model for a Christian Ethic of Territorial Governance | 194

Bibliography | 199

Subject Index | 207

Scripture Index | 217

Foreword

Joel Willitts

DURING MY PH.D. PROGRAM I presented a paper at a conference focused on Matthew's Gospel. The paper's topic, part of my thesis project, was on a similar topic to Nick's book, the territorial restoration of the Land of Israel in Matthew. After I presented my paper, the first questioner, an esteemed Matthean scholar, raised his hand. Fearful that he might pose that one question that singly undermines my whole argument, I was startled by what in fact he wanted to know. He actually asked a personal question: "Are you a Dispensationalist?"

While it was not that "one" question I feared, it was a question I was unprepared to answer. The first set of thoughts that raced through my mind were related to the paper's argument and evidence. Did I unknowingly reference Charles Ryrie, John Walvoord, or Lewis Spere Chafer, the triumvirate of Classic Dispensationalism? Of course I didn't! My topic was early Judaism and the kingdom teaching of Jesus in the First Gospel. The reason the esteemed scholar asked me that question, he went on to explain, was that he was genuinely curious why I was even interested in the question of the Land of Israel in Matthew. He was puzzled not by my argument *per se*, but by my interest. Why was I interested in the Land? It was perhaps a fair question, although it was the only time that week—or ever since, come to think of it—I heard a presenter asked such a thing. It was clear to me, for the first time, that even New Testament scholars steeped in the Jewish context of the New Testament as a rule thought only Dispensationalists raised questions about the land. I'm not a Dispensationalist; and I pretty sure Nick isn't either. Rather we, and a small army of other scholars, are reading the New Testament, and Jesus in particular, disenchanted by the long and deep interpretive ruts that have their origin in unbiblical, christologically deficient, unconsciously held philosophical frameworks.

While the de-turfed view of Jesus' teaching has been questioned in the decade since that academic meeting, not least by me, it remains the default position for both the majority of Jesus scholars and the wider Christian church today. Nick's book then is an extremely important contribution to the discussion of Jesus and Israel's land promise; it's import is much more far-reaching than a single sub-discipline however. I'll briefly name four categories of importance: historical, biblical, philosophical and theological, and ethical.

First, Nicholas's book demonstrates the historical inconsistency of the Third Quest's position that Jesus' word and deeds are inextricably linked to his first century Jewish restoration theology. While maintaining this they equally argue that Jesus redefined Israel's restoration so radically that either Jesus himself of the first generation of Jewish followers of Jesus were quick to jettison a territorial expectation. Nicholas demonstrates that what drives this scholarly ambivalence is not historical or exegetical sources, but an inherited ideology that diminishes materiality for spiritual transcendence and divorces the apostolic teaching from its biblical cultural context.

Second, Nick presents compelling readings of key gospel texts that are are either marginalized or de-territorialized by conventional Christian exegesis. He shows that when read from the perspective of the Jewish Scriptures, in view of the irrevocability of God's covenant with Israel, what one might label a "post-superssionistic" theological hermeneutic, Jesus is very much at home within his Jewish first-century restorationalist milieu. What's more, while Jesus was distinct from the other prophetic and messianic figures of his time, it was not on account of his revision of the inherent territorial aspects of Israel's restoration. Rightly pointed out by Nick is what distinguished Jesus in his time was his unique appropriation of the universal implication of Israel's territorial restorationarticulated in the Hebrew prophets, particularly in his kingdom ethics.

Third, Nick deconstructs the theological and philosophical presuppositions that have supported the commonplace Christian interpretation of Jesus' de-turfed kingdom tracing them all the way back to the very early centuries of the church. Constructively, he argues that a robustChristian anthology which gives proper recognition of the embodied nature of the human animal and theiractual relatedness to the *adam*, and thereby *emplaced* (my word), as well as embodied, is a theological necessity, if it is to be Christian. The interpretation of Jesus decoupled from an interest in place undermine and eventually erode the Christian witness that matter, matters.

Finally, Nick shows the ethical significance of a territorial restoration in the teaching of Jesus. Tracing the continuity between place and ethics in the Jewish prophetsand the teaching of Jesus, this is where the book will make its greatest contribution. The above three points, while important, are theoretical and could leave one to conclude that this is an argument about the irrelevant. However, Nick's book shows that thinking well about Jesus' ministry and message giving full play to the territorial element of Israel's restoration, results in a *habitus* in the world that treats others as embodied differents to be loved. It is an ethic that brings peace without diminishing difference.

It is my prayer that Nick's book is read widely. I wish that all thoughtful Christians would read it with an open mind, willing to consider fully the implication of the dark tendency entrenched deep in the Christian interpretive tradition which has led to anemic kingdom ethic. What's more, through contributions such as Nick's, I hope that the predominantly non-Jewish church reclaim their Jewish roots in order to bear witness to God's universal gift of salvation for both the circumcised and uncircumcised and then regain an appreciation of the messianic ethic of non-violence though self-giving in mutual interdependence.

Introduction

I. Origins of Project

THE GENESIS OF THIS work derived from that most serendipitous and unexpected of conspiracies: being at the right place at the right time. The place was a doctoral seminar exploring the moral significance of recent historical Jesus scholarship for Christian ethics; the time was a discussion of John Howard Yoder's *The Original Revolution*. Having just slogged our way through N. T. Wright's magisterial and formidable *Jesus and the Victory of God*, we were relishing the opportunity to sink our teeth into what we thought was fare of more manageable proportions. Yet like a good Swedish meatball, the comparatively diminutive size of *The Original Revolution* belied the density of its substance. Even those of us who fancied ourselves as seasoned connoisseurs of Yoder were astonished by this volume's kick, and pleasantly surprised by the sheer efficiency with which it enumerated the reasons why the words and actions of a first-century Palestinian Jew living under Roman occupation constituted a robust political ethic that was normative for modern political discourse today.

Yet even as we savored each delectable morsel of this sumptuous Yoderian feast, a bitter aftertaste lingered in my mouth. I came away from *The Original Revolution* more convinced that Jesus' historicity and Jewishness were inextricably tied to and determinative of his powerful political witness, and further persuaded that his repeated invocations of the kingdom of God were brimming with palpable political content. Yet, I still could not shake the uneasy feeling that Yoder's readings of both were punctuated by a subtle yet discernible blindness toward their territorial inflection. I struggled to reconcile Yoder's admonition that we see Jesus as a specifically "Jewish pacifist," who dynamically appropriated and enacted Israel's Scriptures on the one hand, with his resolute insistence that Jesus ultimately decoupled the kingdom of God from Israel's covenantal land promises on the other. How was the latter conclusion borne out by the former? Yoder himself so ably and eloquently demonstrated that Jesus' words and actions were part and parcel of a contentious and ongoing Jewish debate about what it meant to be Israel in the midst of a long narrative of persecution, exile, and ultimately restoration. Why then did Yoder fail to honor the underlying ethic in Jesus' teaching regarding the land?

Initially, I suspected that Yoder's a-territorial reading of Jesus and Jesus' teaching regarding the kingdom were idiosyncratic to his own particular form of biblical interpretation and thus partially the function of the foreclosed hermeneutic that an Anabaptist heritage can bestow upon a reading of the canon. However, other recent historical Jesus scholarship from the likes of W. D. Davies, Marcus Borg, and N. T. Wright follows this disquieting pattern. Not only were most of these scholars in close agreement with Yoder's conclusions but their assessments of Jesus and the kingdom also hewed closely to a similar line of argumentation and analysis. Essentially, they argue that we must recognize Jesus as a political actor, and therefore place his words and actions in the swirling cauldron of first-century Jewish hopes for Israel's national liberation and restoration. However, we must not be tempted to push the political edge of his restorational rhetoric and actions too far, lest we confuse his proclamation of the kingdom of God as in any way suggestive of Israel's territorial restoration. That would dilute Jesus' ethical and political distinctiveness and thus undermine the kind of salvation his gospel and kingdom offer. They seek to wrest Jesus' teachings about the kingdom from a purely spiritual interpretation, and rightly so. Yet they are unwilling to consider the earthy, loamy soil upon which that teaching was proclaimed, and the love Jesus had for the actual land.

Yoder and company had finally wrenched Jesus from the procrustean bed of apolitical and anti-Jewish assumptions, only to re-embed him in one of their own making. Their contextual reading of Jesus as a first-century Jewish prophet who worked within a restorative eschatology put them on an interpretive trajectory that made it troublingly likely, or at least entirely plausible, that Jesus in fact envisaged a territorial restoration of Israel. Troubled and intrigued, I began to investigate three central questions: First, is an a-territorial reading of Jesus and the kingdom of God endemic to or a distortion of the Christian tradition? If it be the latter, what is the etiology of that distortion and how could it be corrected? Second, is it possible and perhaps even more accurate to read the New Testament, particularly the gospels, against the backdrop of Roman occupation and Israel's fervent hopes for restoration and find within them evidence that Jesus proclaimed and anticipated a territorial restoration of Israel? And finally, what impact might that reading have on our re-evaluation of the political and ethical dimensions of Jesus and his teaching about the kingdom of God? How might it inform the construction of a Christian ethic of territorial governance? What follows is an attempt to pursue these questions in the hopes of contributing to the conversation in Christian ethics and New Testament scholarship today regarding land, Jewish identity, and political discourse.

II. Prolegomena and Questions

Of all the investigative trends that have emerged from the recent "Third Quest" into the historical Jesus, few have born as much fruit or generated as much scholarly interest[1] as the decision to (re)locate a reading of Jesus within the eschatological *Weltanschauung* of Late Second Temple Judaism (LSTJ) and its attending constellation of restoration motifs.[2] This interpretive shift has not only precipitated a more textured mapping of Jesus' historical *Sitz im Leben*, but it has also provided a much-needed correction

---

1. For a representative appraisal of which Late Second Temple Judaism (LSTJ) restorational themes are most apposite to a proper historical understanding of Jesus, see Meyer, *The Aims of Jesus*; Meyer, "Appointed Deed, Appointed Doer"; Sanders, *Jesus and Judaism*; Borg, *Conflict, Holiness and Politics in the Teachings of Jesus*; Horsley, *Jesus and the Spiral of Violence*; Beutler, "Two Ways of Gathering"; McCartney, "Ecce Homo"; Meier, *Mentor, Message, and Miracles*; Meier, "Jesus, the Twelve, and the Restoration of Israel," in Scott, ed., *Restoration*, 365–404; Ravens, *Luke and the Restoration of Israel*; Wright, *Jesus and the Victory of God*; Turner, *Power from on High*; Evans, "Aspects of Exile and Restoration in the Proclamation of Jesus and the Gospels," in Chilton and Evans, *Jesus in Context*, 263–96; Evans, *Jesus and His Contemporaries*; Fredriksen, *Jesus of Nazareth, King of the Jews*; McKnight, *A New Vision for Israel*; Newman, *Jesus & the Restoration of Israel*; Pao, *Acts and the Isaianic New Exodus*; Bauckham, "The Restoration of Israel in Luke-Acts," in Scott, ed., *Restoration*, 435–88; Bauckham, *Jesus and the Eyewitnesses*; Freyne, "The Geography of Restoration: Galilee-Jerusalem Relations in Early Jewish and Christian Experience," in Scott, ed., *Restoration*, 406–34; Freyne, *Jesus, a Jewish Galilean*; Bryan, *Jesus and Israel's Traditions of Judgment and Restoration*; Bryan, "Jesus and Israel's Eschatological Constitution," in Holmén and Porter, eds., *Handbook for the Study of the Historical Jesus*, 3:2835–54; Dunn, *Jesus Remembered*; Pitre, *Jesus, the Tribulation and the End*, 31–40; Van Zyl, "The Soteriology of Acts"; Dennis, *Jesus' Death and the Gathering of True Israel*; Fuller, *The Restoration of Israel*; Levenson, *Resurrection and the Restoration of Israel*; Bird, *Jesus and the Origins of the Gentile Mission*; Wenell, *Jesus and Land*; Willits, *Matthew's Messianic Shepherd-King*.

2. This is to acknowledge our decision to follow Sanders in *Jesus and Judaism* and suggest that notwithstanding the plurality of restorational themes present within LSTJ literature, there nevertheless seems to be a coalescence around those of (1) the rebuilding of the temple, (2) the restoration of Jewish exiles from the Diaspora, (3) under the aegis of a Davidic descendent, (4) the reconstitution of the twelve tribes and subsequent parceling out of the land, and (5) the submission/salvation of the Gentiles.

to the lingering anti-Jewish and supersessionist *tendenz* that tainted earlier periods of historical Jesus research.³

In addition to spawning these important methodological rectifications, the move toward a restorational historiography also prompted a vigorous reevaluation of Jesus' normative and socio-political witness.⁴ Whereas previous studies in this vein tended to dilute the viscous pulp of Jesus' moral teachings into a vapid gruel of existentialist and perfectionist principles, thus evacuating them of lasting sociopolitical import, more recent scholars have read Jesus' Sermon on the Mount/Plain,⁵ his parables,⁶ and his eschatological proclamations of the kingdom of God⁷ amidst the

---

3. See Theissen and Winter, *Quest for the Plausible Jesus*, esp. 67-171; and Evans, "Assessing Progress in the Third Quest of the Historical Jesus," 35-54. As the former observe with respect to the predominant use of the "criterion of dissimilarity" in the "Old/First" and "New/Second" historical Jesus quests, "Such a procedure is not reprehensible in itself, but for an understanding of Judaism and the Jewish world of Jesus it promises more than it can deliver, and so leads to false assessments of Judaism" (75).

4. Although by no means exhaustive, the following list of works provides an instructive specimen: Schüssler Fiorenza, *In Memory of Her*; Bammel and Moule, *Jesus and the Politics of His Day*; Horsley, *Sociology and the Jesus Movement*; Horsley, *Jesus and Empire*; Horsley, *Jesus in Context*; Horsley and Hanson, *Bandits, Prophets and Messiahs*; Oakman, *Jesus and the Economic Questions of His Day*; Myers, *Binding the Strong Man*; Sobrino, *Jesus the Liberator*; Yoder, *The Politics of Jesus*; Herzog, *Parables as Subversive Speech*; Herzog, *Jesus, Justice and the Kingdom of God*; Herzog, *Prophet and Teacher*; Malina, *The Social World of Jesus and the Gospels*; Malina, *The Social Gospel of Jesus*; Stegemann et al., *The Social Setting of Jesus and the Gospels*; Stegemann, "Background III: The Social and Political Climate in which Jesus of Nazareth Preached," in Holmén and Porter, eds., *Handbook for the Study of the Historical Jesus*, 3:2291-314.

5. Cahill, "Nonresistance, Defense, Violence and the Kingdom," 380-97; Cahill, "The Ethical Implications of the Sermon," 144-56; Hauerwas, "The Sermon on the Mount, Just War, and the Quest for Peace," 36-43; Greenfield, "The Ethics of the Sermon on the Mount," 13-19; Stassen, *Just Peacemaking*; Stassen, "The Fourteen Triads of the Sermon on the Mount (Matthew 5:21—7:12)," 267-308; Stassen, *Living the Sermon on the Mount*; Hagner, "Ethics and the Sermon on the Mount," 44-59; Pathrapankal, "The Ethics of the Sermon on the Mount," 389-407; Allison, *The Sermon on the Mount*; Parrent, "The Sermon on the Mount, International Politics, and a Theology of Reconciliation," 176-90.

6. See Donahue, "The 'Parable' of the Sheep and the Goats," 3-31; Guevin, "The Moral Imagination and the Shaping Power of the Parables," 63-79; Scott, *Hear Then the Parable*; Rohrbaugh, "A Peasant Reading of the Parable of the Talents/Pounds," 32-39; Herzog, *Parables as Subversive Speech*; Jones, *The Matthean Parables*; Evans, "Jesus' Parable of the Tenant Farmers in Light of Lease Agreements in Antiquity," 65-83; Bock, "The Parable of the Rich Man and Lazarus and the Ethics of Jesus," 63-72; Longenecker, *The Challenge of Jesus' Parables*; Crossan, "The Parables of Jesus," 247-59; DeBorst, "'Unexpected' Guests at God's Banquet Table," 63-79; Garroway, "The Invasion of a Mustard Seed," 57-75.

7. Yoder, *The Politics of Jesus*; Horsley and Silberman, *The Message and the Kingdom*; Wright, *Jesus and the Victory of God*; Hays, *The Moral Vision of the New Testament*;

contextual backdrop of Roman imperialism and the revolutionary ferment of first-century Jewish Palestine. They have convincingly demonstrated that Jesus concretely embodied a Jewish ethic of justice and nonviolent peacemaking, and that this ethic has real moral traction for the organization of social and political life today.

Yet even as the number of scholars laboring within this restorative paradigm has swelled, there remains a cluster of unaddressed questions that are only now receiving focused attention. Two that are of central concern to this study: First, did Jesus envision a territorial restoration of *eretz* Israel that would be concomitant with the eschatological kingdom of God?[8] Second, might such a territorial/national vision play a role in informing a Christian political ethic?[9]

III. Thesis

The purpose of this project is to pursue these queries, attempting to craft credibly affirmative responses to both. Stated simply, I will demonstrate, *pace* the preponderance of scholarly opinion, that it is both historically and theologically plausible that Jesus presupposed an eschatological, territorial restoration of *eretz* Israel and that this presupposition has applicable

---

Borg, *Conflict, Holiness and Politics in the Teachings of Jesus*; Marshall, *Beyond Retribution*; Verhey, *Remembering Jesus*; Horsley, *Jesus and Empire*; Horsley, *In the Shadow of Empire*; Moxnes, *Putting Jesus in His Place*; Stassen and Gushee, *Kingdom Ethics*; Ringe, *Jesus, Liberation and the Biblical Jubilee*; Boyd, "The Kingdom as a Political-Spiritual Revolution," 23-41; Crossan, *God and Empire*; Talbott, "Nazareth's Rebellious Son," 99-113.

8. See Davies, *The Gospel and the Land*; Davies, *The Territorial Dimension of Judaism*; Wright, *Jesus and the Victory of God*; House, *Israel, the Land and the People*; Freyne, "The Geography of Restoration"; Freyne, *Jesus, a Jewish Galilean*; Walker, "The Land and Jesus Himself"; Kim, "Your Kingdom Come on Earth"; Wenell, *Jesus and Land*; Wenell, "Jesus and the Holy Land," in Holmén and Porter, eds., *Handbook for the Study of the Historical Jesus*, 3:2773-800; Laaksonen, *Jesus und das Land*; Pitre, *Jesus, the Tribulation, and the End of Exile*; Fuller, *The Restoration of Israel*; Marchadour and Neuhaus, *Land, the Bible, and History*, esp. 61-77; Willits, *Matthew's Messianic Shepherd-King*; Burge, *Jesus and the Land*; Charlesworth, "Background I: Jesus of History and the Topography of the Holy Land," in Holmén and Porter, eds., *Handbook for the Study of the Historical Jesus*, 3:2213-42.

9. See Yoder, *The Christian Witness to the State*; Yoder, *The Original Revolution*; Yoder, *The Royal Priesthood*; Yoder, *Body Politics*; Yoder, *The Royal Priesthood*; Yoder, *For the Nations*; Yoder, *The Jewish-Christian Schism Revisited*; Yoder et al., *The War of the Lamb*; Hauerwas and Willimon, *Resident Aliens*; Hauerwas, *After Christendom?*; Hauerwas, *Against the Nations*; Hauerwas, *A Better Hope*; Cavanaugh, *Theopolitical Imagination*; Cavanaugh, *Migrations of the Holy*; McClendon, *Ethics*.

normative and theological content for fashioning a Christian ethic of territorial governance.

Thus I shall argue that what made Jesus' vision of the kingdom of God both distinctive and yet consistent with the various messianic schemata circulating in first-century Palestinian Judaism was neither that it anticipated a territorial restoration of Israel nor that it foresaw this restoration as having broader political and ethical ramifications for the Gentile nations and ultimately the cosmos as a whole.[10] Rather, what made Jesus' kingdom vision distinctive yet recognizably Jewish was both his understanding of the nature of the soteriological relationship between a territorially restored Israel and the Gentile nations and the means by which he believed this soteriological program would be enacted. More specifically, I will contend that Jesus' eschatological vision of Israel's territorial restoration elided the theme of Gentile destruction and subjugation that pervaded most (though not all) accounts of restoration in LSTJ literature.[11] The means by which he sought to inaugurate Israel's territorial restoration was not a campaign of militaristic violence, but rather a politico-ethical program of nonviolent resistance.

Having established this historical and theological proposal, I will then endeavor to elucidate its normative implications for current political discourse, particularly as it pertains to the increasingly contentious and nettlesome subject of territorial governance. This type of discourse has come under a mounting wave of criticism from a growing chorus of Christian ethicists and political theorists. Ethicists tend to couch their objections in the themes/tropes of diaspora and/or exile while political theorists invoke cosmopolitanism and post-colonialism. Both are skeptical regarding a territorially delimited nation-state remaining *the* conceptual locus for modern political reflection.

---

10. On this point we concur with Evans's assertion that "what Jesus wanted for Israel was pretty much what most first-century Jews wanted. How this restoration was to be achieved no doubt was a matter of debate, but that restoration of one sort or another was desired was widely held" ("Reconstructing Jesus' Teachings: Problems and Proposals," in Chilton and Evans, *Jesus in Context*, 149).

11. We will have reason to explore this point in much further detail in chapter 2 below. For the time being, however, we defer to Fuller and his astute observation that while a broad survey of LSTJ literature reveals that "*the defeat* of Israel's adversaries" is the most "common . . . motif in early Jewish texts of restoration," this "expectation, however, is far from simplistic and predictable." On the contrary the "various representative texts . . . of how Israel imagined the fate of her enemies demonstrate considerable complexity and diversity in terms of this motif's complex of features, relationships, and interpretations. The various expressions of the enemies' defeat extend beyond possible outcomes of victory, salvation, subjugation, or conversion" (*Restoration of Israel*, 111–12).

Where these critiques ultimately flounder, however, is in their inability to appreciate and recognize the anthropological, ethical and indeed theological significance of territoriality or what Michael R. Curry has rightly called the "normativity of place."[12] For if an essential part of what makes the Christian theological vision unique is its "scandalous" epistemological affirmation that the Lord of the universe is most concretely known and recognized in the birth, life, death and resurrection of a particular first-century Palestinian Jew named *Yeshua*, then it can surely be of no less consequence nor any less scandalous to suggest that the nature and scope of his lordship is most concretely manifested and thus inextricably bound to the territorial remnants of a once powerful ancient Near Eastern kingdom hugging the outskirts of the Mediterranean Basin. To think and act otherwise would be to remember and follow a flimsy flannel board Jesus, hewn from an ideological cloth of our own making, rather than an actual historical figure who occupied real time *and space*.

I shall use the rest of the project to correct this problem by exploring how Jesus' territorial ethic of non-violence and just peacemaking that deeply honors land and its meaning for communities lays the groundwork for articulating a Christian ethic of territorial governance.

---

12. Curry, "'Hereness' and the Normativity of Place."

1

W(h)ither the Land? The De-territorialization of Jesus and the Kingdom of God in New Testament Scholarship

1.1 Introduction

ONE OF THE PRIMARY objectives governing this chapter and the next will be to investigate how and why such a wide swath of contemporary Christian thought, including that whose theological mien has been deeply shaped within the crucible of a post-Shoah sensibility, still remains largely resistant to the proposition of linking Jesus and his proclamation of the kingdom of God to a territorial restoration of Israel.

Toward that end I will attempt to sketch a representative overview of how that linkage has come to be viewed within recent historical Jesus scholarship and Christian social ethics by way of examining how influential voices within each have sought to evaluate the political and moral relationship existing between Jesus' understanding of ἡ βασιλεία τοῦ θεοῦ and what W. D. Davies has aptly termed the "territorial dimensions of Judaism."[1] Furthermore, these chapters will also serve to locate and begin to critically interrogate some of the underlying theological, hermeneutical and moral presuppositions that have underpinned, or more precisely, undermined such efforts and thus made a positive territorial reading of both Jesus and the kingdom extraordinarily difficult, if not impossible, to, as it were, get off the ground.

---

1. Davies, *The Territorial Dimensions of Judaism*.

1.2 Scholarly Incongruities and Puzzling Conundrums

Notwithstanding the significant strides that both these disciplines have made in recovering the political and national substrate of Jesus' mission as well as their repeated demonstration of how that mission is suffused with various elements of Jewish restoration eschatology, to date only a handful of works from either field has formally addressed the question of whether Jesus' own conception of the kingdom of God can be said to meaningfully include a territorial restoration of Israel.[2] That this question has garnered such paltry consideration is a rather remarkable and even somewhat baffling development not only because several texts from the late Second Temple period regularly express the hope that a messianic figure, under Yahweh's aegis, will re-gather Jewish exiles from the Diaspora and return them to Israel in order to re-take possession and rule over the land,[3] but also because acquisition and governance of the land is, as Walter Brueggemann suggests, a "central, if not *the central theme* of biblical faith."[4]

Indeed as Christopher Wright has argued, for Israel the land was never "just a neutral stage where the drama [of redemption] unfolds," but instead has always remained an indispensible "part of the pattern of redemption" since "the social shape of Israel was intimately bound up with the economic issues of the division, tenure and use of the land."[5] Wright then is surely on

---

2. See notes 8 and 9 in the Introduction for a listing of recent works that have addressed the topic.

3. See Horsley, *Jesus and the Spiral of Violence*, 173–77; Bryan, *Jesus and Israel's Traditions*, 107–11. For an excellent survey of how the expectation of Israel's territorial restoration constantly reoccurs in the sundry eschatologies contained within the literatures of both the Hebrew bible and LSTJ period, see Fuller, *Restoration of Israel*, 13–84; and Willits, *Matthew's Messianic Shepherd-King*, 162–68. As Willits notes, while "it is true that beliefs about *Eretz Israel* were diverse... there is no evidence to suggest that these beliefs, however universally they were expressed, were ever untethered from the abiding conviction that YHWH had 'granted' a particular territory to Israel" (167).

4. Brueggemann, *Land*, 3. For additional studies that also explore the theological, societal, political, and ethical centrality of the land for ancient Israel, see Warshal, "Israel's Stake in the Land," 413–20; Harry M. Orlinsky, "The Biblical Concept of the Land in Israel: Cornerstone of the Covenant between God and Israel," in Hoffman, ed., *Land of Israel*, 27–64; Wright, *God's People in God's Land*; Wright, "Theology and Ethics of the Land," 81–86; Wright, *Old Testament Ethics*, esp. 76–99, 182–211; Fager, *Land Tenure and the Biblical Jubilee*; Weinfeld, *The Promise of the Land*; March, *Israel and the Politics of Land*; Habel, *The Land Is Mine*.

5. Wright, *Old Testament Ethics*, 83. It is also important to recognize Bryant's observation that although the symbiotic relationship between holiness and land underwent some further developments and revisions during the Second Temple period, as evidenced for example by the Qumranian innovation that a righteous and *Torah*-observant community could actually atone for those national sins that polluted and

to something when he states that Israel's administration of the land acts as a sort of "covenantal measuring gauge" in that it "reveals both the temperature of the theological relationship between God and Israel, and also the extent to which Israel was conforming to the social shape required of them in consistency with their status as God's redeemed people."[6]

It is quite peculiar then why an eschatological expectation that features so consistently throughout a first-century Jewish worldview and that is of such a vital and integral importance to Israel's theological, political, and moral *gestalt* would merit such scant attention, especially amongst those who are quite insistent that Jesus' words and actions are nigh to inscrutable save for understanding them as the proclamations of a Jewish nationalist working within the framework of a restorative eschatology.

Moreover, it is equally noteworthy that the prevailing consensus reached by those select few who have addressed this topic is decidedly pessimistic. That is all but a tiny minority are sympathetic to the spirit if not the letter of Hans Kvalbein's judgment that despite the fact that some of Jesus' kingdom logia (e.g., Matt 5:5 || Luke 6:20) do betray a certain sense of spatiality, which in light of both the messianic expectations pervading his historical milieu as well as the territorial connotations conjured up by the terms βασιλεία and מַלְכוּת, could reasonably be interpreted as intimating the reconstitution of a sovereign Davidic state, there is nevertheless "no reason to suppose that Jesus meant the land of Israel in a geographical sense when he spoke about the kingdom of God." Rather as Kvalbein counsels and as most of his colleagues have concurred, the "promised land" to which Jesus refers, if he refers to it at all, is but "a *typos* of the coming kingdom."[7] In fact, it has become something close to an article of faith among many to assert that it is precisely Jesus' steadfast refusal to ever explicitly link the kingdom of God with the re-establishment of Israel's territorial borders, which not only most distinguishes him from other first-century messianic figures but which also makes both him and his gospel cut such an attractive and compelling political ethos insofar as both eschew "a politics of superiority that would deny to others the same human rights as those of its members[.]"[8]

---

corrupted the land, the overarching conviction that Israel's purity and vocation as a "holy nation" was intimately and irrevocably tied to its governance of the land still remained intact. For, as Bryan states, "The desire for Israel to remain pure even outside of the cult is driven not by a uniquely Pharisaic or Essenic desire to live like priests in the cult but by the scriptural conviction that the Land and the people as well as the sanctuary and priesthood were holy" (*Jesus and Israel's Traditions*, 148).

6. Wright, *Old Testament Ethics*, 96.
7. Kvalbein, "Kingdom of God," 68.
8. Reed, "Refugee Rights and State Sovereignty," 71.

That these perceived incongruities continue to persist, however—that is between the land's central theological, political and ethical importance within the consciousness of ancient Israel and Second Temple Judaism and its apparent "spiritualization" or even abrogation by Jesus and Paul within early Christianity—poses an interesting conundrum since it raises the important question of whether the current lack of scholarly output and negative sentiment vis-à-vis Jesus' and the kingdom's territoriality is simply an accurate reflection of there being a diminishingly thin and supposedly "typological" historical and textual datum from which to work, or whether it is because, in the words of Matthew's Jesus, we have eyes to see yet do not. In other words is the apparent absence or near absence of ostensible territorial references to the kingdom of God within the gospels, itself dispositive and incontrovertible proof of Jesus finally and unequivocally disavowing the persistent eschatological hope of restoring a sovereign Jewish political kingdom within Palestine? Or is it instead an indication of how that evidence has been (mis)read and handled, namely through a "Christian exegetical tradition [that has] habitually sought to separate the kingdom of God from Jewish territorial expectation."[9]

Each of these questions in turn unveils a set of additional queries that makes the sense of tension surrounding this puzzle all the more acute and thus the need for further exploration and resolution all the more pressing. For suppose one decides to take the side of the majority opinion and stipulate that Jesus did in fact forsake a territorial restoration of Israel in order to embrace a more transcendent and cosmopolitan kingdom unencumbered by the earthly vagaries of geography and ethnic heritage. How does one reconcile that account with the contrary evidence that two of Jesus' most radically different audiences—Pilate and his disciples—both observed him to be speaking and acting in such a politically potent and provocative manner that neither thought it impertinent to ask him whether he was "the King [ὁ βασιλεὺς] of the Jews" (John 18:33)[10] or if he was going to restore

---

9. Allison, *Constructing Jesus*, 175.

10. For an exquisite and deeply penetrating account of how the trial and crucifixion scenes between Pilate and Jesus in John 18:28—19:25 are replete with palpable political content directly relevant to a discussion of Jewish expectations for a restored Israel, see Rensberger's *Johannine Faith and Liberating Community*, 91–100. As Rensberger explains, far from being a sympathetic figure who is a reluctant and at times hapless accomplice to Jesus' false trial and unjust execution, the Johannine Pilate is presented as "an agent of 'the world'" whose chief aim is to "humiliate 'the Jews' and to ridicule their national hopes by means of Jesus" (92). This is especially the case in 19:13–16 when Pilate sardonically asks "the Jews" whether they really want him to follow through on their stated request to "crucify your king." For what "this final thrust elicits from [the Jews]," Rensberger notes, is "an abnegation of their highest national hopes: 'We have

(ἀποκαθιστάνεις) the kingdom of Israel at this time (Acts 1:6)? Moreover, how can one still credibly recognize such a figure as being of first-century Jewish extraction when even as erstwhile a Hellenist and staunchly pro-Diaspora a Jew as Philo never entirely relinquished the hope that YHWH would one day re-gather the Twelve Tribes from the Diaspora and return them to rule over a territorially restored Israel?[11]

---

not king but Caesar'; and Pilate, having heard the only thing that he has been waiting to hear, hands Jesus over with alacrity" (95).

11. In *De Praemis et Poenis*, Philo writes the following concerning the future of Diasporic Jews:

> For even though they may be at the very extremities of the earth, acting as slaves to those enemies who have led them away in captivity, still they shall all be restored to freedom in one day, as at a given signal; their sudden and universal change to virtue causing a panic among their masters; for they will let them go, because they are ashamed to govern those who are better than themselves. But when they have received this unexpected liberty, those who but a short time before were scattered about in Greece, and in the countries of the barbarians, in the islands, and over the continents, rising up with one impulse, and coming from all the different quarters imaginable, all hasten to one place pointed out to them, being guided on their way by some vision, more divine than is compatible with its being of the nature of man, invisible indeed to everyone else, but apparent only to those who were saved, having their separate inducements and intercessions, by whose intervention they might obtain a reconciliation with the Father . . . And when they come cities will be rebuilt which but a short time ago were in complete ruins, and the desert will be filled with inhabitants, and the barren land will change and become fertile, and the good fortune of their fathers and ancestors will be looked upon as a matter of but small importance, on account of the abundance of wealth of all kinds which they will have at the present moment, flowing forth from the graces of God as from ever-running fountains, which will thus confer vast wealth separately on each individual, and also on all the citizens in common, to an amount beyond the reach even of envy. (164–65; 168)

Notwithstanding what appears here to be a rather clear-cut and straightforward affirmation of Israel's eschatological territorial restoration, it should be noted that Philo's larger understanding and interpretation of Israel's land promises as well as the nature of its future restoration is still very much a matter of scholarly debate and disagreement. For a perspective that tends toward a more literal and nationalist reading of the land and restoration within Philo, see B. Schaller, "Philon von Alexandrien und das 'Heilige Land,'" in Strecker, ed., *Das Land Israel in biblischer Zeit*, 172–87; Peder Borgen, "'There Shall Come Forth a Man': Reflections on Messianic Ideals in Philo," in Charlesworth, ed., *Messiah*, 341–61; Scott, "Philo and the Restoration of Israel," 553–75; Barclay, *Jews in the Mediterranean Diaspora*; Gafni, *Land, Center and Diaspora*. For a perspective that favors a more spiritualized and allegorical interpretation, see Betsy Halpern-Amaru, "Land Theology in Philo and Josephus," in Hoffman, ed., *Land of Israel*, 65–93; Richard D. Hect, "Philo and Messiah," in Neusner et al., eds., *Judaisms and Their Messiahs*; Birnbaum, *The Place of Judaism in Philo's Thought*; Fuller, *The Restoration of Israel*. What is important to note here is that even someone like Fuller who is more apt to see

Conversely, suppose one is persuaded that a de-territorialization of Jesus and the kingdom is not just the regrettable and errant by-product of a flawed form of Christian exegesis, but is instead isomorphic to the tradition itself such that it is impossible to construct a landed interpretation of Jesus and kingdom without also seriously compromising and damaging the integrity of one's Christian faith and identity in the process. How does one square that interpretation with the fact that several patristic theologians were vigilantly protective of the chiliastic belief that Jesus would restore a landed kingdom to Israel at the *parousia*?[12] Furthermore how is such an a-territorial reading of Jesus consistent with Christianity's sacramental vision that it is not only "theologically necessary to view created things as real promises of the kingdom [of God]," but also, "to understand the kingdom of God not merely as the historical promises of the world, but of its natural promises as well."[13] And finally, does not countenance of such a supposition lay the foundations for a Gnostic form of Christianity in general and a doceticized interpretation of Jesus in particular since both denude us of the very theological and ethical resources necessary to inform a discussion of territorial governance?

As by now should be evident, what this series of questions clearly indicates is that there is something enormously significant at stock in pondering whether Jesus envisaged a territorial restoration of Israel, not only in terms of ensuring we possess an understanding of him that is historically and theologically accurate, which is to say coeval with the contextual dynamics of late Second Temple Judaism, but also for the sake of deciding to what extent both he and the kingdom can provide substantive moral and political guidance in thinking about territorial governance. What is more, they also indicate that finding a favorable historical and moral relationship between Jesus and a territorially restored Israel will require not just a critical deconstruction of some of Christianity's most cherished and longstanding exegetical habits and theological proclivities, but, paradoxically, a recovery and further buttressing of some of those very same habits and proclivities as well.

For the time being however, it will be necessary to take stock of those works that have engaged this subject, few and skeptical though they may be. Accordingly a further exploration of some of the more formative studies

---

Philo as interpreting the "traditional Jewish symbols of the Land, covenant and even the Jews ... as typologies or inferior symbols of a superior, spiritual reality available to all humanity" still acknowledges that "it cannot be said definitively that Philo forfeits the idea of a real return to the Land" (*Restoration of Israel*, 99).

12. See Wilken, *Land Called Holy*, esp. 46–64.

13. Moltmann, *God in Creation*, 5.

to have addressed Jesus' and the kingdom's historical and theological relationship to Israel's land promises as well as that relationship's correlative normative and political implications is in order and provided under the respective headings of "Historical Jesus Scholarship" and "Christian Social Ethics" below.

1.3 Texts for Examination

In order to create a representative sampling of how recent historical Jesus scholarship has come to view Jesus' and the kingdom's territoriality, I have chosen to examine three texts in particular: W. D. Davies's *The Gospel and the Land: Early Christianity and Jewish Territorial Doctrine*; Marcus Borg's *Conflict, Holiness and Politics in the Teachings of Jesus*; and N. T. Wright's *Jesus and the Victory of God*. The reason I have selected these particular works is because they have come to be widely recognized as some of the most influential and seminal within historical Jesus research over the past four decades, particularly as each has helped to recover Jesus' identity as a first-century Palestinian Jew as well as show how that identity underwrites a political and social reading of the kingdom. Therefore an analysis of their arguments should provide both a suitable an emblematic specimen.

1.4 W. D. Davies: *The Gospel and the Land: Early Christianity and Jewish Territorial Doctrine*

Although by no means the first New Testament scholar of note to explore the question of how Jesus' pronouncements about the kingdom of God impinged upon Israel's hopes for national restoration,[14] W. D. Davies's

---

14. One thinks here especially of Reimarus's *Von dem Zwecke Jesu und seiner Jünger* (1778; *The Goal of Jesus and His Disciples*, trans. G. W. Buchanan [Leiden: Brill 1970]), which argued that Jesus sought to liberate the Jews from Roman rule and is largely credited as beginning the whole field of historical Jesus research as well as G. B. Caird's short but insightful treatise *Jesus and the Jewish Nation*. In a closing missive one sees as having an especially deep and formative impact on two of his more prominent pupils—N. T. Wright and Marcus Borg—Caird writes, "Here then, in conclusion, is the picture of the ministry of Jesus I have been trying to put before you. Jesus believed that Israel had been called to be God's saved and saving nation, the agent through whom God intended to assert sovereignty over the rest of the world, and that the time had come when God was summoning the nation once for all to take its place in his economy as the Son of Man. His teaching was something more than individual piety and ethics, *it was a national way of life through which alone God's purpose could be implemented*" (22, emphasis added).

Davies, of course, was not unaware of Caird's proposal and thought it significant

monumental *The Gospel and the Land* is still considered by many to be one of the most significant, if not *the* definitive account on the subject. Thus his status as being something of an *eminence gris* in this area remains very much intact and for good reason.

For the significance of *The Gospel and the Land*, both for today and when it was originally published, lies not only in the fact that it is one of the first modern volumes of New Testament scholarship to adumbrate a comprehensive exploration of the role of the land (אֶרֶץ/γῆ) within both early Jewish and Christian sources, but also, operating as it was at the cusp of the Third Quest, in its dogged resolve that a proper historical interpretation of early Christianity is ultimately inseparable from a reading of Judaism.[15] For as Davies so eloquently and perceptively writes,

> As did Judaism itself, so also the Church understood itself in the light of a particular history; it placed itself in the same stream of revelation as Judaism did; it bound itself not only to the God of Abraham and Isaac and Jacob but to the concrete history of His dealings with Israel, to Moses, Elijah, the Prophets, the sweet singers of Israel and its priests. The history of Judaism became part of the history of the Church. This also meant that, in a Christian view, Judaism made the Christian faith an inseparable part of its own history. Christianity is in a specific stream of

---

and persuasive enough to merit at least a partially sympathetic endorsement insofar as it helped expose and deconstruct the fallacy of an a-political interpretation of Jesus that was being promulgated by Bornkamm and others (347–48). Nevertheless he ultimately dismisses Caird's argument on the grounds that he "too easily equates the Jewish community addressed by Jesus with a nation and the will of God with the slings and arrows of history, so that . . . the eschatological language of Jesus becomes . . . a way of interpreting the national present future" (348). Thus "Caird has sacrificed the personal and transcendent dimensions of the Kingdom of God," says Davies, "to an exaggerated politico-national concern" (348).

15. Despite the fact that I take issue with several of the exegetical and theological assumptions that undergird Davies's a-territorial interpretation of Jesus and the kingdom, I am nevertheless aware and chagrined that not enough attention or credit has been given to him for being one of the first prominent Anglo New Testament scholars to consistently and vocally criticize the persistent diminution of Judaism within European and North American New Testament scholarship well before it was in scholarly vogue to do so. Along those lines it is important to remember that Davies essentially presaged the so-called New Perspective on Paul when he wrote the following lines in his *Paul and Rabbinic Judaism: Some Rabbinic Elements in Pauline Theology*, which first appeared in 1948: "Both in his life and through, therefore, Paul's close relations to Rabbinic Judaism has become clear, and we cannot too strongly insist again that for him the acceptance of the Gospel was not so much the rejection of the old Judaism and the discovery of new religion wholly antithetical to it, as his polemics might sometimes pardonably lead us to assume, but the recognition of the advent of the true and final form of Judaism, in other words, the advent of the Messianic Age of Jewish expectation" (324).

history; it can never be detached from it without ceasing to be itself.[16]

Subsequently Davies uses the first four chapters of *The Gospel and the Land* to engage in a sweeping but careful delineation of the land's theological and ethical significance within major blocks of early Jewish literature—specifically the Hexateuch, the Prophets and Late Second Temple Jewish writings—in order to provide a solid historical and textual foundation from which to answer the more programmatic question of "[h]ow did [the Early Church] react to the hope that dealt with the land of Israel?"[17] As one might expect the result of this ambitious survey is to show that there was "no one doctrine of the land" that was determinative for early Jewish thought, but rather "a multiplicity of ideas and expectations variously and unsystematically entertained."[18]

In particular Davies enumerated the existence of no less than eight such expectations, which in short order were:

1. Rejection of a "nomadic ideal"—Notwithstanding the elevation and perhaps even the valorization of Israel's post-exodus wilderness wanderings within certain sections of early Jewish thought, the place of the wilderness, both geographically and conceptually, was at best theologically ambiguous. For while Israel's time in the wilderness could "boast of the divine succor and guidance, of the revelation of the [YHWH], of the election of the people, [and] of the giving of [*torah*]," it was still ultimately "only a transitional period" and thus "its value was preparatory and not final."[19] Consequently even though we see the theme of the wilderness "reappea[r] in the eschatology of Judaism, which is thought of, among other things, as a new exodus which would witness a new Moses and the return of the manna, etc. . . . the wilderness is not the goal but a stage on the way to the land[.]"[20]

2. Maccabean and Zealot devotion to the land despite textual silence—Davies cautions that although territorial references are few and far between within Maccabean and Zealot sources, it can nevertheless not "be doubted that [loyalty to the land] was a primary axiom of the rebels" and parenthetically adds that "(our deepest axioms or assumptions

---

16. Davies, *Gospel and the Land*, 381.
17. Ibid., 161.
18. Ibid., 157.
19. Ibid., 85.
20. Ibid., 90.

are often most unexpressed)."²¹ What accounts for this virtual silence about the land, Davies contends, is that in both the Maccabean and Zealot revolts devotion to the land "took a religious form, so that in the sources it is loyalty to the Torah and to the Temple that receive the accent."²²

3. Absence of the Abrahamic covenant (ברית בין הבתרים) in early Jewish sources—Analogous to the point made above, Davies acknowledges that outside of the Hexateuch there are only a handful of references in the rest of the *Tanak* and early rabbinic sources to YWHW's covenant with Abraham (then Abram) in Gen 15:18–21 to "give this land (יְהָאָרֶץ אֶת־ נָתַתִּי) from the river of Egypt to the great river, the river Euphrates, the land of the Kenites, the Kenizzites, the Kadmonites, the Hittites, the Perizzites, the Rephaim, the Amorites, the Canaanites, the Girgashites, and the Jebusites" to Abraham and his descendants. However, this covenant "with Abraham was [still] at the foundation— assumed and unexpressed—of the people of Israel," and therefore "like the foundation of a building it was often hidden from view and not actively discussed."²³

4. Ancient Israel understood and saw itself primarily as a covenant religious community and not as a political state as such—Here Davies notes that while discussion of themes (1) and (2) "may have created the impression that Israel in the Old Testament is to be understood as a community bound to a land and governed by a law, much as a modern national state might be so tied and governed[,]" such an impression is nevertheless misleading since Israel's *torah* "[was] not related primarily to the political organization of a state, but rather to a community of men [*sic*] in which the common allegiance to Yahweh was the constitutive element."²⁴ This in turn "explains why it is impossible to discover an Israelite idea of the State."²⁵

---

21. Ibid., 98.
22. Ibid.
23. Ibid., 108.
24. Ibid., 108–9.
25. Ibid., 109. For a perspective that is nearly directly opposite that of Davies, see Gottwald's *The Tribes of Yahweh* and *The Politics of Ancient Israel*, both of which proceed on the supposition that it was actually ancient Israel's social and political configuration as an Ancient Near Eastern state, and more precisely a state uniquely committed to a program of socio-economic and political egalitarianism, which proceeded and eventually gave rise to the religious cult of Yahwism. Or as Gottwald puts it, "It cannot escape our attention that, instead of many gods, Israel projected one God, in symbolic complementarity with the determined way in which, in place of the many strata of Cannanite

5. A recognizable relocation of interest away from the land to larger universal concerns in post-exilic literature—As a direct result of both the Assyrian and Babylonian exiles Davies notices that "the land of Israel as such hardly plays any part" in writings of Job, Proverbs, Ecclesiastes, Song of Songs, Esther, Jonah, and portions of Daniel, which is somewhat surprising since "loss of control over the land . . . might have been expected to lead a concern with, if not concentration upon it."[26] What we find instead however is "a concern with broad human, rather than specifically Israelitish problems" although this shift is not, Davies warns, "necessarily to be understood as precluding attachment to the land."[27]

6. An internalization and individuation of religion in the post-exilic period—Concomitant with the shift away from *eretz* Israel to a broader humanistic focus comes also a post-exilic "awareness of the dimensions of specifically personal religious experience."[28] Both Deutero-Isaiah's transference of the national promise of "entry into the land' to "the just man, the saint" (Isa 57:13b; Isa 65:13–16) and Daniel's eschatological emphasis on the vindication of the persecuted martyrs

---

society, Israel projected a strataless society, which is to say: one indivisible God for one indivisible people. The cultural-material hypothesis begins with the assumption that Yahwism as the symbolic side of Israelite social relations *had no existence whatsoever independent of the thoughts of these particular socially egalitarian Israelite people*" (*Tribes of Yahweh*, 648; emphasis added).

Despite this disagreement, however, over whether Israel's uniqueness first lay in its politics or its religion it is important to see that both Davies's and Gottwald's analyzes make the same functionalist categorical error of artificially separating politics and religion. In other words, Davies would have us believe that because the "context or setting in life in which Israel had received the Law was the covenant' both the law and its issuing are to be seen as purely religious phenomenon and "not related primarily to the political organization of a state." Conversely, Gottwald maintains that the most "fruitful course for recovering the ancient Israelite political scene" is to investigate "the course of Israel's political life" without "the premature closures of interpretation imposed by the moral and religious judgments of biblical writers . . . whose viewpoints, while they must be carefully considered, dare not be uncritically canonized as the final word on the subject" (*Politics of Ancient Israel*, 13). Both these assessments, however, fly in the face of Milbank's apt observation that "Jews have always insisted on the connection between their religious and social distinctiveness: this is what the centrality of *torah* implies" (*Theology and Social Theory*, 113). Thus notwithstanding their sounding the alarm about anachronistically retrojecting modern interpretive categories back onto early Judaism, both Davies and Gottwald appear to unwittingly disobey their own sound advice.

26. Davies, *Gospel and the Land*, 110–11.

27. Ibid., 111, 115.

28. Ibid., 115.

via resurrection are both emblematic of this turn inwards although once again Davies hastens to add that "concern with the fate of the individual as such ... was not exclusive of concern with the land" especially since "the resurrection itself came to be tied to the land."[29] Nonetheless, this undeniable process of internalization and individuation 'could not help but lead to a relocation of emphasis' away from the land.[30]

7. The supplanting of the Temple by the synagogue in Rabbinic thought—Notwithstanding a continued longing for a return to the land and Jerusalem, the prolonged diasporic experience of "living outside the land ... could not help but tend to detach Jews from it."[31] The most concrete manifestation of this is found, says Davies, in the creation of the synagogue, which "had almost certainly emerged in the Babylonian exile and developed throughout the Dispersion to supply for Jews a rallying point other than the Temple, which was in the land."[32]

8. The transcendentalizing of the land in Hellenistic and Palestinian sources—Here Davies points to the writings of Philo as well as to the more obscure *Testament of Job* both of which illustrate how "Judaism was being penetrated by Hellenism before the Christian era, and was in some circles, gradually clothing traditional Jewish *realia* in a Hellenistic dress, so that the immortality of the disembodied soul could be substituted for the reunion of soul and body in the resurrection in the land."[33]

With this typology in hand and its varying and at times contradictory perspectives on the land in view,[34] Davies next seeks to inquire what explanatory light they might shed on the important historical and theological question of how the "earliest Christians, Jews convinced that the 'end of the ages' had come upon them and that the promises of God were being

29. Ibid., 118.
30. Ibid.
31. Ibid., 119.
32. Ibid.
33. Ibid., 126.
34. I will speak more to this below but for now at least we should make it clear that although Davies's typology provides a useful heuristic that helps trace the different perspectives and interpretations of land extant within early Judaism, it should not be seen nor understood as mere objective reportage. More to the point, both the construction of the categories themselves as well as the trajectory of how they are positioned betrays a set of unspoken axioms all of which tend toward the conclusion that early Judaism itself was progressively moving away from a territorial understanding of Israel.

fulfilled" responded to ancient Israel's land promises. More specifically, he asks, "[d]id they simply ignore or suppress or reject [them]? Did they confront them deliberately, to sublimate them or transcend them? Or did they at times succumb to them?"[35]

Efforts at untangling these knotty questions lead Davies to begin his search for answers not first with a reading of the canonical Gospels as one might expect but instead to an extensive analysis of the Pauline epistles since, as he asserts, these are the "earliest extant documents produced by primitive Christianity."[36] Moreover, it is not only their early provenance and close historical proximity to the historical Jesus that makes Paul's letters an attractive investigative entry point for Davies but also the fact that "their author, before he joined the Christian community was a Jew" who because of his refusal to share in the "lax conformity of so many in the Dispersion and the lofty coldness of the established priesthood" would have "*felt* the full force of the doctrine of the land, Jerusalem, and the Temple."[37]

This opting for Pauline priority by Davies and its attendant rationale are no small points and therefore should not be overlooked. For what both essentially do is cast Paul, or rather a subset of the Pauline corpus, as a sort of definitive historical and theological barometer by which we can then transitively gauge and extrapolate how early Christianity viewed Israel's land promises. For as Davies himself affirms the "measure of the seriousness with which [Paul] regarded the doctrine may well be safely taken as a *fair indication of the reaction of Christians to it*, because few would be likely to deal with more emphatically, even passionately, than he."[38] Thus by Davies's lights if there is an early Christian affirmation of Israel's territoriality to be had, it is primarily Paul, and not the earlier Jesus traditions, which offers us our best historical bet.[39]

---

35. Ibid., 161.

36. Ibid., 164.

37. Ibid., 164, 166. It is interesting to note Davies's choice of verb tense in this sentence—i.e., that Paul *was* a Jew before he joined the Christian community, which carries with it the implication that after his conversion experience Paul did not consider himself a "Jew" to the extent that he disowned or jettisoned its territorial elements even while retaining other important signifiers of Jewish identity (see note 8 above).

38. Ibid., 166; emphasis added.

39. To be sure there is a persuasive methodological rationale to support, at least initially, Davies's decision to opt for Pauline priority not only for the same reasons he adduces (e.g., historical proximity to Jesus and Paul's palpable Jewish identity) but also because we agree with the so-called maximalist position espoused by David Wenham and other Pauline scholars that there is an overwhelming amount of textual evidence within the Pauline Epistles—whether authentic or authored under Paul's influence—to suggest that "far from being peripheral, . . . the Jesus-tradition is central to Paul's

Yet despite repeatedly lowering his bucket deep into the Pauline well, Davies comes up dry. More specifically he finds there is no mentionable evidence within Paul's epistles to entertain seriously the notion that he ever re-affirmed ancient Israel's land promises much less any suggestion that he understood Jesus to be announcing a territorial kingdom of God. On the contrary it is Davies's conclusion that what we find in Paul is still a deep devotion to an "eschatological Israel" to be sure, but "an Israel, which, through Christ, transcends the connection with the land and with the Law attached to that Land."[40] This is corroborated not only by the fact that Davies finds no explicit references to *eretz* Israel or direct appropriation of the Abrahamic land promises within Paul's writings, but also more importantly by what he observes to be a noticeable evolution in Paul's thought, namely what he describes as a "*deliverance* from traditional Jewish apocalyptic forms of

---

theology" (Wenham, *Paul*, 399). Hence to read Paul's view of Israel's territoriality is also to vicariously peer into Jesus.

Nevertheless we cannot help noticing that there is also a set of unspoken historical and theological assumptions tacitly at work here as well. Specifically, apropos to Davies's discussion of land ideas/expectations (2) and (3) above, although there are few direct references to the Jesus tradition within Paul, it is nevertheless clear that both he and his audience are clearly working from and guided by that tradition. In other words, both Paul and his successors are clearly addressing and responding to a group of early Christian audiences while presupposing they are already conversant with and operating within the Jesus tradition much in the same way that the Maccabeans and Zealots as well as the authors of the *Tanak* and early rabbinic literature would have assumed their audiences to be conversant with and operating within the tradition of ancient Israel's land promises despite referring to them only occasionally if at all. Thus while Davies is technically right that as a matter of textual provenance the Pauline Epistles are indeed closer to the historical Jesus than are the Gospels, in terms of historical and theological development these texts are nevertheless secondary to and therefore dependent upon previously existing Jesus traditions, traditions we believe offer a much more penetrating glimpse into early Christianity's evaluation of Israel's territoriality and thus are more important since they are directly engaging the question of how Jesus and his kingdom proclamations relate to Israel's eschatological restoration.

Additionally, and as will become more apparent in our analysis of his engagement with Paul below, Davies has a tendency to abstract and conceptualize Paul's interpretations of those earlier Jesus traditions, especially regarding the eschatological relationship between Jesus and Israel, such that he reads Paul's letters not as specific responses to a particular set of questions arising out of disagreements over what Israel's eschatological restoration would look like, but instead as transcendent and sweeping philosophical treatises. Hence his decision to follow Charles and Dodd's lead in shifting the interpretive center of gravity for Paul away from the Jewish apocalyptic and towards the more philosophical categories of "the personal, the intellectual and the ecclesiological," (209).

Thus it would appear that Davies's decision to begin with Paul rather than with the Gospels ultimately helps create a hermeneutical and theological lens that cannot help but automatically predisposes one toward an a-territorial reading of Jesus and the kingdom.

40. Davies, *Gospel and the Land*, 217.

thought . . . to a more *refined* Hellenistic eschatology."[41] In particular Davies notes that there is a discernible trajectory in Paul's epistles whereby "Paul's [later] epistles are less concerned with apocalyptic imagery" than with the more existentialist and personalist concepts of "'[being] in Christ,' 'dying and rising with Christ,' [and] '[being]in the Spirit.'"[42]

Three realities in particular, the personal, the intellectual and the ecclesiological, stand out as being especially expressive of this sea change in Paul's thought and with it a move away from a Jewish apocalyptic framework and "the *realia* of Judaism[.]"[43] With respect to the personal dimension, Davies, leaning heavily on the work of his mentor C. H. Dodd, notes that the delay of Jesus' *parousia* "chastens" Paul and thereby causes "a gradual diminution of apocalyptic dualism, a growing appreciation of this world and, we may add, an unconcern with geographic apocalyptic."[44] As evidence of this point Davies offers up Paul's words in Phil 3:20–21 with its language that "the commonwealth of Christians" is already "in heaven" and deduces that Paul understands that "[t]o be 'in Christ' in the present and to be with Christ in the world to come has *replaced* any hope that Paul may ever have cherished of dwelling in the land."[45] Moving to the intellectual dimension Davies largely concurs with Lucien Cerfaux's and W. L. Knox's views that what a reading of Paul's later epistles show is that he has "abandoned Jewish eschatology with its geographic structure, and embraced the perspectives of Hellenistic dualism."[46] A newly Hellenized Paul thus "speaks of being 'in Christ' and being 'with Christ,'" with the upshot being that "Christ has become for Paul the 'locus' of redemption here and in the world to come." Thus "the land" has "been for him 'Christified'" meaning that it "is not the promised land much as he loved it that became his 'inheritance,' but the Living Lord, in whom was a new creation."[47]

Yet to be "in Christ," Davies admits, can never entirely mean for Paul to exist in a "solitary state of individual possession[.]" Instead, it always has to refer to "a life shared with those, who with him, had responded to Christ."[48] This statement thus leads Davies to finally reflect on Paul's ecclesiology and

---

41. Ibid., 210–11; emphases added. For similar evaluation of how Hellenistic sources influenced Paul's thought and especially his scriptural hermeneutic, see Boyarin, *A Radical Jew*.

42. Davies, *Gospel and the Land*, 208–9.

43. Ibid., 209.

44. Ibid., 210.

45. Ibid.

46. Ibid., 212.

47. Ibid., 213.

48. Ibid.

see perhaps if it contains the one last remaining vestige of a residual Jewish territorial sensibility. Davies's diagnosis, however, holds true to form. For he agrees with D. Georgi's conclusion that what Paul's reflections on his collection efforts for the Jerusalem church reveal is "that, despite its apocalyptic framework (that is, the geographic, eschatological structure centering in Jerusalem), the centre of gravity of Paul's ministry has shifted away from geographic eschatology."[49] Thus Davies once again maintains that for Paul "[t]o be 'in Christ'—interpreted in terms of the eschatological 'people of God' and salvation-history or more 'locatively' in terms of the Body of Christ—has replaced being 'in the land' as the ideal life."[50]

That Paul and early Christianity steadily abandon a Jewish apocalyptic and geographical framework, should not however, Davies claims, be seen as matter of Pauline invention or innovation. On the contrary it is but the organic and in some respects inexorable outgrowth of Jesus himself. For as he asserts "the Gospel, as Paul understood it, in itself implied such a development."[51] Hence while Paul may have been instrumental in fanning the flame of the kingdom's de-territorialization, it is ultimately Jesus who ignited the spark.

That this is the case, Davies asserts, is not only evident from a broad reading of the canonical Gospels themselves,[52] but also by focusing upon a key set of pericopes that are directly pertinent to establishing Jesus' aims and intentions regarding Israel's restoration. And what according to Davies were those aims and intentions?

In answering that all decisive question, Davies argues that one of the fundamental problems plaguing modern New Testament scholarship has been a consistent tendency to de-politicize Jesus' aims and actions for fear that such a reading would be anachronistic and eisegetical. To be sure such a concern is not without merit since Davies concedes that "the peril of modernizing Jesus is real." At the same time however, he also cautions that "such

49. Ibid., 217.
50. Ibid.
51. Ibid., 219.
52. Unfortunately, neither time nor space allows us to fully engage Davies's extensive analysis (more than one hundred pages) of Matthew, Mark, Luke, and John and the absence of territorial motifs found there within. The following summation, however, encapsulates the thrust of that analysis quite nicely: "Our examination of the major documents of the New Testament, with the deliberate limitation of avoiding discussion of the transcendentalizing of the land in the Heavenly Jerusalem . . . is over. We have discovered in the New Testament, alongside the recognition of the historical role of the land as the scene of the life, death, and resurrection of Jesus, a growing recognition that the Christian faith is, in principle, cut loose from the land, that the Gospels demanded a breaking out of its territorial chrysalis" (ibid., 336).

a suggestion should be allowed only as a warning not as a norm[.]" For in the end "we cannot completely anachronize Jesus either."[53] Thus while Davies is quick to join the growing chorus of those who have disavowed S. G. F. Brandon's now widely discredited thesis that Jesus aligned himself with the Zealots, he is nonetheless appreciative for what that thesis has done, namely "it compels the recognition of burning nationalism in first-century Judaism" and that Jesus' ministry "was conducted in an atmosphere of great tensions."[54] Accordingly the proper historical question to be asked vis-a-vis discerning Jesus' intentions and actions is not whether they somehow possessed a national political valence but rather how, "if he rejected the nationalist [Zealot] movement" did "he come to terms with the political realities of his day?"[55]

He did so, Davies responds, by concerning himself "to gather a community of people to share in his ministry."[56] Yet it is "not to the nation of Israel that Jesus sent his disciples," but "to *the lost sheep* of the house Israel (Matt. 10:6, our italics), that is, of the *people* of Israel."[57] In other words Davies holds that while Jesus' aims were political and even restorational to the extent that it is "impossible to rule out Jesus' concern with his own people," they are nevertheless also "non-political" insofar as Jesus is "concern[ed] with his own people not as constituting a national entity . . . over whose political destiny as such he agonized, but his own people as intended to be the 'Israel' of God and, therefore, as the matrix within which he could hope to reconstitute the Chosen People, 'Israel,' that is to create the community of the People of God."[58] Thus in the final analysis Davies believes the most accurate and plausible way to make sense of the interaction between Jesus' restorational intentions and actions is as follows:

> The activity of Jesus, then, was not aimed directly at changing any national policy, but by teaching, preaching, and healing, at creating a community—not a nation—"aware of the presence of God as an urgent reality" and at inducing "them to give the appropriate response, so that they might become effectively members of the new people of God which was coming into being." This explains two other frequently discussed aspects of his ministry. First, his intense concern with individuals. The

53. Ibid., 344.
54. Ibid., 344-45.
55. Ibid., 344.
56. Ibid., 349.
57. Ibid.
58. Ibid.

disciples whom he called were challenged to a personal decision: insofar as they committed themselves personally to him and accepted his demands, the people of God was being formed. And, secondly, Jesus' assertions that, after the new people of God had emerged in Israel, there would also be an incursion of Gentiles into it. Jesus confined his mission to the people of Israel: his dealings with Gentiles were peripheral: even when he left the borders of "Israel" he only visited outposts of Israelite population. But at the same time he rejected any idea of divine vengeance on the enemies of Israel, and included Gentiles in salvation and contemplated that the distinction between Jew and Gentile would disappear. Not political organization and policy were his concern, but human community, loving serving and ultimately inclusive.[59]

So while Davies is certain that Jesus, like Paul, "knew the love of his native land" and perhaps may have even been initially motivated and inspired by it,[60] his "concentration on a loving, universal community" nonetheless "suggests that the land itself played a minor part in his mind."[61]

Conclusive confirmation of this point, Davies contends, is to be found in four specific Gospel passages—the parable of the fig tree (Luke 13:6-9); the parable of the hidden talent (Matt 25:14-30); Jesus' beatitude about the meek inheriting the land (Matt 5:5); and Jesus' appointment of the twelve apostles to rule and judge over Israel (Matt 19:28 || Luke 22:30)—which, according to Davies, are the only passages where "the question of the land

---

59. Ibid., 353.

60. Davies obliquely acknowledges this point deep in one of his footnotes when he writes, "Were it not for such a passage [Matt 8:11] and the evidence provided by Jeremias concerning Jesus' concerns with the Gentiles, it would be tempting to find Jesus sharing in the doctrine of the land which we traced" (ibid., 353n51). There are two significant points about this statement that deserve further comment. First, Davies's invocation of Matt 8:11 and Jesus' pronouncement that "many will come from east and west and will eat with Abraham and Isaac and Jacob in the kingdom of heaven" shows him to be following the lead of several other New Testament scholars in understanding that language to be applying to Gentiles. Thus it never seems to occur to Davies that those coming "from east and west" may well be a reference both to Gentiles and to Jewish exiles who are still living in the diaspora. We will probe this point further in chapter 3 below. Second, it is interesting to note that save for Jesus possessing a self-conscious mission to the Gentiles, Davies thinks that Jesus would in fact be guided by Israel's land promises. Yet because Jesus does include Gentiles in the kingdom, this is all the more confirmation that he could not have envisioned a territorial restoration of Israel. In other words, Davies presupposes that a territorial restoration of Israel effectively precludes the possibility of a Gentile mission by Jesus.

61. Ibid., 354.

directly emerges" for Jesus.⁶² A brief synopsis of Davies's exegesis of each is therefore in order:

The Parable of the Fig Tree (Luke 13:6–9)

In reading this parable Davies is particularly struck by the wording of the conclusion of verse 7—"Cut it down! Why should it be wasting the soil?"—not only because it is peculiar to the Lukan tradition⁶³ but also because it legitimately raises the question of whether Jesus believed Israel's judgment would "includ[e] or would incur separation from the land."⁶⁴ "Certain considerations" he believes "favour an affirmative answer."⁶⁵ Among these considerations is what he observes to be the presence of a "typical Aramaic asyndeton," which lends the verse particular "forcefulness." Hence Davies believes the interrogative "Why should it be wasting the soil?" can be read to metaphorically imply that the "land on which Israel grows, the vineyard, is the land of Israel," and thus that Israel will be cut off or down from the land.⁶⁶

However, even if the interpretive grain of the verse cuts in that general direction, Davies cautions that there are still enough exegetical ambiguities within the verse such that it "affords little light on Jesus' attitude to the land."⁶⁷ In particular he acknowledges that although the preposition εκ usually means "out of" or "out from," there is little lexical support to render the Greek verb ἔκκοψον as meaning to cut the fig tree (i.e., Israel) out of or from the land. Furthermore, there is also no textual evidence in either the Hebrew Bible or the LXX to suggest that verb καταργεῖ, which is translated as "wasting" or "using up," is "evocative of any theology of the land" although he does make the point that one of its possible meanings—"to do nothing" or "to be fruitless" in connection with observing the Sabbath—could perhaps show that Jesus is "ironically saying that the conduct of Israel is to bring the land the rest of desolation such as Lev. 26:27–39 had spoke of[.]"⁶⁸ Finally,

---

62. Ibid.

63. Davies notes that the parallels of the parable in Mark 11:12–14, 20–21, and Matt 21:18–19 are different not only in terms of emphasis and timing—"the judgment on Israel is already accomplished" in both, whereas in Luke "the emphasis is on the forbearance or patience of the judge"—but also because "only in Luke is there a direct reference to the earth or the land on which the fig tree (Israel) grows" (355).

64. Ibid.
65. Ibid.
66. Ibid.
67. Ibid., 357.
68. Ibid.

Davies acknowledges that we cannot be sure if Jesus means the phrase τὴν γῆν ("the land") to refer to the specific land of Israel (אֶרֶץ) itself or instead to a more generic sense of the earth or soil (הָאֲדָמָה).

The Parable of the Hidden Talent (Matt 25:14–30)

As with the Lukan passage above, Davies's attention is immediately drawn to a specific verse—25—which describes the slave informing his returning master that he "hid your talent in the ground" (ἔκρυψα τὸ τάλαντον σου ἐν τῇ γῇ). Noting how insufficient attention has been paid to the difference between Matthew's phrasing of ἐν τῇ γῇ and Luke's ἐν σουδαρίῳ or "in a piece of cloth" in the parallel Parable of the Pounds (Luke 19:11–27), Davies argues that the appearance of the latter Lukan phrase should be seen as an indication of the "creeping in of a Latinism" and therefore contends that Matthew's version is most likely the more authentic since it "would fit the context admirably."[69] As to how this more authentic tradition relates to Jesus' perspective on Israel's territoriality the best that Davies can manage is a series of rhetorical and hypothetical questions all of which point in the direction of Jesus indicating that analogous to the selfish servant squandering his talent by foolishly burying it in the ground, so too was Israel squandering the gift of God's love and grace by confining it to the land. For as he suggestively asks, "May Jesus have been concerned not only to point out that the pious Jews, who were seeking personal security in a meticulous observance of the Law, were denying the knowledge of God entrusted to them not only to simple people, publicans and sinners within the land, but also to Gentiles and people 'outside the land'?"[70] That said, Davies still hedges his bets and admits that the phrase may not be related to Israel's territoriality at all but simply to the Pharisaic practice and Palestinian custom of burying money in the ground.

Jesus' Beatitude of the Meek Inheriting the Land (Matt 5:5)

Davies warns against putting too much stock in this saying for two reasons. First, and perhaps foremost, he seriously and repeatedly questions whether it can be authentically attributed to the historical Jesus.[71] As evidence against

---

69. Ibid., 358.

70. Ibid., 358–59.

71. In the span of less than two pages Davies reiterates his assertion against authenticity no less than three times with one of the most forceful coming at the very end of his exegesis of Matt 5:5 and thus acting as a sort of definitive coda lest the two previous

its authenticity, Davies offers the following arguments: (1) the diminishment of *"peculiarity"* (read dissimilarity) of Jesus' teaching if he *is directly* appropriating Ps 37: 11—"But the meek shall inherit the land and delight in abundant prosperity" (אֶרֶץ יִירְשׁוּ־ שָׁלוֹם: רֹב עַל־ וְהִתְעַנְּגוּ אֶרֶץ יִירְשׁוּ־ וַעֲנָוִים;); 2)) the location of the beatitude as second and not third in various extant manuscripts; (3) the upsetting of Matthew's penchant for sevenfold groupings if Matt 5:5 is included; (4) since the term for "poor" (πτωχοί) in Matt 5:3 and "meek" (πραεῖς) in Matt 5:5 are both derived from the same Hebrew verb עָנָה (to humble, be put down) Davies wonders why Jesus would say an additional beatitude about the "meek" in 5:5 if the "poor" had already been addressed in 5:3. Thus while no single one of these items is persuasive in and of itself for Davies, their cumulative force is nevertheless convincing and thus it "is at least dubious whether Jesus uttered 5:5."[72]

Second, even if we allow that this beatitude is authentic there is still good reason in Davies's mind not to ascribe it a territorial reading. This is because it "is the Kingdom of God that transcends geography as Jesus proclaimed it, not the geographically concentrated 'promise' of the Old Testament that Matt. 5:5 is concerned with." In order to recognize this, however, Davies maintains that it is "necessary to divorce Matt. 5:5 from its meaning in Ps. 37:11."[73] Grounds for doing so are found in the fact that the "'inheritance' of

---

mentions went unheeded.

72. Ibid., 361. Despite Davies's insistent skepticism there is actually good reason to believe that Matt 5:5 is authentic. Along those lines it is therefore important to bear in mind what Meier has said in *A Marginal Jew* regarding how to adjudicate the authenticity of Matthew's special beatitudes—i.e., 5:5, 7, 8, 9, and 10. Noting how their vocabulary is unique to the Matthean Gospel and even distinct to this particular section of Matthew, Meier concludes that "there are no strong reasons for attributing the special Matthean beatitudes to Matthew's redaction, while there are some indication of M tradtion" (335). Moreover a comparison of the structure between these special Matthean beatitudes and those of the Q tradition reveals some striking similarities, "[n]amely both the Q beatitudes and the M beatitudes began with a beatitude about the ⬛[set ayin]ă[set breve over a]nāwîm ('poor' or 'meek'), listed a number of beatitudes, and then concluded with a beatitude on persecution." Thus it is at least possible that "these Q and M lists represent but two surviving examples of various lists of beatitudes that circulated in the early church and were attributed to Jesus" (335). And while Meier agrees that none of this definitively "prove[s] that the historical Jesus did speak some or all of the M beatitudes" there is at least a plausible basis for claiming their authenticity inasmuch "they reinforce the basic point seen in the Q beatitudes: Jesus did look forward to a definitive salvation from God. The M beatitudes sees this salvation more in terms of God's faithful reward of the faithful members of his covenant people, but the final M beatitude on persecution maintains at least implicitly the tone of eschatological vindication of the unjustly oppressed—and so of eschatological reversal" (336).

73. Ibid., 362.

Christians in other parts of the New Testament is supra-terrestrial."[74] Hence the choice that lies before the exegete, Davies contends, is that we can either mistakenly follow Ps 37: 11 and "hold that Matt. 5:5 refers to inheriting, not the earth, but the land of Israel in a transformed world, in the Messianic age or the Age to Come," or we can take the more sensible and probable route and see "that for Matthew [and by implication, Jesus] 'inheriting the land' is synonymous with entering the Kingdom and that this Kingdom transcends all geographic dimensions and is spiritualized."[75] And again we can have a high degree of confidence in doing so since "we have previously recognized that in Judaism itself, as elsewhere in the New Testament, the notion of 'entering the land' has been spiritualized."[76]

Jesus' Appointment of the Twelve Apostles to Rule and Judge over Israel (Matt 19:28 || Luke 22:30)

Davies quickly dispatches with the Lukan passage by noting that it is nestled in a larger argument among the disciples as to who was to be the greatest in the coming kingdom of God (Luke 22:24–27). Hence the function of Luke 22:28–30 is to serve as a "corrective comment" whereby Jesus informs this unruly group of would be rulers "that the one criterion of greatness is service."[77] Thus Davies believes the larger context of this passage "makes it clear that the kingdom in which they are to [rule] cannot be compared with the kingdoms of this world" by which he means to say that the disciples are "to rule in a new kind of kingdom—in another dimension of existence."[78]

The Matthean passage, however, proves itself to be much more formidable since Davies acknowledges that Jesus' use of παλιγγενεσίᾳ to explain the "renewal of all things" may well describe a situation wherein "there would be a restored Israel with twelve tribes and twelve thrones[.]"[79] Even so, there is ample room for dismissal. For once again Davies claims that although there is nothing to rule out the authenticity of this saying *per se*, it is nevertheless wholly unlikely that it comes from the historical Jesus "in view

---

74. Ibid.

75. Ibid.

76. Ibid. Davies can only mean Paul since this is the only other New Testament source he has engaged with at length. Therefore, he is once again advising us that we should read Jesus' gospel pronouncements of the kingdom through the hermeneutical grid of what he believes to be Paul's non-territorial and Hellenized eschatology.

77. Ibid., 363.

78. Ibid.

79. Ibid.

of Mark 10:35ff."[80] "But even if it be regarded from Jesus himself," Davies continues, "what it asserts of the future is bare. There is no specific reference to the land on which the restored Israel is to dwell, although such is assumed."[81] What is more, although παλιγγενεσίᾳ "may have a geographical connotation in 19:28," it more frequently "evokes a cosmic renewal, so that in 19:28 also probably the restoration of the twelve tribes is understood not so much in terms of a restored land of Israel as of a renewed cosmos."[82]

Therefore, in light of reading these pivotal Gospel passages, Davies asserts that the only meaningful summation we can surmise from them is that "Jesus . . . paid little attention to the relationship between Yahweh, and Israel and the land."[83] However, he is not content to simply let the matter rest there. For the overarching conclusion of his study of Paul's and Jesus' views of the land inescapably pushes us towards is this:

> The person of a Jew, Jesus of Nazareth, who proclaimed the acceptable year of the Lord only to die accursed on a cross and so to pollute the land, and by that act and its consequences to shatter the geographic dimension of the religion of his fathers. Like everything else, the land also in the New Testament drives us to ponder the mystery of Jesus, the Christ, who by his cross and resurrection broke not only the bonds of death for early Christians but also the bonds of land . . . If it was the Hellenists and Paul who broke asunder the territorial chrysalis of Christianity, they did so in the name of Christ, to whom all space, like all time, was subordinated . . .[84]

---

80. Ibid., 365. It is unclear why Davies thinks the Markan version of this story undermines its authenticity. To be sure there are some noticeable departures from Matthew's version with one of the most significant being the mentioning of twelve thrones. However, the fact that James and John seek Jesus' permission to "sit, one at your right hand and one at your left, in your glory" (v. 37) in Mark still indicates that the disciples are interested in ruling over Israel (sitting presupposes there is somewhere to sit) and that this appointment is bound up with a restorational eschatology (in your glory). Moreover, Jesus' response in v. 40—"but to sit at my right hand or at my left is not mine to grant, but it is for those for whom it has been prepared"—does nothing to invalidate the idea that James and John as well as the other disciples will be sitting in judgment of Israel at the eschaton but only the notion that it is up to Jesus who will sit where. Hence, we suggest that rather than undermine its historicity Mark 10:35ff. actually bolsters the authenticity of the Matthean story since it appears to confirm the basic contours of Matthew's version.

81. Ibid.
82. Ibid.
83. Ibid.
84. Ibid., 375.

1.5 Marcus Borg: *Conflict, Holiness and Politics in the Teachings of Jesus*

Before delving into how Borg's own historical project interprets the territorial relationship between Jesus and the kingdom of God and how that interpretation comports with and differs from Davies's, it is first worth noting the extent to which the former's historical methodology is indebted to and inspired by the latter. Not surprisingly the ledger runs deep and Borg admits as much in an autobiographical essay when he states that it was only after taking a New Testament seminar with Davies during his first semester at Union Theological Seminary in the early 1960s that the historical "Jesus moved [to the] center stage" of his thinking.[85] More specifically, Borg credits Davies with disabusing him of "the popular image of Jesus as the divine savior who knew himself to be the Son of God and who offered up his life for the sins of the world" and instead imparting him with two formative interpretive convictions that have guided his historical reading of Jesus ever since, albeit in varying degrees. First, Borg posits that any historical retrieval of Jesus must come to terms with the fact that he "was an eschatological figure" who literally expected "the coming kingdom of God 'in power', the gathering of the elect and judgment" and that this expectation "was central, not peripheral, to shaping and animating Jesus' ministry and message."[86] Second, it must also acknowledge that Jesus' "central message was the imminent coming of the kingdom of God, understood eschatologically."[87]

One need not probe very deeply into *Conflict, Holiness and Politics* to see elements of both these convictions at work since they form the backbone of Borg's larger attempt to try and reconstruct the source and objective of Jesus' political aims and actions. For like Davies Borg is also similarly concerned that three major misconceptions about understanding eschatology in general and Jesus' appropriation of it in particular, have consistently thwarted efforts by New Testament scholars to accurately comprehend and explain the explicit political nature of his ministry.

The first misconception is the erroneous supposition that because Jesus did not explicitly align himself with the militarism of the Zealots or because his focus was supposedly "on eternal religious and moral principles quite divorced from the vagaries of the historically conditioned conflicts of his time," then his words and actions should therefore be considered devoid of

---

85. Borg, "Me & Jesus—the Journey Home."
86. Ibid.
87. Ibid.

any political content.[88] Such could be the case, Borg allows, if by 'political' we put forward the rather pinched and narrowly circumscribed idea that "Jesus did not seek a seat on the Sanhedrin or serve in the civil service or become involved in palace intrigues or guerilla warfare, all of which is correct."[89] But if one expands the definitional aperture of 'politics' to encompass all that falls within the broader "concern about the structure and purpose of a historical community," which Borg insists that it must do, then it surely cannot be the case that either Jesus or the kingdom were politically inert.

Quite the opposite, in fact, for there is ample reason in Borg's estimation for why it is not only plausible but indeed necessary to see Jesus as a forceful political actor. Firstly, while the conceptual bifurcation between what is 'political' and what is 'religious' may still enjoy a peculiar hermeneutic credibility within Western modernity, it is hardly appropriate or applicable to a proper contextual reading of Jesus' historical and cultural milieu. Indeed while those beholden to the artificial strictures this worldview foists may think it perfectly reasonable to suggest that "Jesus may have transcended the interrelationship of politics and religion," such a figure, Borg reminds us, "would virtually cease to be a first-century Jewish religious figure if he did."[90] Furthermore, not only would an apolitical Jesus be an implausible historical aberration, but he would also cease to remain, in a real and fundamental way, the Christ of Christian dogma insofar as "incarnation" means "precisely that God in Christ did become enmeshed in the circumstances of human life in a particular time and place, which need not (and perhaps cannot?) exclude the turbulent political questions of that time and place."[91]

A second means of depoliticizing Jesus that Borg identifies comes in the form of misreading his eschatological pronouncements about the kingdom of God. This has occurred mainly in one of two ways. Either one chooses to follow Johannes Weiss's and Albert Schweitzer's reading of Jesus in which case his pronouncement about the imminent coming of the kingdom are seen to render all "concern with the structures and historical fate of Israel" superfluous, or one can "use implications deriving from eschatology in the sense argued by Weiss to discredit those understandings of the teachings of Jesus which speak of politics[.]"[92] In either case the sense of timing these interpretations have precluded scholars from asking a whole host of important historical and political questions such as "[h]ow was Israel to

---

88. Borg, *Conflict, Holiness and Politics*, 22.
89. Ibid., 23.
90. Ibid.
91. Ibid., 24.
92. Ibid., 29.

live? What as to be its relationship to Rome? Or, if it was the purpose of Jesus to create a new community, what was to be its relationship to Israel?"[93] Yet once one comes to see that Jesus' eschatological pronouncements about the kingdom of God stem from and mirror the same social motivations that animated Israel's prophets and their concerns "about the historical present future of Israel,"[94] then it becomes clear that Jesus saw and spoke of a kingdom as "a decisive act of God in history, even though it may have some continuity with the past and does not obviate a historical future."[95]

Finally, Borg addresses the existentialist reading of Jesus put forward most (in)famously by Rudolph Bultmann's demythologizing hermeneutic and notes that while such an interpretation of the kingdom is not illegitimate *per se* since it does help "account for the element of crisis and the urgency of decision"[96] in Jesus' kingdom teachings, it is nevertheless problematic when it attributes "the ahistorical and individualistic characteristics of existentialism to Jesus."[97] Such an attribution not only "dehistoricizes the New Testament in general" but also "Jesus in particular."[98] This is because, as Borg states, "the ministry of Jesus did not consist of articulating timeless moral principles or religious doctrines intended for generations yet unborn, but brought a decisive crisis to those who heard him, i.e. Israel."[99] In particular, Jesus' focus and teachings on the kingdom of God "refer to impending historical events and which pertains to the structures and institutions of Judaism."[100] Thus as Borg finally perorates, "[a]ny understanding of Jesus' mission and teaching," which fails to see that it was concerned primarily with the crisis and urgency surrounding "the structures and historical destiny of the people of God" cannot ultimately do justice either to properly understanding that crisis and urgency or to Jesus himself.[101]

If then both Jesus and his eschatology are irreducibly political, and both are addressing a particular historical crisis within the national life of Israel, the question then becomes what was that crisis? It is in responding to this question that we begin to see Borg's understanding of Jesus' mission part ways with Davies's. For up until this point, both have been in essential

---

93. Ibid., 27.
94. Ibid., 30.
95. Ibid., 27.
96. Ibid., 32.
97. Ibid., 31.
98. Ibid., 31–32.
99. Ibid., 32.
100. Ibid.
101. Ibid.

agreement that Jesus' mission was directed toward the pivotal question of how the nation of Israel was to be restored in the midst of Roman occupation and subjugation. However, as seen above, whereas Davies held that Jesus' intentions were political but not explicitly national insofar as they focused exclusively on restoring the *people* but not the actual territorial kingdom of Israel, Borg by contrast contends that it is only by placing Jesus within the larger historical and social matrix of Jewish national resistance to Rome, and in particular the post-exilic quest for national holiness, that we are able to most fruitfully reconstruct and understand Jesus' politics. For as he states, "[d]uring the postexilic period, the content of the *imitatio dei*, the paradigm in conformity with which [Israel's] national community developed, was *holiness*, understood as separation from everything impure."[102] Thus "the political program of postexilic Judaism," of which Jesus was fully enmeshed, "was the permeation of national life by holiness, a program undergirded by the twin institutions of Torah and Temple."[103]

To see how this is so, Borg studiously analyzes and compares how two of Jesus' more notable contemporaries—the Essenes and the Pharisees—envisioned and put into practice their own respective campaigns for restoring Israel's national holiness. With respect to the former Borg notes that Essenic program was premised on separation from the broader society such that they lived "in isolated self-sufficient communes" while fastidiously avoiding "contact with the impurity of the *amme ha aretz* and Gentiles."[104] Thus while the Essenes's posture of withdrawal may not have been as overtly a confrontational and pugnacious approach than that taken by either the Pharisees or Zealots, they nevertheless still "harbored the expectation that Rome would soon be expelled from the land in the final apocalyptic battle between the children of light and the children of darkness."[105]

The Pharisees' program, by comparison, also aimed at separation but it was "a separation *within* society" and they did so by eating "unconsecrated food as if they were Temple priests" and also by practicing meticulous tithing, both of which were intended to "insulate and isolate Israel from practices of the heathen" and "to protect it against assimilation and corruption."[106] In this way then, the Pharisees "did not intend to be a party within Israel but intended to be Israel itself."[107]

102. Ibid., 66.
103. Ibid., 68.
104. Ibid., 72.
105. Ibid.
106. Ibid., 73–74.
107. Ibid., 74.

Despite these differences in tactics, however, Borg is nevertheless insistent that both the Essenes and the Pharisees were still driven by the same strategic goal of achieving national holiness. Furthermore, this quest was inextricably bound with a desire to retake and purify Israel's land, and thus expunge of any corruptive source(s) that might profane it. The unsavory history of the Roman occupation of Jewish Palestine during the first century only underscored the urgency of this commitment since everywhere the Essenes and Pharisees looked, they observed the Romans wantonly desecrating their most cherished and sacred of national institutions, whether it was Caligula trying to erect a statue of himself within the Temple precincts around 40 CE or the refusal of the Romans to pay a tithe. Thus as Borg states this constant threat to *torah* must have meant that the yearning to be free from Roman rule would have been "persistent" among all first-century Jews.[108]

Yet Borg is also quick to point out that this quest for holiness not only precipitated national animus towards the Romans, but also fomented internal cleavages within "Jewish society itself." For although the Essenes, Pharisees and other Jewish holiness parties may have all coalesced around the unifying goal of purifying Israel from Roman rule and occupation, each nevertheless "had its own program for the internal reform of Judaism" that was commensurate with that task.[109] Consequently each group "in effect, generated its own antithesis" whereby even fellow Jews who subscribed to a different notion of what it meant to be 'true Israel' were castigated by their co-nationals as either 'sons of darkness' or as traitorous collaborators.[110] Paradoxically then, the shared commitment to national holiness actually had the divisive effect of creating "greater 'intracultural differentiation'" and "increasing division within Jewish society" over competing "visions of what Israel should be."[111]

It was therefore within this seething cauldron of intense internal rivalry and the rising tide of rebellious sentiment against Rome that Jesus' own program for holiness and national restoration emerged and took shape. Therefore as Borg states "the key to understanding the politics of Jesus cannot be examined simply by asking about his attitude toward Rome, but must [also] be treated by inquiring about his stance vis-à-vis the quest of holiness."[112]

---

108. Ibid., 79.
109. Ibid., 83.
110. Ibid., 84.
111. Ibid., 83.
112. Ibid., 86.

How did Jesus' own quest for national holiness compare and contrast with those of the Essenes, Pharisees and Zealots? According to Borg the answer lies with an understanding of how Jesus radically replaced and redefined Israel's tradition of holiness. For in contrast to other Jewish holiness parties, whose own conceptions of holiness were steeped in notions of separation, Jesus instead insisted that a quest for national renewal and holiness should be "subordinated to a concern over justice, compassion, and faithfulness."[113] Evidence for reorienting holiness's *telos* in this manner is clearly manifested, Borg believes, in a variety of Gospel accounts including Jesus' subversive practice of sharing table fellowship with Jewish tax collectors and the ritually impure, his decision to heal on the Sabbath, and perhaps most tellingly, in his public demonstration against the Temple.

Borg's interpretation of the Temple incident is worth singling out for further discussion not only because of the way it nicely encapsulates his own thinking about the decisive shift that occurred in Jesus' views about holiness, but also, as will be seen in our discussion of E. P. Sanders below, because of the formative influence it has had on subsequent New Testament scholars.

According to Borg, the full import of Jesus' indictment of the Temple cannot be properly interpreted or appreciated apart from recognizing just how much the Temple came to symbolize and propel the early Jewish quest for holiness. For as he states, "the place of God's presence, a sign of Israel's election, and the sole locus of sacrifice where atonement was made for sins and impurity, it was an institution substantive to the definition and existence of Israel."[114] Thus an affront of the Temple would have been seen by most of Jesus' contemporaries as tantamount to a treasonous assault on the prevailing mood of what it meant to be Israel itself.

With that in mind Borg proceeds to tease out the full political freight of the phrases "den of robbers" and "a house of prayer for all nations" in Mark 11:15–19. In regards to the former phrase Borg argues that in accordance with its predominant usage and meaning in the LXX, Apocrypha, Josephus as well as the New Testament as a whole, the Greek word for "robber"—λῃστής—"cannot refer to economic dishonesty on the part of the merchants, or to the inappropriateness of commercial activity in the Temple precincts" but instead "is more appropriately translated as 'violent ones,' or 'brigands.'"[115] That this is the proper translation of λῃστής and what Jesus implied by that word is further confirmed by the fact that the exact

---

113. Ibid., 116.
114. Ibid., 174.
115. Ibid., 185.

phrase "den of robbers" comes from Jer 7:11 wherein the Hebrew word for "robbers"—פָּרִצִים—"refers to those [Jews] who blissfully trusted that the Temple provided security against Babylon despite their violation of the covenant."[116] Thus both the political connotation of λῃστής itself as well as Jesus' intertextual reference to Jer 7 makes it clear that Jesus' description of the Temple as a "den of robbers" can "be understood in either a specific or general sense." If specifically, "the reference might be to the Temple as the scene of actual military violence during the life of Jesus and/or the warning notice [in the outer court of the Temple] which promised a violent death to any Gentile who crossed into forbidden territory."[117] If generally, then just as the פָּרִצִים "in 586 BCE trusted the Temple to guarantee their impunity vis-à-vis Babylon" then so also "for many elements in first-century Judaism the Temple was both a guarantor of security and a focal point of liberation hopes."[118] In either case, Jesus' message was straightforward and cutting: the Temple had been wrongfully co-opted into the holy iconography of separatism such that devotion to it was inextricable from a willingness to commit revolutionary violence against the Romans.

This then makes Jesus' use of the phrase a 'house of prayer for all the nations' all the more poignant and evocative in Borg eyes for as he notes Jesus is quoting Isa 56:7, which suggest that he, like Isaiah, anticipated and envisioned a time when the Gentiles "would have the same privileges as Israel."[119] What is more the bite of these phrases becomes all the more sharp when one locates them within the broader narrative context of their being uttered on the cusp of celebrating the Passover, and after Jesus' triumphant entry into Jerusalem while riding an ass, which was a direct fulfillment of the messianic vision of Zech 9:9 in which "the coming king mounted on the foal of an ass was to be a king of peace who would banish the war horse and the warrior's bow from Jerusalem and speak peace to the nation[.]"[120] Thus when viewed against this larger backdrop, it is obvious to Borg that both Jesus' words and actions against the Temple were nothing short of a full scale "political demonstration" whose chief objective was to "appeal to the nation to abandon the quest for holiness and follow a different politico-religious policy[.]" Moreover, they also served to warn

---

116. Ibid.
117. Ibid., 186.
118. Ibid.
119. Ibid., 187.
120. Ibid., 188.

his fellow Jews that if they failed to heed his warning and adopt his program of inclusive compassion, then as was the case during the time of Jeremiah, "the consequence of uncritical trust in the Temple would be [its] destruction" by the Romans.[121]

Therefore what this episode and all the other accounts of conflict between Jesus and the Pharisees and Romans in the Gospels point towards, Borg contends, are two major conclusions about his political aspirations. First, they show that Jesus' concern was not just with renewing a particular subsection of Israel, that is, its *people*, but the nation as a whole, including its leading national institutions of Torah and Temple. That this is so, Borg claims, is further established by the fact that Jesus' statement about directing his mission to the "lost sheep of the house of Israel" (Matt 10:6) is not a partitive genitive but instead an explanatory genitive that means then that "the sayings of crisis and the criticisms directed against his contemporaries point to a mission of all of Israel, not simply to a part."[122]

Moreover, these narratives also demonstrate that Jesus believed Israel's central national vocation as it pertained to embodying holiness was not to insulate, separate and protect itself, but rather was to become "a compassionate community" that was to be "[an] active dynamic power that overcame uncleanness."[123] As such he was not only calling upon his fellow Jews to repent and display compassion toward those internally marginalized groups within Israel, but even more radically, to embrace Gentile outsiders as well, including and especially Israel's arch enemies, the Romans—an exhortation Borg believes is clearly the subtext of Jesus' command to "love your enemies" in Matt 5:43–44 || Luke 6:27.

That Jesus wanted to include the Romans and all other Gentiles within Israel's compassionate orbit can be verified, Borg believes, in two ways. First, Borg convincingly explains that both Matthew and Luke's use of ἐχθροὺς for "enemies" in their respective accounts of Jesus' Sermon on the Mount/Plain denote "both personal *and* national enemies."[124] Consequently, it cannot be the case, as Richard Horsley has tried to argue, that Jesus is simply referring here to quelling a situation of interpersonal conflict amongst fellow Jewish peasants. Instead what Jesus was announcing was nothing short of a "public policy at a particular time in history toward a particular state," which entailed "eschew[ing] acts of terrorism and revenge."[125] Furthermore, when

---

121. Ibid., 189.
122. Ibid., 109.
123. Ibid.,148.
124. Ibid., 143; emphasis added.
125. Ibid., 244.

one couples this irenic and conciliatory exhortation with Jesus' additional commands to be "peacemakers" (εἰρηνοποιοί) in Matt 5:9 and his statement that God showers rain upon both the just and unjust in Matt 5:45 it becomes obvious that

> All these traditions were directly pertinent to one of the central issues facing Israel and the renewal movements operating within it. These traditions flow out of compassion understood in an inclusive sense. Contrary to the "holiness code" which undergirded resistance, the "compassion code" urged love of enemies and the way of peace. Thus the compassion code strikes a new but complementary note. Whereas the other substitutions of compassion for holiness were concerned primarily with shaping the internal corporate life of Israel in the direction of greater inclusiveness, this material points specifically to the consequences of the shift of paradigms for Israel's relationship to Rome.[126]

Second, Jesus' redefinition of holiness and its expansion of compassion also helps illuminate why it would have been so threatening to both Roman and fellow Jew alike. For while a commitment to enemy love in particular and greater compassion in general were certainly not on the same order of calling for a violent revolution against Rome, they were nonetheless no less audacious or subversive in their political intent insofar as they were both based "on the conviction that in the political affairs of the world the judging activity of God was at work."[127] Hence, by calling his fellow Jews to steer clear of hatred for the Romans, Jesus was in no way offering "a positive evaluation of Roman imperial order" but instead was showing that he was intensely "concerned about the institutions and historical dynamic of Israel" and thus speaking to "the issue of resistance to Rome."[128]

Conversely, Jesus' call to compassion would have been similarly disruptive to the separatist elements of Jewish national consciousness as well since it "called for a departure from the established structures which had shaped and nurtured the existence of those who heard Jesus to a new understanding of Israel as a community of compassion, and to face a future that was largely unknown, with only the promise that ultimately God would vindicate them."[129] Of course, as Borg rightly acknowledges, adopting such a program ran its fair share of significant risks not the least of which was that the "Torah and Temple *as institutions preservative of Israel's cohesive-*

126. Ibid., 145.
127. Ibid., 246.
128. Ibid., 245, 246.
129. Ibid., 246.

ness would largely disappear if they were subordinated to the paradigm of compassion." Hence what seemed threatened by Jesus' call to show greater compassion was nothing less than "national identity and national survival itself."[130] However, Borg hastens to add that Jesus' deconstruction and redefinition of holiness need not nor should it indicate that he somehow jettisoned his Jewish identity or forsook a fealty to *torah*. Rather, it shows that Jesus' "disputes with his opponents concerned the *interpretation* of the *torah*, not the validity of the Torah itself."[131] Accordingly, Jesus' "substitution of compassion for holiness need not have meant the dissolution of Israel, even though it burst the limitations of holiness as a corporate ideal."[132]

At this point we have traced the main contours of Borg's historical reconstruction of Jesus' political program for Israel's restoration. At the risk of being redundant, the following paragraph sums up Borg's position well:

> Jesus' conflict with the Pharisees centered upon the adequacy of the quest for holiness as a program for Israel's national life. His choice of terrain upon which to do battle concerned those subjects (table fellowship, sabbath, Temple) important to Israel's survival and integral to its quest for holiness. Much of his teaching propagated an alternative paradigm with identifiable political consequences as a course for Israel. No less prominent were his action in the Temple as an indictment of Israel's course of separatist resistance, his undercutting of the Temple ideology as a pillar of resistance, and his portrayal of the future as one filled with Roman threat. All of this provides evidence that Jesus' ministry concerned what it meant to be Israel in the setting of Israel's conflicts with Rome.[133]

On its face at least, there is nothing within this proposal that immediately forestalls the possibility of Jesus envisioning a territorial restoration of Israel. In fact, it is generally congenial to such a reading given that Borg consistently affirms that Jesus is directly concerned with preserving and sustaining Israel as a *nation*, even if he also at the same time acknowledges that Jesus subscribed to a brand of Jewish nationalism that differed radically from what most of his contemporaries had come to expect and believe.

Such might very well be the case were it not, however, for the stubborn and curious fact that what is conspicuously absent from both this summary as well as its more detailed exposition above is any explicit reference by Borg

---

130 Ibid.
131 Ibid., 150.
132. Ibid., 151.
133. Ibid., 239.

to Jesus' repeated invocation of the kingdom of God. In fact notwithstanding his earlier assertions that the kingdom of God must occupy a central place in any historical reconstruction of Jesus, we must wade over 250 pages into *Conflict, Holiness, and Politics* before we finally find Borg addressing the subject at any sustained length. Ironically, the reason this is so is because despite his earlier warnings about not misreading the kingdom's eschatological nature as being divorced from concrete political realities, the kingdom of God does not in Borg's judgment provide a good starting point for a study of the teachings and intention of the historical Jesus since he believes it is extraordinarily difficult to pin down with any reasonable degree of certainty whether Jesus thought the kingdom to be already present and therefore active, or instead whether it was to arrive in the future and therefore needed to be awaited.[134]

Accordingly rather than try to sort through and make sense of these apparent interminable temporal aporias, Borg thinks it best to begin with other points of interpretation for the kingdom of God since "it is a sound principle of interpretation to begin with what is clearest and then move to that which is more opaque[.]"[135] Among those points he believes offer a firmer interpretive footing are the following: (1) "Jesus as a Spirit person initiated a renewal movement in the midst of a profound socio-religious crisis within Judaism, calling his people to the imitation of God's compassion as a program for life within the community and for their relationship to those outside of the community"; (2) "As a prophet, [Jesus] warned [his fellow Jews] of the consequences of following their present course"; and (3) "As a sage, he taught that the way to a transformed heart, to purify heart, was the path of death and rebirth."[136] Consequently, the question then becomes whether there is "an understanding of the Kingdom of God that is compatible with this overall picture."[137]

---

134. One is baffled by how it is that Borg can make this kind of argument when he earlier chastised other New Testament scholars for failing to recognize that a proper understanding of eschatology is contingent upon the recognition that it can "refer to an act of God of history, whereby something new enters and decisively changes history, even though it may have continuity with the past and does not obviate a historical future" (ibid., 29–30). In other words how can Borg see Jesus' announcement of the kingdom of God as simultaneously possessing both a present and future orientation without this diminishing the political nature of his mission in the slightest yet suddenly pivot and then assert that kingdom's temporal "ambiguity" makes it an untrustworthy dock from which to launch the ship of historical investigation into Jesus?

135. Borg, *Conflict, Holiness and Politics*, 258.

136. Ibid.

137. Ibid.

There is, Borg maintains, once we follow Norman Perrin's assertion that the kingdom of God "is a symbol in the teachings of Jesus and not a concept," by which Borg means to say that the "phrase points to something beyond itself[.]"[138] Of course this then begs the question to what larger reality does the kingdom point us toward, to which Borg responds that "we must pay careful attention to the linguistic home of the symbol 'Kingdom of God' in the proclamations of Jesus and in particular 'the cultural-religious traditions in which Jesus stood, and the specific contexts in which, according to the Gospels, he used the phrase."[139]

Regarding Jesus' cultural-religious heritage, Borg observes that although the specific phrase "Kingdom of God" is relatively uncommon in the Hebrew Bible, its "correlative notions of God's kingship and Kingdom are widespread" and largely associated with Israel's "myth of salvation history," which "affirms that visible reality has its origin, sustenance, and destiny . . . in God" and that "God as king created all that is, restores it yearly in the annual cycle of nature, and will one day effect a final restoration."[140] Borg calls this Israel's version of the "classic cosmogonic-eschatological myth" and notes that it was seen as operating not only in the realm of nature "but also in [Israel's] history, 'a history that was destined to eventuate in the everlasting Kingdom of God, marked by righteousness, justice and peace."

Beginning with the emergence of apocalyptic thought and literature in the late postexilic period, however, Borg contends that this myth underwent a noticeable modification wherein apocalyptic writings began to exacerbate the distinction between the realms of nature and history into an antithesis.

---

138 Ibid. Borg's linguistic distinction between the kingdom of God being a "symbol" rather than a "concept" is borrowed directly from Perrin's own work in his formative *Jesus and the Language of the Kingdom*, in which he explains that Jesus' description of the kingdom of God conforms more to the definition of a "*tensive* symbol" rather than a "*steno*-symbol" since the meaning of the kingdom was polyvalent (i.e., it could simultaneously refer to not only a kingdom but also God acting as a king as well as God being declared king) and not confined to any single interpretation (29–33). While there is certainly much to commend to Perrin's argument, there are nevertheless a variety of factors, as Moore has recently cogently outlined in her volume *Moving beyond Symbol and Myth*, which make it problematic. In regard to this last criticism, Moore offers a point about what makes Jesus' understanding of the kingdom of God distinct, which not only highlights a major shortcoming of Perrin's and Borg's mythical-symbolic interpretations, but also further confirms the thesis of this study. For as she writes, "if Christian Origins scholars are seeking a distinctive element to the historical Jesus' interpretation of the 'God is king' metaphor, it is in his preference for 'kingdom' over other forms of expression. This distinctive interpretive spin implies that Jesus *has shifted focus from the type of relationship that exists between the divine king and his subjects to the 'place' in which this relationship occurs*" (284–85; emphasis added).

139. Ibid., 259.

140. Borg, *Conflict, Holiness and Politics*, 259.

As a result the "present age was seen as the realm of evil, devoid of the divine" whereas the "dawning of the new world—the Kingdom of God—necessitated the end of the old, the purgation of all evil through judgments and destruction, and re-creation."[141] Consequently, Borg believes that "for much apocalyptic thought, the other realm [i.e. the kingdom of God] and this realm were linked at the beginning and end of history, but not *within* history (emphasis added)." Nevertheless, he still maintains that "apocalyptic expression continued to . . . affir[m] that the two realms were not *ultimately* separated, and that the destiny of creation was the Kingdom of God."[142]

With this historical background in place Borg next addresses Jesus' own specific appropriation of the kingdom of God and states that these sayings can be roughly grouped together into one of three main categories: "in connection with exorcisms, as something which could be entered or possessed, and in passages which refer to the future."[143] Regarding the first group Borg cites the story of Jesus healing the blind-mute demoniac in Matt 12:28 || Luke 11:20 as being especially illuminative since it explicitly links Jesus' performance of an exorcism and his proclamation of the kingdom of God together. However, he also notes that another connection of signal importance this passage supplies and that often gets glossed over is how it "joins Jesus' use of [the] Kingdom of God to the religious experience of a Spirit person," which has, in Borg's view, the following immediate implication:

> "Kingdom of God" here is Jesus' designation or "name" for the primordial beneficent power of the other realm, an energy which can become active in ordinary reality and which flows through him in his exorcisms. Expressed in language drawn from the religious history of Judaism, Jesus' exorcisms were the Kingdom (or kingship) of God manifested in the world of history. Expressed in language drawn from the intellectual tradition of the history of religions, his exorcisms were the "power of the holy" entering the profane world.[144]

Consequently by inviting his listeners to enter the Kingdom of God, Borg believes Jesus was not calling them to participate in a historical reality within time and space, i.e. territorial Israel, but instead, like the "Jewish mystic" Ezekiel, was encouraging them "to enter the place of God's presence,

---

141. Ibid., 260.
142. Ibid.
143. Ibid.
144. Ibid., 261.

the realm outside of time and history, the 'time' before and beyond time."[145] More precisely, he was calling people "to the end of the world of ordinary experience, as well as the end of the world as one's center and security."[146]

This understanding that the kingdom of God is not anchored to any one specific time and place, let alone historical Israel, but is instead "a symbol pointing to an experiential reality known in Jesus' subjectivity" in turn provides a hermeneutical clue for how Borg thinks we should understand the large number of Jesus' sayings that speak of entering, being in, or possessing the Kingdom of God.[147] For although these sayings do imply some spatial meaning in that Jesus says that one may be in it or outside of it, they are nevertheless "best understood," Borg claims, in one or both of two ways: either we can see the kingdom as referring "to the mystical experience of God, the return to the paradisal experience of life in the presence of God, the experience of communion with God as *Abba*," or as "entering [into] a community" albeit "not to an institutional community but to a spiritual community, i.e., a community of those who know 'spirit,' who know the embracing compassion of God in their own experience."[148]

Finally Borg addresses Jesus' kingdom sayings that appear to speak of a coming future reality and notes that the assumption that "language employing future imagery necessarily implies temporal futurity is unwarranted."[149] As evidence contradicting this mistaken assumption, Borg refers to the language of the Lord's prayer in Matt 6:9–13 ǁ Luke 11:1–4 and its request that 'thy kingdom come' and states that although the "petition *may* refer to a temporally future consummation visible in the external world," it could just as easily be "a petition for the *internal* experience of entering God's presence, of having God's presence come upon one (emphasis added)."[150] He also examines the narrative of Jesus appointing the twelve disciples to rule over Israel in Matt 19:28 ǁ Luke 22:29–30 and strikes a chord nearly identical to Davies above when he states that even if some early Christians interpreted these proclamations to mean that "the other realm would one day be externalized in the visible created world, and that Jesus would be the lord of that Kingdom," Jesus' focus was nevertheless clearly elsewhere in that "he emphasized a path of transformation *for the individual* by means of which entry into the Kingdom of God could be experienced, and a path

---

145. Ibid., 262.
146. Ibid., 263.
147. Ibid.
148. Ibid., 264–65.
149. Ibid., 265–66.
150. Ibid., 266.

of transformation for the people of God, whose collective historical life was to embody compassion (emphasis added)."[151] Furthermore it is Borg's belief that it is only by existing outside the actual warp and woof of history, and therefore presumably outside the land of Israel as well, that the kingdom of God becomes the inclusive and reconciliatory locus between Jew and Gentile. For as he explains in relation to Jesus' eschatological announcement that "many will come from east and west to sit at table with Abraham, Isaac and Jacob in the Kingdom of God" (Matt 8:11-12 || Luke 13:28-29), "If instead we understand Kingdom as a symbol for the experience of God in the other realm which is outside of time, then this passage affirms that the experience is accessible to all, and that the realm entered in that experience transcends the polarity of the living and the dead as well as the polarity of Jew and Gentile."[152]

In sum, then, what all of these appropriations of the kingdom of God by Jesus ultimately reveals is that

> Jesus used the phrase "Kingdom of God" within the framework of what we might call an eschatological mysticism—a mysticism which used language associated with the end of the world. Or we might call it a mystical eschatology—an eschatology in which the new age was the other realm of mystical communion. Within that framework, Kingdom of God symbolized the experience of God, an experience known by Jesus himself. The Kingdom of God as the experience of God accounts for Jesus' teaching concerning the way of transformation and the course for Israel. Out of that experience flowed an awareness of a way other than the normative ways of the other renewal movements, one open to the outcasts and not dependent on holiness, but on self-emptying and dying to self and the world.[153]

It is difficult to read this statement in light of all that has preceded it and not be struck by the same kind of lingering question as that posed by N. T. Wright: "What happened to the solid rejection of existentialism

---

151. Ibid., 268. It is incredible how in interpreting this logion and its explicit reference to restoring the twelve tribes of Israel, Borg could be almost completely oblivious to its nationalist and territorial overtones, especially in light of how he has consistently and emphatically stated that Jesus political mission was focused on the renewal and restoration of Israel's national institutions. This leads one to wonder why, if Jesus primarily saw the kingdom as the mystical in-breaking of an a-historical primordial reality, would he go to the trouble of couching it in concrete language of tribes and thrones?

152. Ibid.

153. Ibid., 269-70.

with which [Borg's] book opened?"[154] For not only does Borg's account of the kingdom of God as a sort of inner subjective trans-historical mysticism run afoul of the very same kind of mistaken eschatological dualism he so persuasively inveighs against in dismissing all those non-political interpretations of Jesus' mission, but it also inexplicably omits, as Wright also perceptively notices, "precisely that Israel-dimension which makes the rest of his book so striking."[155] As a result, Borg's interpretation of the kingdom and therefore of Jesus cannot help but effectively rule out the possibility of Israel's territorial restoration since such a restoration is inconceivable apart from it occurring within the context of an actual historical and institutional community, that is, Israel. In the end then, despite Borg's earlier emphasis that we see Jesus' political program of inclusive compassion as aimed at nothing less than the *national* renewal of Israel, there is little within his accompanying discussion of the kingdom of God to bear that claim out, nor for that matter distinguish it from Davies' thesis that Jesus ultimately relocated the kingdom to the *people* of Israel. In fact, one could even suggest that Davies' personalist interpretation of the kingdom actually offers a more hospitable territorial reading of the kingdom than does Borg's in as much as he concedes that Jesus sought to 'Christify' all physical and historical spaces, and not just the land of Israel itself. Borg's mystical and individualist interpretation of the kingdom, by contrast, abjures even this attenuated possibility and thus leaves us with a somewhat *schizoid* Jesus who works tirelessly for and eagerly anticipates Israel's national restoration only to have that restoration be finally transmogrified into an ethereal and a-territorial experience of a-historical individualism.

1.6 N. T. Wright: *Jesus and the Victory of God*

My analysis of Wright's *Jesus and the Victory of God* will be considerably shorter than those supplied thus far but hopefully no less informative. It is important to note, however, that this abridgement is intended neither as a slight against Wright's far-reaching influence, nor for that matter is it meant in any way to diminish the scope of this voluble work. On the contrary even the shortest of précis could never fully suppress what even his fiercest critics have repeatedly conceded: that few can equal Wright's stature for the manifold ways he has fundamentally re-oriented and improved (mostly)

---

154. Wright, "Foreword to the New Edition," in Borg, *Conflict, Holiness and Politics*, xx.

155. Ibid., xxi.

perceptions about the historical Jesus.[156] And by weighing in at a hefty and densely packed 662 pages, the only thing that is even remotely brief about *Jesus and the Victory of God* is its title.

Instead the real reason for this work's shortened analysis is because many of the main theses it sets forth—that is, seeing Jesus as a political actor; as working within the framework of Jewish restoration eschatology; as proclaiming a kingdom that is intimately bound to Israel's sense of national identity and mission—are ones we have already encountered and thus are well versed.

That said, there are nevertheless enough distinctions with Wright's reiteration of these common themes to warrant further scrutiny. A case in point is his description of Jesus as a political actor. Echoing Davies's and Borg's points above, Wright agrees that it is simply inconceivable to ever credibly sustain an apolitical interpretation of Jesus given the sheer volume of contradictory evidence to be found both within his historical context and the Gospels. In particular, he points to (among other things) the tumultuous and revolutionary atmosphere of first-century Jewish Palestine,[157] the numerous convergences between Jesus' career and Israel's traditions of "oracular" and "leadership" prophecy,[158] his announcement of the kingdom of God,[159] the unmistakable political subtext of his parables and teachings,[160] and his numerous conflicts with the Pharisees and Romans,[161] as not only being confirmatory of a concrete political mission and praxis, but as also lending further credence to Borg's additional claim that Jesus' chief political aim was to directly confront and challenge Israel's bellicose sense of national entitlement. For as he explains,

> It is not that Jesus' agenda was not about "politics." That would be a half-truth, and wrong at that. It is that Jesus in his teaching, and his challenge to Israel, aimed precisely at telling Israel to repent of—her militaristic nationalism. Her aspirations for national liberation from Rome, to be won through a great actual battle, were themselves the tell-tale symptom of her basic disease, and had to be rooted out. Jesus was offering a different way to liberation, a way which affirmed the humanness of the

---

156. See, for example, the set of essays assembled in Newman's edited volume *Jesus and the Restoration of Israel: A Critical Assessment of N. T. Wright's Jesus and the Victory of God*.

157. Wright, *Jesus and the Victory of God*, 150–60.

158. Ibid., 162–74.

159. Ibid., 221, 242–44.

160. Ibid., 174–82, 279–96.

161. Ibid., 390, 547.

national enemy *as well as* the destiny of Israel, and hence also affirmed the destiny of Israel as the bringer of light to the world, not as the one who would crush the world with military zeal.[162]

However, even while heartily endorsing the main contours of Borg's political reading of Jesus, Wright is nevertheless certain that subscription to such an interpretation precludes the possibility of whittling down his kingdom proclamations into a mystical expression of an a-historical and a-spatial kind of existentialism.[163] Rather, he agrees with Sanders that for reasons of historical, contextual and theological continuity, Jesus' kingdom teachings must have had the national restoration of historical Israel firmly in view, and in particular Wright contends that Jesus' parable of the Prodigal Son (Luke 15:11–32) paradigmatically encapsulates his belief that he "aimed . . . to reconstitute Israel around himself, as the true return-from-exile people; to achieve the victory of Israel's god over the evil that enslaved his people; and, somehow, to bring about the greatest hope of all, the victorious return of YHWH to Zion."[164]

At the same time though, Wright cannot abide by Sanders's contentions that Jesus preached a non-national form of repentance and conjoined such a call to an apolitical vision of the kingdom of God. He finds the former proposition untenable on account of the fact that a Jewish conception of repentance as understood all the way back to the prophetic tradition into the first century CE had always focused on what Israel as a nation must do before YHWH would return it from the exile and restore it to the land.[165] Accordingly, as he states, "'[r]epentance' in Jesus' context, then, would have carried the connotations of 'what Israel must do if YHWH is to restore her fortunes at last.'"[166]

Furthermore, he also thinks it methodologically foolhardy to dismiss, as Sanders does, Jesus' pronouncements of a call to repentance as being editorial revisionism by the early Church. Not only does this dismissal ignore how these sayings conform to the pattern and form of national repentance as expressed by Amos, Jeremiah, and John the Baptist, but it also fails to see how Jesus' welcoming of sinners, his call to live by a different set of ethical principles and norms, of renewing one's heart, and the call to follow him nonviolently on the way to the cross all implicitly reveal "*a summons to*

---

162 Ibid., 450.
163. Ibid., 223.
164. Ibid., 473–74.
165. Ibid., 248.
166. Ibid., 249.

repentance."¹⁶⁷ Consequently, Wright thinks it fairly certain that Jesus "was acting as a prophet of Jewish restoration, speaking on behalf of Israel's god, summoning the nation, in view of impending judgment, to repent of nationalist violence, and offering to all those who did the promise that they would emerge as the vindicated people of Israel's god."¹⁶⁸

This point in turn casts serious doubt on the notion that Jesus envisioned an apolitical and "otherworldly" kingdom of God separate from a national restoration of Israel. For if Jesus' call to repent was not merely nationalist in tone but eschatological as well, and if we understand eschatology to mean, as Jesus did, "not the end of the world, but the rescue and renewal of Israel and hence of the world,"¹⁶⁹ then it is nearly impossible to avoid the conclusion that "Jesus' intention was to . . . reform Israel, not to found a different community altogether."¹⁷⁰ Thus as Wright sees it, the real question to be asked regarding Jesus is not whether he ever linked a national call to repentance with a political vision of the kingdom, or more precisely a restored Israel. Both Jesus' historical context and the Gospels make it clear that he did, albeit a national restoration that shunted the pernicious tendencies of ethnocentrism and militaristic violence and therefore brought with it "both the hope for the gentile world, and a dire warning for those who failed in their vocation to be the light of the world."¹⁷¹ The real question then becomes "whether or not one responded to this challenge."¹⁷²

Thus when Wright holds that Jesus "set his face against the central institutions and symbols of Israel" like the Temple and the Land, we should not interpret him to be saying that Jesus was admonishing his audience to repent from them. Rather, his aim "was to call Israel back to what he saw the true meaning of those traditions."¹⁷³

If Wright is correct on this point, and I believe there is plenty of evidence to suggest that he is, then we can see why he would find attaching a territorial component to Jesus' vision of the kingdom to be so problematic. For although the symbol of the land had been partially demoted behind the Temple in the Jewish hierarchy of national iconography by the Second Temple period, it nevertheless still remained a potent emblem of national

---

167. Ibid., 254.
168. Ibid., 253.
169. Ibid., 279–80.
170. Ibid., 275.
171. Ibid., 310.
172. Ibid., 258.
173. Ibid., 428.

pride and fervor, even if it was only an instrumental one.[174] Thus for Jesus to re-invoke expectations of a territorial reclamation under the mantle of restoration would be tantamount, in Wright's mind, to inviting the very same kind of ethnocentrism that had originally caused Israel to stray away from its Isaianic vocation in the first place. And so it was, according to Wright, that Jesus transmuted Israel's "expectation of the restored land" onto "restored human beings" instead.[175] For what Jesus did, Wright continues, in a manner highly reminiscent of Davies above, was offer

> people "inheritance," and greater possessions than they would have abandoned; but he regularly construed this in terms of human lives and human communities that were being renewed and restored through the coming of the kingdom. The pearl of great price was available for those who sold everything else; among the things that would have to be sold was the traditional symbol of sacred land itself. It was swallowed up in the eschatological promise. YHWH was now to be king of all the earth.[176]

1.7 Conclusion

Having now examined at some considerable length how these influential works of historical Jesus scholarship address the question of whether Jesus' proclamation of the kingdom of God entails the hope for a territorially restored Israel, it now seems appropriate to offer some kind of summary and evaluation. As I have tried to demonstrate throughout, each of these volumes offers a distinct approach and response to this question and each therefore needs to be appreciated on its own merits lest the rough edges of their uniqueness is indiscriminately smoothed over by the relentless sander of harmonization. Nonetheless I also think it is safe to say that while substantive points of difference between them remain, a similar pattern of interpretation and response nevertheless emerges that holds fairly consistently across their variances.

In order to demonstrate what that pattern is and how it is evident, I would like to borrow a page from how these texts regularly summarize and present their findings about the historical Jesus by specifically ranking their assessments of Jesus' political aims and the kingdom's political nature according to a scale of authenticity:

---

174. Weinfeld, *Promise of the Land*, 201.
175. Wright, *Jesus and the Victory of God*, 429.
176. Ibid.

Certain:

- Jesus was a first-century Palestinian Jew working within and guided by a paradigm of Jewish restoration eschatology. As such, he saw his mission as somehow addressing the nation of Israel as a whole.
- As a result of appropriating and laboring within this eschatological framework, Jesus consistently invoked the kingdom of God in his teachings and saw its arrival—whether imminently or in the not too distant future—as being inextricably linked to the restoration of Israel and return of the exiles from the Diaspora. Furthermore, he saw both himself and his twelve disciples as playing a central role in governing a newly restored Israel.
- Jesus' teachings about the kingdom and his actions anticipating its impending arrival therefore take on a concrete political/social hue and were a major source of conflict both between himself and other first-century Jewish groups (i.e., the Pharisees and Saducees) as well and the Romans.

Probable:

- Jesus' triumphal entry into Jerusalem and subsequent demonstration in the Temple were most likely the key precipitants that set into motion his trial by the Sanhedrin and eventual crucifixion by the Romans.
- While difficult to pinpoint the precise motivation behind these events, it seems plausible to suggest that Jesus used them as platform to publically express his belief that YHWH would soon be ushering in a sovereign national kingdom of God
- Although uncertain as to the precise means by which it would manifest itself, Jesus nevertheless saw the arrival of the kingdom and Israel's restoration as having some kind of salvific effect for the Gentiles.

Doubtful:

- Jesus saw the arrival of the kingdom of God and Israel's restoration as possessing a territorial dimension. Instead he either saw the kingdom's arrival and Israel's restoration as being fulfilled or subsumed within Israel's people, or as somehow transcending the physical parameters of space and the political artifice of territorial borders.

Thus the results are easy to observe and the pattern of their interpretation is fairly easy to detect as it goes something like this: If we are to remember Jesus accurately as an actual historical figure possessive of credible aims and intents, then it is incumbent that we recognize him as a first-century Jewish prophet who actively worked for, anticipated, and proclaimed Israel's national restoration through the kingdom of God. At the same time it is just as incumbent to see him as someone who is extremely critical of those traditions of Jewish nationalism and restoration that perpetuated violence and ethnocentrism. Accordingly Jesus sought to unmoor the kingdom of God and Israel's hopes for national restoration from the land, not only because he sought to make all lands holy (Davies), but also because the re-establishment of Israel's territorial borders would be a major impediment if not abortive to his political vision and praxis of justice and peace (Borg and Wright). Thus Jesus is an eschatological Jewish nationalist, but he also represents something unique just to the extent that he disavows Israel's land in order to extend God's kingdom to encompass all peoples and all lands.

As I shall discuss in a more detailed fashion below in chapter 3, there is a good deal to commend and support in this historical reading of Jesus. At the same time however, I also think there is much to be criticized particularly with respect to the way it seems to pit Jesus' political hopes for a more inclusive and compassionate Israel as being diametrically opposed to a territorial kingdom of God. At present however, we need only be aware that this a-territorial interpretation of Jesus and the kingdom persists within recent historical Jesus scholarship and that it continues to have an impact within other fields as well. For as will be demonstrated in the next chapter, it is a line of interpretation that has gained traction in recent Christian ethical thought as well.

2

From a Territorial State into State of Ethical Praxis: Discerning the Roots and Structure of the Kingdom's De-territorialization in Christian Ethics

2.1 Introduction

IN THE PRECEDING CHAPTER I examined the recent trend in Third Quest scholarship toward recovering a thicker contextual understanding of Jesus' proclamation of the kingdom of God. In particular I analyzed the work of W. D. Davies, Marcus Borg, and N. T. Wright and highlighted their efforts to re-read Jesus' kingdom logia against the restive political backdrop of first-century Palestine and the eschatological matrices of Late Second Temple Judaism. This effort proved fruitful on several fronts, but was especially helpful in illuminating a pair of conclusions that seem conflicting if not at times contradictory.

First, not only have these studies retrieved the kingdom's subversive political subtext, they have also demonstrated its strong thematic comportment with Jewish restoration eschatology. Indeed each has established why Jesus' kingdom pronouncement must be read as a prophetic call for Israel's national restoration. And while such an interpretation may not be exhaustive, its hermeneutical necessity is undeniable nonetheless. Thus as Ben Meyer declares "disassociation of the 'reign of God' . . . from the 'restoration of Israel' is *a priori* implausible."[1]

---

1. Meyer, *Aims of Jesus*, 133.

At the same time, however, each of these projects has also disputed the claim that Jesus envisaged and/or proclaimed a *territorial* restoration of Israel. More to the point, all have rejected it as a highly dubious proposition that runs afoul of three countervailing arguments.

The first and most trenchant rebuttal is the conspicuous absence of explicit territorial references to the kingdom within the Gospels. Had Jesus truly sought a restoration of *eretz* Israel, then one would naturally expect his kingdom to incorporate logia with the appropriate land motifs. After all, as their ubiquitous presence and restorative significance throughout the Hebrew Bible and Second Temple literature readily attests, there certainly was no shortage of such territorial topoi for Jesus to draw upon. Nor for that matter did Jesus lack for suitable place or occasion to exploit their resonance. The demonstration in the Temple, for instance, stands as one of the most obvious if not tempting of moments.[2]

2. For example, see Evan's essay "Jesus and the 'Cave of Robbers,'" 93–110. In addition to verifying this narrative's historical authenticity, Evans also asks why Jesus' Temple protestations would provoke a lethal response by the Romans. Part of the answer, he suggests, lies with the fact that Jesus' actions caused him to be "viewed as a royal messianic claimant of some sort," a perception verified by the *titulus* affixed to his cross (105). As such, Evans notes the parallels between Jesus' actions in the Temple and the messianic figure described in the *Psalms of Solomon* 17, which reads in part:

> Behold, O Lord, and raise up unto them their king, the son of David, At the time in the which Thou seest, O God, that he may reign over Israel Thy servant; And gird him with strength, that he may shatter unrighteous rulers, And that he may purge Jerusalem from nations that trample (her) down to destruction. Wisely, righteously he shall thrust out sinners from (the) inheritance, He shall destroy the pride of the sinner as a potter's vessel. With a rod of iron he shall break in pieces all their substance, He shall destroy the godless nations with the word of his mouth; At his rebuke nations shall flee before him, And he shall reprove sinners for the thoughts of their heart. And he shall gather together a holy people, whom he shall lead in righteousness, And he shall judge the tribes of the people that has been sanctified by the Lord his God. And he shall not suffer unrighteousness to lodge any more in their midst, Nor shall there dwell with them any man that knoweth wickedness, For he shall know them, that they are all sons of their God. And he shall divide them according to their tribes upon the land, And neither sojourner nor alien shall sojourn with them anymore. He shall judge peoples and nations in the wisdom of his righteousness. Selah. And he shall have the heathen nations to serve him under his yoke; And he shall glorify the Lord in a place to be seen of (?) all the earth; And he shall purge Jerusalem, making it holy as of old . . . (21–30)

While it remains doubtful that Pontus Pilate was himself familiar with this tradition and cognizant of its territorial and political implications, he was most certainly aware of popular Jewish animus at the time and therefore sensitive to the ways in which Jesus' actions in the Temple could stoke further revolutionary sentiment and unrest. Furthermore, it is also quite certain that Jesus' Jewish audience was well acquainted with this

That Jesus consistently eschewed these territorial tropes however, especially when their invocation was sure to maximize his restorative mission, is considered telling and thus serves as but one dispositive sign that his was a landless kingdom.

Another is the paucity of gospel pericopae addressing the kingdom's territoriality either directly or metonymically (e.g., Luke 13:6–9; Matt 25:14–30; Matt 5:5; Matt 19:28 || Luke 22:30). Aside from their obvious dearth and brevity, the value of such references is further underscored by their possessing insufficient exegetical warrant to establish a Palestinian locale.

Thus Davies gainsays the possibility of reading Israel's land into the semantic orbit of Matt 5:5 based on the supposition that the Matthean Jesus is clearly describing a spiritualized and non-territorial age.[3] The same holds true for Davies's interpretation of the παλιγγενεσία in Matt 19:28 and its parallel in Luke 22:30. The Lukan account is quickly dispatched as "symbolic" and thus devoid of any territorial content in general, let alone of Israel's in particular.[4] Matthew's parallel narrative, by contrast, is not only deemed historically authentic but also indicative of some distinct territorial setting. Nevertheless, because "what it asserts of the future is bare," Davies cautions there is "no specific reference to the land on which the restored Israel is to dwell[.]"[5] As such the Matthean restoration of the twelve tribes is best understood "not so much in terms of a restored land of Israel as of a renewed cosmos."[6]

Finally, Davies, Borg and Wright all emphasize the reciprocal relationship between the kingdom's centrifugal geographic arc (Matt 28:16–20) and Jesus' benign posture toward Gentiles even if they were not his primary audience.[7] And while this connection leads Davies, Borg and Wright to differ on whether Jesus re-locates the kingdom to within himself, a transcendent

---

tradition and therefore eagerly anticipatory of its territorial implications even if they were not specifically (re)enunciated by Jesus. Thus as Yoder observes when writing on this episode in *The Politics of Jesus*, "Jesus is now in control of the course of events. It would be but one more step to consolidate that control, riding the crest of the crowd's enthusiasm and profiting from the confusion as the liberated cattle stampeded from the court and the traffickers scramble across the cobblestones after their money. The coup d'etat is two-thirds won; all that remains is to storm the Roman fortress next door" (43).

3. Davies, *Gospel and Land*, 359–62.
4. Ibid., 360.
5. Ibid., 365.
6. Ibid.
7. For a substantive treatment of how Jesus' posture toward Gentiles is reflective of first-century Jewish attitudes, see McKnight, *A Light among the Gentiles*; and Bird, *Jesus and the Origins of the Gentile Mission*.

cosmological realm, or a new human community, they all agree he does so in order to repudiate the jingoistic sentiments espoused by his contemporaries, especially those harbored by the Pharisees and Zealots. Consequently this buttresses a landless interpretation of the kingdom insofar as the advent of a peaceful reconciliation between Jews and Gentiles is thought to preclude, perforce, the reconstitution of a Jewish territorial state.

Any one of these arguments is reckoned persuasive enough in its own right to invalidate a territorial interpretation of the kingdom. When considered *en bloc*, however, as is customary, the imbricating logic of their synergy becomes incontrovertible.

Steven M. Bryan therefore offers a typical coda when stating that while it is clear that Jesus' kingdom proclamation evinces Israel's national restoration, such a restoration need not, and indeed in light of the mitigating evidence adduced above, should not be construed to portend a concomitant restitution of Israel's territorial borders. Instead what the Gospels show is that "*Jesus differs from others in the band of Israel's prophets . . . in his steadfast refusal to cast this new social and political order into the familiar forms of Israel's theocratic past and to gauge the assertion of God's rule on Israel's behalf in terms of the emergence of those forms.*"[8] Consequently, as this canvassing of Third Quest scholarship confirms, to be certain of the kingdom's nationality is, *mutatis mutandis*, to be equally sanguine of its a-territoriality.

To be sure, such a verdict sets into motion an array of significant conclusions. But few reverberate with as much force or resonance as those emanating from an ethical appraisal of the kingdom. For as Bryan also argues,

> If the kingdom of God is in some sense not yet, it is *not* because the kingdom now present for Jesus has become a formless abstraction, still awaiting the real coming of the kingdom in concrete form. Rather, in the wake of the *failure of Israel and its constitutional features* to conform to the terms and conditions of the eschaton, new forms are coming into existence, among them the form of Israel itself. *This is why Jesus' ethical teaching remains the best index of the degree to which Jesus' eschatology may be said to be realized.* If a people conformed to the eschatological expression of God's will was already coming into existence, then Israel's restoration was already to that degree a reality—a reality effected by John and extended by Jesus.[9]

---

8. Steven M. Bryan, "Jesus and Israel's Eschatological Constitution," in Holmén and Porter, eds., *Handbook for the Study of the Historical Jesus*, 3:2852.

9. Ibid., 2853; emphasis added.

In other words Bryan would have us believe that because Jesus judges the territorial morphology of Israel's restoration to be too provincial, bellicose, and outmoded a skin in which to pour the new wine of a more inclusive and irenic kingdom, he therefore effects its eschatological transformation, namely from a Jewish territorial state into a state of ethical praxis. And so it was and is that Israel's kingdom has been restored.

2.2 From a Territorial State to a Non-territorial Religious Ethic: A Historical and Theological Etiology of the Kingdom's De-territorialization

Aside from gaining currency amongst other Third Quest scholars, the argument that Jesus transformed or reconfigured the kingdom of God from a Jewish territorial state into a state of ethical praxis is a significant development for two other reasons.[10]

The first concerns how such an argument resolves the discrepancy I hinted at above, mainly the discomfiture between Jesus' wish to restore Israel as a nation while simultaneously rejecting its territoriality. For while today's post-structuralist geography regularly countenances and indeed celebrates a dis-integration of national identity from territoriality,[11] retrojecting such a cleavage into the political imaginary of first-century Judaism invites an immediate and pressing question: given the pivotal albeit fluctuating role that Israel's territoriality played in Second Temple constructions of Jewish national identity, under what set of political and theological circumstances could the proclamation of a landless kingdom still be viewed as Israel's national restoration?[12]

---

10. See, for example, Chilton and McDonald, *Jesus and the Ethics of the Kingdom*; and McKnight, *A New Vision of Israel*. It should be noted that neither of these volumes fails to address the national dimensions of Jesus' kingdom proclamations especially as it relates to the restoration of Israel. Nevertheless in discussing what kind of ethical content can be culled from Jesus' kingdom vision both tend to focus their attention on the character and performance of social relationships irrespective of how those relationships are situated in and defined by the particular territorial space of Israel.

11. See Arjun Appadurai's essay "Sovereignty Without Territoriality: Notes for a Postnational Geography," in Low and Lawrence-Zúñiga, eds., *Anthropology of Space and Place*, 337–50.

12. See Grosby, *Biblical Ideas of Nationality*, esp. 52–68. Grosby considers Albrect Alt's thesis that ancient Israel existed as a national tribal union prior to the institution of a Davidic territorial state. In doing so he takes note that Alt's analysis rests upon a fundamental assumption, namely, "a separation of an image of a 'people' from an image of a bounded area of land, in the formation of a society, specifically the nation" (55). Grosby finds this assumption to be questionable however inasmuch as it cuts against

Two recent works may provide a partial answer. I stress their limitations since neither formally addresses this question *per se,* or at least my specific articulation of it. That said their investigations do encompass a set of topics directly pertinent to its purview, not the least of which is the evolving relationship between Jewish national identity and territorial sovereignty in the late Second Temple period. Both therefore deserve a more careful perusal.

The first is Doron Mendels's much-discussed volume *The Rise and Fall of Jewish Nationalism.*[13] According to Mendels, the dégringolade of Jewish sovereignty over Palestine, beginning with Pompey's invasion in 63 BCE and ending with the violent suppression of the *Bar Kokhba* rebellion in 135 CE, precipitated yet another acute crisis of Jewish national identity.[14] For not only did the successive series of territorial incursions marking this period put into stark relief just how impotent the Jews were in defending their land against the Romans, it also constituted a stark and deeply troubling affront to *torahnic* practice. For as Mendels perceptively notes, the annexation of Judean territory by Rome "was a [direct] transgression of [Israel's] scriptures, because in it the Land was considered to be one holy entity."[15]

The severity of this threat to Jewish national identity becomes even more palpable once it is understood in light of the *mitzvot Ha'teluyot Be'aretz* (מצוות התלויות בארץ) or the 26 or so *torahnic* commandments

---

the territorial grain of the Deuteronomic code as clearly evidenced, for example, by Deut 12:1, which reads, "Now these are the laws and customs you must keep and observe *in the land* that Yahweh the God of you fathers has granted you to possess, for as long as you live *in that land*" (55; Grosby's emphasis). In light of this passage Grosby observes the following:

> The Deuteronomic code was not only the law of the "status community" of the worshipers of Yahweh-it was a law to be applied throughout the territory of the promised land of Israel. It was a law to be obeyed by all those who dwelled within the land; thereby unifying the inhabitants of the land, as subjects of the law, into the "people" of Israel, and unifying the land, the extent of the jurisdiction of the law, into the territory of Israel. The misleading consequences of the separation of kinship from territoriality in the history of ancient Israel and the worship of Yahweh are immediately obvious if the belief in the people of "all Israel," understood as encompassing the twelve tribes, was predicated upon (or cannot be disassociated from) an image of the bounded territory of the "land" of Israel." (61–62)

13. Mendels, *The Rise and Fall of Jewish Nationalism.*

14. Two others being of course the Assyrian conquest and exile of Northern Israel in the eighth century BCE followed by the subsequent Babylonian exile in the sixth century.

15. Mendels, *Rise and Fall of Jewish Nationalism,* 246.

From a Territorial State into State of Ethical Praxis 59

whose application and fulfillment are directly predicated upon Israel's land.[16] Among those customs over which these *mitzvot* had specific jurisdiction were maintenance and regulation of the Temple's sacrificial economy as well as the Sabbatical Year (שביעית) and Jubilee (יובל)—two traditions that delineated exacting standards on how land holdings were to be tended and re-distributed in order to preserve a lasting modicum of ecological sustainability and socio-economic equality.[17]

Accordingly the Roman expropriation of Jewish land would not only have made it practically impossible to observe these *mitzvot*; it also would have fundamentally compromised the very theo-political grammar from which both they and indeed Israel itself, derived their *raison d'être*. Thus as Mendels states, when "[v]iewed from the standpoint of a Jew living during this stormy era, the outrageous treatment of the Land by the Romans . . . . meant the loss of this Land as an entity and the shattering of it as a national symbol."[18]

As the severity of this crisis grew, Mendels believes two divergent perspectives concerning the restoration of Jewish territorial sovereignty came into fruition. The first, which would eventually crystallize into Zealotism, had as its main goal the militant reconstitution of a Jewish territorial state, purged of all Gentile presence and influence, and the reestablishment of a Jewish hegemony. The second perspective, by contrast, became increasingly disillusioned with and even hostile toward territorial reclamation. For Jews of this latter persuasion "the Land gradually ceased to be an important factor of Jewish political awareness." As a result "their energy and interests [were diverted] into other spheres."[19]

One such sphere into which these displaced nationalist energies were sublimated was the concept of holiness (קֹדֶשׁ), or more precisely the quest to preserve its integrity and practice amidst Roman occupation and corruption. As is often the case in such intractable situations, Mendels believes necessity became the mother of invention. For once Palestine ceased to exist as an independent Jewish state, it became increasingly apparent and thus acceptable to some Jews that "the concept of holiness, namely, the observance of the ordinances concerning the land such as the tithe, pilgrimage, sabbatical year, and the political sovereignty of the Jews over the land were not

---

16. For further discussion of the *mitzvot Ha'teluyot Be'aretz*, see Harrington's *Holiness*, esp. 101–3.

17. Ibid.

18. Mendels, *Rise and Fall of Jewish Nationalism*, 246.

19. Ibid., 252.

necessarily [to be viewed as] one and the same thing."[20] Instead "[r]eligous [sic] Jews in this period were forced to make a clear distinction between the Holy Land and an Israelite State" and thus adopt a posture analogous to that of Diaspora Jewry whereby the "Land—or rather parts of it—could be holy without necessarily having a Jewish sovereign."[21]

The rise of such a perspective, Mendels contends, goes a long way toward explaining Jesus' own ambivalent posture toward the land. For even though Mendels thinks it highly unlikely that Jesus ever called for an independent Jewish state, he is nonetheless confident that Jesus sought to make Palestine a Holy land. This feat was to be accomplished, however, not by virtue of armed resistance but through *torah* compliance *tout court*, irrespective of Jewish territorial sovereignty. For as Mendels argues, Jesus

> had no political aspirations concerning the Land of Israel; he was beyond and above such mundane ambitions. The Land in its political aspects was irrelevant to him, and in many ways was against his mission ... The whole idea of the conquest of the Land as well as the concept of statehood on it is greatly toned down in the New Testament. It is not simply that the later Evangelists decided not to mention the heroes of the Old Testament who were associated with the conquest and holding of the Land; it is, rather, part of the whole concept of early Christianity, going back to Jesus and his disciples, that the Land as part of an earthly Jewish state had no political importance for the New Israel.[22]

Thus what Mendels proposes is a reading of Jesus whereby his interest in restoring a sense of Jewish national identity is largely subjected to, if not altogether swallowed up, by a quest for maintaining holiness, an interpretation that not coincidentally is highly compatible with Borg's assessment of holiness discussed in the previous chapter.

This perspective also coheres with another argument that notes the existence of a whole array of non-territorial indica through which first-century conceptions of Jewish nationhood were expressed, including those that elevated Jewish religious practice as an identifying criterion. Along those lines, as Love Sechrest has cogently demonstrated in her work *A Former Jew: Paul and the Dialectics of Race*,[23] an extensive cataloging of *ethne*'s references in early Jewish literature reveals that *torah* observance and cultic

---

20. Ibid., 258.

21. Ibid. One wonders here what to make of Mendels's qualifier "religious" since the idea of a "non-religious" or "secular" Jew would be nonsensical at the time.

22. Ibid., 262.

23. Sechrest, *A Former Jew*.

practice became stronger indicators of Jewish national identity in the first century than did inhabiting a Judean geographic locale.[24] In fact, as Sechrest argues, this reorientation of Jewish national identity around religious practice instead of territorial placement comprises a significant distinction between it and contemporaneous conceptions of Gentile autochthony insofar as the latter tended to emphasize geographic location as a more salient and determinative criterion of national identity.[25] In light of this evidence Sechrest thinks it probable that the physical displacement of territorial Diaspora precipitated a concomitant migration in *ethne*'s meaning such that a coherent and viable sense of Jewish national identity could still exist and flourish apart from living in and/or ruling over territorial Israel.[26]

Consequently, what both these arguments show is that Jewish religious practice played a far stronger role in defining and preserving a sense of Jewish national identity in the early first century than did inhabiting and/or exercising sovereignty over a plot of Palestinian geography. With that locative and theo-political shift in view, it therefore does seem plausible to stipulate, as Bryan and others do, that Jesus recalibrated questions of Jewish national identity along a non-territorial trajectory such that it was possible and even necessary to re-conceive Israel's national restoration in terms of a renewed Jewish religious praxis rather than a reconstituted sovereign Jewish state.

Furthermore since the bifurcation between "ethics" and "religion" is a modern contrivance with no conceptual legitimacy in a pre-modern worldview, especially one as interpenetrating and holistic as Judaism, it seems equally plausible to conclude that Jesus viewed "religious" observance of *torah* and compliance with its "ethical" precepts as coterminous.

Accordingly Jesus' desire to restore the ἔθνη of Israel by way of restoring/renewing its religious identity may have been an unconventional, and indeed, judging by the level of controversy and consternation it elicited, a convoluted political program. But it was not, as Mendels's and Sechrest's arguments serve to show, so completely incongruous with a first-century Jewish imagination as to be incomprehensible. On the contrary, Jesus' move toward an ethical/religious restoration of Israel was in some ways the inexorable and organic outgrowth of a shift that had already occurred.

Consequently the perceived dissonance underlying Jesus' move to transform the kingdom of God from a territorial state into a state of ethical praxis can be satisfactorily resolved and set aside once it is recognized

---

24. Ibid., 173–75.
25. Ibid., 179–80.
26. Ibid.

how such a transformation represents a form of dis-similarity *within* first-century Judaism and not a deviant aberration *from* it.

And indeed Bryan seems to assume as much when addressing the question of what makes Jesus' kingdom vision distinct from yet contiguous with a first-century Jewish worldview. For on the one hand Bryan acknowledges that

> the perception that Jesus differed from the teachers of the law was correct inasmuch as his ethical teaching is not easily categorized as a new law or as an exposition of the law of Moses (Matt 7:29). However, this fact should not be taken to mean that Jesus' intent was to inaugurate a denationalized kingdom. Rather, the significance of the fact that Jesus' ethical teaching does not function as a legal code or exposition is that the nature of Israel's national existence has been conceived on entirely different terms.[27]

And yet as Bryan also notes,

> This construal of Israel's restoration along ethical lines which did not condition or associate the kingdom's arrival on the emergence of certain specific constitutional elements may be directly traced to John the Baptist. In one striking saying Jesus suggests Israel's restoration, understood as its ethical reconstitution, had already been accomplished: "Elijah is indeed coming first to restore all things . . . But I tell you that Elijah has come, and they did to him whatever they pleased, as it is written about him" (Mark 9:12–13). Jesus thus rejects an understanding of Elijah's restoration as the future regathering of the twelve tribes as in Sir 48:10 and associates this restoration instead with the ethical renewal initiated by John's call to repentance.[28]

A similar kind of dissimilar logic can also be detected in N. T. Wright's arguments as well. For on the one hand Wright firmly holds that "Jesus belonged thoroughly within the complex and multiform Judaism of his day. His protests were classic Jewish protests-from-within. His claims . . . were parallel in form, though different in content, to those of many other Jewish leaders of his day. His activities made sense, and were intended to make sense, within a Jewish worldview."[29] And yet he is equally positive that

> [Jesus] summoned [his fellow Jews] to follow him in a way of being the people of YHWH which was, according to him, the true

---

27. Bryan, "Jesus and Israel's Eschatological Constitution," 2848.
28. Ibid., 2850.
29. Wright, *Jesus and the Victory of God*, 472.

though surprising fulfillment of the whole scriptural story. He aimed to bring about a radical shift within, not an abandonment of, the worldview of his hearers. They thought of themselves as Israel, as expecting the fulfillment of YHWH's promises, particularly concerning the great redemption, the restoration, the return from exile, the "forgiveness of sins." Jesus offered exactly that; but as his own stories made clear, what he offered did not look like what they had been expecting . . . He aimed then to reconstitute Israel around himself, as the true returned-from-exile people.[30]

Furthermore Wright contends the most significant way Jesus "reconstitute[d] Israel" around himself was by articulating and demonstrating a renewed ethical vision. For as he states, "The Sermon on the Mount . . . suggest[s] an answer. Evil would be defeated, not by military victory, but by a *doubly* revolutionary method: turning the other cheek, going the second mile, the deeply subversive wisdom of taking up the cross. The agenda Jesus mapped out for his followers was the agenda to which he himself was obedient. This was how the kingdom would come, how the battle would be won."[31]

In addition to further corroborating the claim that Jesus transformed the kingdom of God from a territorial state into a stateless religious ethic, there is a second formative conclusion lurking within Bryant's and Wright's comments as well. For not only do they presuppose that this transformation became the dominant paradigm through which the kingdom of God should be interpreted in its historical context; they also, *mutatis mutandis*, suggest it should become the template for its current interpretation as well. Indeed it is not uncommon to find several Third Quest projects buoyed by the tacit admonition that Jesus' kingdom vision could serve as the normative framework for contemporary Christian political identity and practice.

Wright for one has certainly worked hard to make that admonition more explicit and operational. For as he has written in another context,

> In particular, the story of Jesus compels us to work out, better than we normally do, the hermeneutical principle by which we get from the penultimate act—his life and death—to the final one, in which we find ourselves still. The whole world view of Israel provides the clue: when Israel's hopes are fulfilled, then the world will be blessed, or at least ruled properly at last. If Jesus is bringing to its climax the destiny of the people of God, then this is bound to have earth-shattering implications for the whole

30. Ibid., 473.
31. Ibid., 465.

world. The hermeneutical rule of thumb, then, is that Jesus' mission to Israel becomes the basis, and the model, for the church's mission to the world. His call to Israel to repent, his summons to her to join him in a new way of being Israel, is to be translated into the church's call to the world to a new way of being human.[32]

And Borg offers something similar when he writes, "So what is the political meaning of the Kingdom of God? In a sentence: it is what life would be like on earth if God were the king and the rulers of this world were not. The Kingdom of God is about God's justice in contrast to the systemic injustice of the kingdoms and domination systems of this world."[33]

What these comments reveal then is a firm conviction that Jesus' kingdom vision, by virtue of both historicity and political nature, is emblematic of a social ethic that is normative for (post) modern Christian political behavior. Furthermore they also assert such an ethic is instantiated most perspicaciously in a set of political practices that inveighs against injustice and violence.

And yet even as these convictions about the kingdom have illuminated its socio-ethical purchase, they have done little to prompt a corresponding discussion of what role, if any, the kingdom's territoriality plays in forging such a political ethic. In fact if recent Christian ethical discourse serves as any guide, then the overwhelming presumption seems to be that outside of its abnegation and/or transformation into a new political community or set of socio-political and economic practices, the kingdom's territoriality has no role to play whatsoever.

Here then lies a penetrating glimpse into how the kingdom's historical de-territorialization engenders an attendant ethical de-territorialization as well. For once it is decided that Jesus' transformation of the kingdom into a non-territorial religious ethic is the kind of ethic to which Christian political identity must be conformed, then the stage is set for subsequent appropriations of kingdom to assume a non-territorial gloss.

The remainder of this chapter will explore this declension further, albeit from the gaze of Christian ethics itself. For as we shall see, there are several currents within its stream that reinforce and even expand the kingdom's de-territorialization.

---

32. Wright, "The New Testament and the 'State.'"
33. Borg, *Heart of Christianity*, 132–33.

2.3 The Ethical De-territorialization of the Kingdom in Three Acts: Praxification, Ecclesiofication, and Typofication

In surveying, as it were, the landscape of recent Christian ethical reflection, there are at least three distinct ways the kingdom has been de-territorialized. In short these are through its *praxification*, its *ecclesiofication*, and/or its *typofication*. A fuller explication and illustration of each follows below.

2.3.1 Praxification: The Kingdom of God as a Place-less Ethical Performance

One of the chief ways the kingdom has been ethically de-territorialized is through its *praxification*. By "praxification" I refer to a process whereby the kingdom gets extruded though a hermeneutical prism that is so highly attuned to its socio-political performance that its normative content is ultimately dirempted from Israel's territoriality. A good illustration of this interpretation can be found in Glen Stassen and David Gushee's highly regarded volume *Kingdom Ethics: Following Jesus in Contemporary Context*.[34]

One of the central arguments Stassen and Gushee put forward in *Kingdom Ethics* is that rather than becoming mired in impenetrable and often abstruse academic debates resolving the kingdom's inscrutable eschatological chronology, Christians are far better served instead to identify and put into practice its salient moral characteristics within a theology of God's delivering action.

Toward that end Stassen and Gushee use Bruce Chilton's research on the Isaiah targum to demonstrate how Jesus' description of the kingdom is deeply immersed in and influenced by an Isaianic moral vision.[35] More

---

34. Stassen and Gushee, *Kingdom Ethics*.

35. It should be noted that, although Stassen and Gushee find Chilton's reading of the Isaiah *targum* persuasive in terms of illuminating Jesus' own kingdom vision, they differ with his conclusion that the Psalms provides the best source to clarify that vision. Instead, they assert that there are "seven clues" that point to Isaiah and not the Psalms as providing the best "background of Jesus' teachings on the kingdom" (*Kingdom Ethics*, 22). These are (1) Jesus' strong identification with the "Suffering Servant" tradition and its hopes of saving and delivering of Israel's people; (2) the parallel between Isaiah's and Jesus' emphasis on how the coming kingdom will deliver and save the oppressed; (3) Jesus' (and the Gospels') frequent citation of Isaiah; (4) the frequent citation of Isaiah in Qumran literature; (5) the frequent appropriation of Isaianic language in Jesus' kingdom proclamations; (6) the linking of the "kingdom of God" with the "kingdom of the Messiah" in the Isaiah *targum*; and (7) the way Isaiah acts as a programmatic script for Jesus throughout the Gospels (ibid., 22–24).

specifically Stassen and Gushee note that Isaiah's vision of the kingdom is marked by seven distinct ethical/political characteristics of God's coming reign. These are deliverance or salvation; righteousness/justice; peace; joy; God's presence as Spirit or Light; healing; and return from exile.[36]

What a careful comparison between these seven Isaianic characteristics and Jesus' own kingdom proclamations reveal, say Stassen and Gushee, is an uncanny resemblance insofar as "Jesus inaugurates the long-promised kingdom and thus offers holistic deliverance to the sick, the poor, the guilty and the rejected; incarnates and demands justice and righteousness; practices and teaches the way of peacemaking; and both experiences and imparts joy."[37]

Accordingly, the proper task for contemporary Christian political ethics, say Stassen and Gushee, is to re-appropriate these theological-ethical marks, especially as they are articulated in the transforming initiatives of Jesus' Sermon on the Mount, and use them as a practical guide for Christian political formation. For as they state,

> We believe that Jesus offered not hard sayings or high ideals but concrete ways to practice God's will and be delivered from the bondage of sin. In other words, he taught his followers how to participate in God's reign. He taught what the kingdom is like, what its characteristics are, and therefore what kinds of practices are done by those who participate in it and are ready for it. We believe that this approach to Christian ethics is most faithful to the biblical witness about what God in Christ intends to do in us and in the world.[38]

Nevertheless, despite clarifying how Jesus' kingdom vision provides a template for Christian political engagement, Stassen and Gushee ignore how this template is intimately intermeshed with Israel's territoriality. In fact, both adopt a line of interpretation similar to that of Bryan above insofar as their ethical assessment of the kingdom is largely divorced from Israel's land.

A manifestation of this tendency is first apparent when Stassen and Gushee agree with Chilton's and J. I. H. McDonald's assessment that "the kingdom of God is not about what God does while humans stand by passively; nor is it about our effort to build the kingdom while God passively

---

36. Ibid., 25.
37. Ibid., 30.
38. Ibid., 31.

watches. The kingdom of God is [instead] *performative: it is God's performance in which we actively participate.*"[39]

Admittedly there is nothing in this statement to suggest as Bryan's does above that Jesus transforms the kingdom from a landed historical nation into a non-territorial ethical praxis. Nor does it assert, as does Bryan, that the latter now serves as the best metric by which to confirm and observe the kingdom's partial eschatological manifestation. Instead, Stassen and Gushee's emphasis on performance is clearly a function of their desire to remedy a troubling yet persistent predilection within Christian ethical reflection that has all too often imbrued Jesus' kingdom pronouncement with spurious metaphysical and social dichotomies between soul and body and individual and community.

As such their emphasis on performance offers a helpful and much-needed corrective. And yet even as they work diligently to suture these destructive wounds, Stassen and Gushee inadvertently open up another by unwittingly separating the kingdom's ethical/political performance from the territorial location upon which that performance is inextricably predicated. Their grammatical and thematic emphasis on the kingdom's ethical *performance* to the virtual exclusion of its *place* all but assures the notion that what matters most about Jesus' kingdom proclamation is not so much a cognition of its *where*—i.e., within the land of Israel—but instead a focus on its *how* and *what*—i.e., the distinct set of transforming initiatives delineated and exemplified by Jesus—as though the latter can and should be discretely disconnected from the former.

And indeed, Stassen and Gushee's interpretation of Matt. 5:5 bears out this elevation of place-less performance. For nowhere in their reading of this Beatitude is Jesus' reference to the kingdom's territoriality ever mentioned or probed save for their fairly generic affirmation that "[i]f [Christians] are poor and surrendered to God, [they] are blessed, because in Christ God is delivering [them] and [they] shall inherit the earth."[40] Instead Stassen and Gushee focus the bulk of their exegetical energies on teasing out the moral nuances of πραεῖς and note how this term connotes both a sense of utter dependence upon God as well as a practical commitment to nonviolent peacemaking.[41] Thus when these dual connotations of humble are juxtaposed, the ethical upshot of their amalgamation becomes clear: "In a nutshell, *blessed are those who are surrendered to God, who is the God of peace.*"[42]

39. Ibid., 21; emphasis added.
40. Ibid., 40.
41. Ibid., 40–41.
42. Ibid., 41.

What is missing from this interpretation, however, as illuminating and instructive as it is, is a comparable exegetical attentiveness to how Jesus identifies the land, and more precisely Israel's land, as the particular territorial location within which the powerless are to be blessed, and wherein they are to cultivate and concretely inhabit the political practices of divine dependency and nonviolent peacemaking. Instead for Stassen and Gushee, it is the kingdom's ethical performance *in se* that is the jewel of Jesus' moral vision, not the territorial fitting in which it is placed. As a result of this occlusion Israel's land is excised from their ethical aperture altogether.

A second manifestation of this *praxifiying* tendency is also apparent in Stassen and Gushee's reading of the Isaiah Targum. When reading Isa 24:23 and Isa 31:4, both note how the Targum's Aramiac text renders the first passage as "*The kingdom* of the Lord of hosts will be revealed on Mount Zion" and the second as "*The kingdom* of the Lord of hosts will be revealed to settle upon Mount Zion." In light of this phrasing Stassen and Gushee make the following observation: "What seems clear is that all these passages announce that God is being revealed, being disclosed before our very eyes. But Jewish piety so highly revered the revelation of the Lord that the Targum did not want to say directly, 'God is revealed.' Instead it said, 'The kingdom of God is revealed.' This means that the kingdom of God was understood as referring to the self-revelation of God and God's dynamic reign. *It was not a place but an action.*" [43]

What is itself revelatory about this statement is not only Stassen and Gushee's contention that the kingdom was understood to act as a kind of synecdoche for God, but also their idea that this theophany was, and indeed remains a place-less action. In other words, their interpretation gives credence to the idea that the arrival and manifestation of God's kingdom is best authenticated by the performance of its ethical characteristics, not its territorial coordinates. This is asserted, moreover, even though the very Targumic verses that Stassen and Gushee both cite refer to *Mount Zion* as the definitive territorial location upon which the kingdom, and thus God's delivering presence, will be most fully revealed!

Hence what one finds in Stassen and Gushee is a forceful argument for why Christians must incorporate the transforming initiatives of Jesus' kingdom vision into their own political repertoire. For it is only through that kind of incorporation that Christians become faithful denizens and emissaries of his kingdom. However, as I have also illustrated, it also a mode of incorporation that ultimately displaces the kingdom's territoriality, both exegetically and politically.

---

43. Ibid., 25; emphasis added.

2.3.2 Ecclesiofication: The Kingdom as a "Churchified" Spatial Reality

A second way Christian ethics has de-territorialized the kingdom of God is through its *ecclesiofication*. *Ecclesiofication* occurs when the Church, read both as an alternative political body as well as a correlative socio-political posture, comes to supplant territorial Israel as the spatial locus within which Christian political identity is forged. A particularly illuminating example of this interpretation can be found in Stanley Hauerwas's and Mark Sherwindt's essay titled "The Reality of the Kingdom: An Ecclesial Space for Peace," in Hauerwas's text *Against the Nations: War and Survival in a Liberal Society*.[44]

Like Stassen and Gushee, both Hauerwas and Sherwindt think it imperative that Christians recover the political substance of Jesus' kingdom vision in order to thicken their ethical reflection and political practice. All too often however, they see these efforts stymied by the lingering residue of a Social Gospel mentality that reduces the kingdom's concrete political meaning into a thin set of abstract and universal principles. As a result Hauerwas and Sherwindt view Walter Rauschenbusch's legacy with a high degree of ambivalence. For on the one hand both credit Rauschenbusch with articulating how the kingdom provides "not only a glimpse of God's future, but also the vision and a program for concrete change in human history."[45] On the other hand, however, they are especially critical of the way Rauschenbusch "transform[s] the theocratic image of the Kingdom of God into the democratic ideal of the brotherhood of man."[46] For what makes this kind of transformation both anachronistic and theologically problematic is that

> [s]cripturally there seem to be no good grounds to associate the kingdom of God with any form of political organization and/or assume that it is best characterized by any one set of ethical ideals such as love and justice. As a platitude it may be unobjectionable to claim that God's kingdom must surely be one of love and justice, but that does little to help one understand what is the meaning of love and justice. Indeed, when the content of such ideals is spelled out, as we see in the case of Rauschenbusch, we begin to suspect that the language of the kingdom is being used to underwrite ethical commitments and political strategies that are determined prior to the claims about the centrality of the kingdom for Christian ethics.[47]

44. Hauerwas, *Against the Nations*.
45. Ibid., 109.
46. Ibid., 111.
47. Ibid.

Thus the main error besetting a Rauschenbuschian interpretation of the kingdom is that it ends up abstracting "the kingdom ideal from the [very] concrete community [it] presupposes."[48]

Given this critique, one might suppose the "concrete community" to which Hauerwas and Sherwindt refer is Israel. And indeed when considering the ethical/political importance of not just the kingdom itself, but Jesus' specific articulation of it, Hauerwas and Sherwindt write that

> theologically and ethically the significance of Jesus for determining the meaning and content of the kingdom implies that history assumes an importance that cannot be ignored as it often is by other forms of ethical reflection. For the particularity of Israel, Jesus, and the Church must be taken up constitutively into what those who proclaim Jesus as Lord and Christ regard as true and good and right. The kingdom does not start with nature, with the notion that the perfection implicit in creation be reformed by divine assistance; rather the kingdom starts as the hope of a people called by God, which for Christians is defined by the life and death of the crucified Christ. The universal scope of the Kingdom is rooted in the universal scope of God's reign. What we can know of this God and his kingdom is always given through the history of Israel filtered through the light of Jesus' cross.[49]

Thus, like Stassen and Gushee, Hauerwas and Sherwindt are mindful that a proper ethical and theological interpretation of the kingdom must be rooted in the firm particularity of a historical datum, namely Jesus and Israel. Moreover, both view the practices of justice and nonviolent peacemaking as central expressions and continuations of that kingdom.

Nevertheless, despite observing these linkages between Jesus, Israel and the Church, a further examination of Hauerwas's and Sherwindt's position reveals some elements of this triptych to be of greater normative weight and importance than others.

For instance, when further emphasizing why an ethical interpretations of the kingdom must be rooted in the particularity of history, Hauerwas and Sherwindt write that

> the kingdom of God is the hope of the *people whom God has called out among all the nations. The question of ecclesiology, therefore, precedes strategy for social action.* Without the kingdom ideal, the church loses its identifying-forming hope; *without*

---

48. Ibid.

49. Ibid, 114–15.

the church, the kingdom ideal loses its concrete character. Once abstracted from the community it presumes the kingdom ideal can be used to underwrite any conception of the just society.[50]

On one level, this statement is simply a recapitulation of the interdependence that obtains between the kingdom's historical and socio-political expression and its ethical/political witness. What my italicizations serve to indicate, however, is the remarkable degree to which Hauerwas and Sherwindt's interpretation of the kingdom is filtered through an exclusive lens of ecclesiology. For no longer in their view does the kingdom presuppose *both* the Church *and* Israel as a distinct yet complementary pair of historical communities from which a concrete set of ethical and political practices can be inhabited. Instead both elevate the Church and only the Church as *the* political locus from which the kingdom's ethical and political concreteness is derived. As a result, their ethical and political interpretation of the kingdom becomes *extra Ecclesiam nulla salus* both descriptively *and* prescriptively.

Furthermore, their language is also suggestive of an even bolder claim, namely that the Church, that is the social and political strategy opened up by the practice of going out of rather than into the nations, has replaced Israel, perhaps not historically but certainly territorially, as the kingdom's primary spatial referent. For as Hauerwas and Sherwindt state when speaking of the political significance of the Church, "within a world of violence and injustice Christians can take the risk of being forgiven . . . As a result, *some space*, both psychological and *physical*, is created where we can be at rest from a world that knows not who is its king."[51]

Thus for Hauerwas and Sherwindt the kingdom, through its historical connection to Jesus and Israel, retains a sense of concrete political spatiality via the Church. And this spatiality is inherently suffused with ethical and political content inasmuch the Church embodies a political counter-space and practice from which it is possible to critique and embody a viable political alternative to the violent-tinged spatiality of the modern nation-state. But once again what Hauerwas and Sherwidnt ultimately end up proposing is an ethical conception of spatiality that is bereft of any concrete connection to *territorial* Israel. Indeed, their emphasis on withdrawing from the nations, actively rejects it.

---

50. Ibid, 112–13; emphases added.
51. Ibid, 117.

2.3.3 Typofication: Israel's Land as a Provisional Paradigm for Holy Space

Finally, there is a third kind of ethical de-terrorialization that arises from what I would call the kingdom's *typofication*. As opposed to its *praxification* and *ecclesiofication*, a *typofied* interpretation of the kingdom can actually be more amenable to its territoriality and therefore sensitive to the idea that the specificity of Israel's land retains an inherent political and normative integrity that cannot be subsumed into either an ethical performance or an ecclesiology. In this respect then, it offers, at least initially, a more robust and positive assessment of the kingdom's territoriality.

What is built into this positive assessment, however, is a latent assumption that while ethically significant and instructive in its own right, the kingdom's original territoriality is nevertheless nothing but a provisional *typos* that proleptically prefigures Jesus. Therefore even though it remains necessary to immerse one's self in the particularity of Israel's territoriality in order to discern and understand the kingdom's ethical and political practices, the eschatological fulfillment of those practices in the person of Christ ultimately renders that territoriality theologically and politically moot. A good example of this kind of argument can be found in Christopher J.H. Wright's discussion of what role Israel's land should play in Christian ethical reflection in his *Old Testament Ethics for the People of God*.[52]

Wright begins this discussion by first identifying a three-part hermeneutical stratagem for assessing the ethical significance of Israel's land in the Old Testament. The first of these is to read the Old Testament *paradigmatically*. As its name indicates a paradigmatic hermeneutic looks at Israel and sees that its "overall social shape, with all its legal and institutional structures, ethical norms and theological undergirding ... becomes the model or paradigm that Israel provides as a priesthood for the nations."[53] Accordingly by "seeing how [Israel] addressed, within [its] cultural and historical context, problems and issues common to humanity in principle or practice, [Christians] are helped to address (if not always solve) the ethical challenges [they] face in [their] different contexts."[54]

In explaining this paradigmatic method Wright is also careful to distinguish it from a principled hermeneutic. For the problem with principlism is that it "can lead to the eventual discarding of the specific realities of the Old Testament text, the concrete earthy history of Israel, the good the

---

52. Wright, *Old Testament Ethics for the People of God*.
53. Ibid., 65.
54. Ibid., 69.

bad and the ugly. Once you have a principle in your pocket why keep the wrapping?"[55] Reading the Hebrew Bible as paradigmatic, by contrast, forces one to "observe all the non-reducible hard edges [of Israel's history], all the jarring tensions and all the awkward corners of earthy reality within them."[56] Consequently, one is also forced "constantly to go back to [the] hard given reality of the Bible itself and imaginatively to live with Israel in their world ('inhabiting the text'), before returning to the equally hard given reality of our own world, to discover imaginatively how that paradigm challenges our ethical responses there."[57]

To further comprehend Wright's point about just how problematic a principled hermeneutic can be, it will be helpful to consider Oliver O'Donovan's discussion of possession in his seminal treatise *The Desire of the Nations: Rediscovering the Roots of Political Theology*.[58]

One aspect of this discussion that distinguishes *Desire of the Nations* as a whole from other recent works of so-called political theology is O'Donovan's explicit desire to sink his project in the political and historical substratum of ancient Israel. Indeed, even critics who are otherwise un-persuaded or even scandalized by O'Donovan's *apologia* for a modified form of "Christendom" are nevertheless appreciative of his premise that "Israel's [political] forms" provide a "a normative critical standard" to which "[a]ny question about social forms and structures must be referred."[59] Moreover, they also sympathize with his critique that it is "failure to attend to Israel" that has caused Christian political thought to haplessly "oscillat[e] between idealist and realist poles."[60]

So that perpetuation of this fallacy may be remedied, O'Donovan proposes a hermeneutical course correction whereby Christians are entreated to re-read the Hebrew Bible not simply as a prolegomenon to a yet-to-be-completed *Heilsgeschichte*, but instead as a fully constituted "public tradition" in its own right wherein "Israel carries [within it] an unrealized promise for the full socialization of God's believing people[.]"[61] In doing so, Christians can thus distill a densely populated constellation of normative political concepts, all of which orbit around ancient Israel's central affirma-

55. Ibid., 70.
56. Ibid., 71.
57. Ibid.
58. O'Donovan, *The Desire of the Nations*.
59. Ibid., 25.
60. Ibid., 27. For a sympathetic yet critical assessment of O'Donovan's argument in *The Desire of the Nations*, see Hauerwas and Fodor, "Remaining in Babylon," 30–55.
61. O'Donovan, *Desire of the Nations*, 25.

tion that "YHWH reigns." These include salvation (also power/triumph), judgment, and possession (also tradition/community identity).⁶²

And yet, even as he advocates abstracting these political concepts from ancient Israel, O'Donovan is also careful to preserve its integrity and uniqueness, lest Israel itself become an epiphenomenal abstraction. For as he writes in a passage that strongly echoes Wright's sentiments above,

> If political theologians are to treat ancient Israel's political tradition as normative, they must observe the discipline of treating it *as history*. They may not plunder the Old Testament as though it were so much raw material to be consumed, in any order and in any variety of proportions, in the manufacture of their own theological artifact. They are dealing with a disclosure which took form in a succession of political developments, each one of which has be weighed and interpreted in light of what preceded and followed it. To dip into Israel's experience at one point ... and to take out a single disconnected image or theme from it is to treat the history of God's reign like a commonplace book or a dictionary of quotations.⁶³

In light of this consideration, one would presume O'Donovan's conceptual schema would display a comparable sensitivity in preserving Israel's particularity. And yet, as Scott Bader-Saye has ably demonstrated in *Church and Israel after Christendom*,⁶⁴ there are actually several instances in *Desire of the Nations* where O'Donovan's discourse falls noticeably short of his own exacting standard.

One of the most telling and troubling of these discrepancies occurs in O'Donovan's explication of the concept of *possession*. The discussion begins promisingly enough with O'Donovan noting the way in which ancient Israel's own understanding of possession centered around the dyadic structure of its law (*torah*) and land.⁶⁵ This prompts the incisive insight that there actually exists a deeper interdependence between these two than initially meets the eye, inasmuch as ancient Israel understood that "[p]ossessing the land was a matter of observing that order of life which was established by [*torah*]," while "possessing the law was a matter of enjoying the purchase on the conditions of life which was YHWH's gift."⁶⁶ Thus for the ancient

---

62. Ibid., 86.
63. Ibid., 27.
64. Bader-Saye, *Church and Israel after Christendom*.
65. O'Donovan, *Desire of the Nations*, 41.
66. Ibid.

Israelite "[t]he material and spiritual aspects" of possession were forever and always "inseparably held together."[67]

Furthermore, an analysis of *nachlaha* (נַחֲלָה) and *cheleq* (חֵלֶק)—the two Hebrew terms the Hebrew Bible most commonly uses for "possession"—reveals a similar interdependence to be operative within Israel's possession of the land itself. For on the one hand both terms indicated that "Israel as a whole possessed the land as a whole."[68] Yet both also make it clear that "each tribe and family has its share, its own way of participating in the gift of God to his people."[69] Accordingly, YHWH's "gift" of the land was understood to be "both collective and distributive."[70]

Up to this point O'Donovan's analysis of possession provides a deft blend of identifying the unique principles undergirding ancient Israel's understanding of possession while also hinting how such principles might be extrapolated to a broader political basis. And such might be the final verdict were it not for O'Donovan's peroration.

For once it is combined with the concepts of salvation and judgment, O'Donovan concludes that Israel's understanding of possession ultimately provides "a point of disclosure from which the nature of all political authority comes into view. Out of the self-possession of this people in their relation to God springs the possibility of other peoples' possessing themselves in God."[71]

Although certainly illuminating in some respects there are nevertheless two aspects of this summation that weaken Israel's socio-historical particularity.

The first is how this articulation of "possession" liquidates its original territorial content. For whereas before O'Donovan stressed that it was possession of a specific land that literally grounded Israel's spirituality and thus endowed its political and economic life with a complementarity between individual and collective ownership, now the object of Israel's possession has mysteriously become a sense of *self*, and a decidedly non-territorial one at that.

Moreover, it is also a construction or rather a disclosure of self that is so generic and abstract as to render Israel's unique covenant relationship with YHWH entirely inconsequential. As a result Israel's understanding and practice of possession can no longer be considered *sui generis*, but instead

67. Ibid.
68. Ibid.
69. Ibid.
70. Ibid.
71. Ibid., 45.

discloses a deeper universal political reality wherein all peoples may acquire a sense of self-possession irrespective of their covenantal status.

Accordingly, as Bader-Saye states, by "abstracting general concepts that can then be applied either directly or analogously to other nations, O'Donovan makes Israel into a paradigm, a model, or an archetype of political authority."[72] And in so doing, he threatens to reduce Israel "to *only* a model or an archetype or a political order that can in principle be embodied by another (nonelect) people."[73]

Thus explains the pitfalls associated with a principled hermeneutic and the urgency behind Wright's rationale for wanting to use a paradigmatic approach instead. Yet even this interpretive vigilance does not prevent Wright himself from indulging in the very same type of interpretive abstractions. For just like O'Donovan, so too does Wright effectively efface the historical and political particularity of Israel's land once he transitions into a discussion of Christian ethics. But before demonstrating how this is so, however, let us resume our review of the two remaining components comprising his hermeneutical method.

The second way Wright proposes reading the Old Testament is *eschatologically*. Again, this mode of interpretation is fairly self-explanatory as one is to read the historical events of the Hebrew canon through a prism that point towards Israel's ultimate redemption and restoration. However, Wright posits that there is a broader and more cosmic dimension of redemption and restoration at play here as well. For as he explains, "God's acts of redemption for the people—their deliverance from the control of the Egyptians, the guidance to the promised land, and establishment there—typically viewed as 'historical' acts, are presented according to the paradigm of creation. These events are thus given cosmological significance. Israel's redemption is part of God's new act of creation."[74]

Finally, there is the *typological* method whereby one reads the Hebrew canon in light of "Jesus as the Messiah who fulfilled and embodied the mission of Israel."[75]

In formulating and distinguishing these different hermeneutical strategies Wright insists that we not view them as manufactured constructs artificially imposed onto the text. Rather they emerge organically from Scripture itself with the paradigmatic and eschatological methods extant in the Hebrew canon and the typological method present in the New

---

72. Bader-Saye, *Church and Israel after Christendom*, 89.
73. Ibid.
74. Wright, *Old Testament Ethics*, 91.
75. Ibid., 187.

Testament. Moreover, it is also important to recognize that even though they are distinct in both tone and focus, these methods are not "mutually exclusive, nor are they relevant in every case."[76]

To wit Wright contends that Israel's land provides a "particularly interesting example" for Christian ethical interpretation since it "can be taken up into Christian reflection and application in all three ways."[77] As such, Christians "should not think that if we speak of the land in the Old Testament having significance for the eschatological new creation, we thereby exclude it from economic relevance in the present social order."[78] Nor should they think that "if we speak of it as finding typological fulfillment in Christ, we thereby 'spiritualise' it out of any paradigmatic relevance to earthly issues of peoples and territories today."[79]

Keeping this interpretive interdependence in mind, Wright proceeds to illuminate the ethical contours of Israel's land in light of each of the hermeneutical methods he identifies. With respect to the paradigmatic method, Wright contends that Israel's land can be read as an instructive microcosm for Yahweh's prelapsarian intentions, "[o]r, to be more precise, God's involvement with Israel in their own land was God's redemptive address to the fracturing of his creative purpose for human beings and the earth."[80] Viewed from this perspective, Christians "are justified, therefore, in taking the social and economic laws and institutions of Israel and using them as models for own ethical task in the wider world of modern-day secular society," all the while recognizing that these economic and social models "provide us with *objectives,* without requiring a *literal* transposition of ancient Israelite practice into twentieth-century society." [8]

Thus when pondering what ethical content can be culled from Israel's tradition of the jubilee (יוֹבֵל), for instance, Wright discerns an applicable set of economic and social practices. Economically the jubilee shows that what "God required for Israel reflects in principle he desires for humanity; namely, broadly equitable distribution of the resources of the earth, especially the land, and a curb on the tendency to accumulation with its inevitable oppression and alienation."[81] More specifically the jubilee did not "entail a redistribution of land" but a "restoration to family units of *the opportunity and the*

---

76. Ibid., 182.
77. Ibid., 182–83.
78. Ibid., 183.
79. Ibid.
80. Ibid.
81. Ibid., 207.

resources to provide for themselves again."⁸² Hence a modern application of the jubilee "calls for creative thinking as to what forms of opportunity and resources would enable people to do that, and to enjoy the dignity and social involvement that such self-provision entails." ⁸³

Socially, the jubilee addressed the economic fragility of the Israelite kinship structure and therefore aimed to "restore social dignity and participation to families" by "legislating for specific structural mechanisms to regulate the economic effects of debt."⁸⁴ In doing so Israel understood that the "economic collapse of a family in one generation was not to condemn all future generations to the bondage of perpetual indebtedness."⁸⁵ Accordingly, "[s]uch principles and objectives are certainly not irrelevant to [modern] welfare legislation or indeed any legislation with socio-economic implications," nor are they irrelevant "to the massive issues of international debt" between lender and heavily indebted countries.⁸⁶

Thus what Wright's paradigmatic interpretation of Israel's land provides is a sophisticated and nuanced act of analogical imagination whereby the economic and social principles underpinning the governance and distribution of Israel's land vis-à-vis the Jubilee are sympathetically transposed onto a modern landscape, all the while recognizing and preserving the contextual uniqueness and limitations of each. The ethical performance of the Jubilee is not detached from Israel's land any more than it is re-spatialized into an ecclesiology. Israel's land remains irrevocably Israel's while modern lands remain modern. However, the contextual and historical gap between the two does not remain so vast as to be unbridgeable. The constancy of economic deprivation and social marginalization as well as the sources that produce them—whether it be loss of actual land or denial of health care access, for instance—ensures that there is just enough continuity and overlap between Israel's world and our own to safely transport its ethical freight across the divide.

However, whatever sense of ethical and geographic distinctiveness Israel's land retains in Wright's paradigmatic interpretation of the Old Testament all but vanishes in his typological reading of the New. For as he states with respect to a panoramic reading of the latter, what "the New Testament

---

82. Ibid.
83. Ibid.
84. Ibid., 208.
85. Ibid.
86. Ibid.

teaches is that there can no longer be such a thing as a 'holy land' or a 'holy city[.]' Instead Christians are told that they now 'have Christ.'"[87]

More specifically Wright argues that instead of communicating a continuous and expanded form of land governance predicated upon ancient Israel, both the Gospels and Pauline Epistolary instead proclaim that "Christ and the kingdom he proclaimed and inaugurated" actually "fulfill" it (i.e. –that form of land governance) thereby "*transforming* it into something that can be the experience not just of a single nation in a small slice of territory but of anyone, anywhere in Christ."[88] Hence the "promise of Jesus to be present wherever his people meet, effectively *universalizes* the Old Testament promise of God's presence among his people in the land[.]"

But how can such a universal transformation of Israel be possible given Wright's previous adamancy of not wanting to run roughshod over its historical and socio-political particularity? The answer, ironically enough, lies in an inability for Wright to follow through on the very interpretive implications his paradigmatic hermeneutic so assiduously prescribes.

Recall from above that the main distinction differentiating a *paradigmatic* reading of the Old Testament from one that is *principled* is, according to Wright, the way the latter "lead[s] to the eventual discarding of the specific realities of the Old Testament text, the concrete, earthy history of Israel, the good the bad and the ugly."[89]

A paradigmatic reading, by contrast, Wright maintains, "forces us constantly to go back to the hard given reality of the text of the Bible itself and imaginatively to live with Israel in their world, before returning to the equally hard given reality of our own world[.]"[90]

Consequently when attempting to ascertain what normative implications Israel's governance of the land holds for Christian ethical and political reflection, Wright insists that Christians must first address the historicist question of "[w]hat did the land signify for the Old Testament Israelite?"

Quite a bit, as it happens. For as Wright explains,

> for an ancient Israelite, the land was above all else *God's gift*. It had been given in fulfillment to his promise to Abraham, and received in the course of their redemptive history. The land was therefore a huge, symbolic, tangible proof to every Israelite householder that he, his family and his people had a special covenantal relationship with the Lord. Deuteronomy links the

---

87. Ibid., 193.
88. Ibid., 196.
89. Ibid., 70.
90. Ibid., 71.

land repeatedly with the assurance of their election in Abraham. They were the Lord's people because they lived in the Lord's land, which he had given to them. The individual enjoyed his personal share in the land through the kinship network and his inalienable family inheritance—his "portion" in the land. Deuteronomy also speaks of the land repeatedly as Israel's inheritance, which invokes family images. Israel was, as Exodus 4:22 stated, the Lord's firstborn son, and the land was again tangible evidence of that relationship of sonship. Thus to belong to an Israelite household living in God's land was to experience secure inclusion within the covenantal relationship: the land was the place of *life* with God. But it also meant to accept the demands of that covenantal relationship: the land was also the place of a specific moral and spiritual *lifestyle* before God. To possess the land was to share in the inheritance and the responsibility of all God's people. The land, in short, for an Israelite, meant security, inclusion, blessing, sharing and practical responsibility.[91]

Notice how closely in both tone and content this disquisition tracks with O'Donovan's appraisal of possession discussed above. For just as O'Donovan argues that it is possession of a specific land that codified Israel's unique covenantal status with YHWH, so too does Wright cite Israel's land as "tangible evidence" and "proof" of its "special covenantal relationship with the Lord."

Moreover both O'Donovan and Wright are keen to observe how the sense of giftedness suffusing Israel's land imparts its governance with a concomitant sense of moral obligation inasmuch as the gratuitous blessing of the land by YHWH correlatively commends that it be administered and allocated in such a manner that not only no single Israelite citizen or household be deprived of its socio-economic security but indeed even resident aliens as well.

These insights coupled with a paradigmatic desire to safeguard Israel's "concrete, earthy history" would seemingly put Wright in a much stronger position to speak to how Israel's socio-economic governance of the land can be imaginatively re-purposed for non-Israelite lands while still preserving and honoring its unique territorial identity.

Yet as has already been indicated above, such does not prove to be the case. Instead Wright makes the argument that "as we move" from the exilic prophets toward the New Testament, we are able to "discern a loosening of, almost a dispensing with, the ancient land-kinship basis of the covenant, in

---

91. Ibid., 142.

visions of the future constitution of the relationship between God and his people."[92]

"In other words," Wright continues, what the prophetic and restorative visions of Jeremiah, Ezekiel, and Isaiah all foreshadow is that "the theological themes of security, inclusion, sharing and responsibility, which were once linked to [Israel's] land, remain valid; but they are loosened from their literal, territorial moorings, as the scope of salvation is widened to includenon Israelites."[93]

What is important to notice here is the degree to which Wright's expansionist interpretation of Israel's land is still constrained and circumscribed by a stubborn historicity. For even though he detects a prophetic "loosening" of Israel's original "territorial moorings," he is nevertheless mindful that neither Jeremiah, Ezekiel nor Isaiah ever fully decouple their eschatological visions of universal inclusion and security from the particular restoration of *eretz* Israel. In fact all remain steadfast with the idea that the blessings of security and inclusion are universally attainable only insofar as they are first instantiated in a territorially restored Israel.

Yet whatever remains of Wright's erstwhile albeit tenuous connection between Israel's land and the blessings of universal inclusion and security is finally and irrevocably dissolved by Jesus in the New Testament as most prominently and definitively evidenced by Paul.

For in describing how the crucifixion of Christ effects an eschatological reconciliation between Jews and Gentiles that ultimately incorporates the latter into God's covenantal fold (Eph 2:11—3:6), Paul, Wright explains, describes Gentiles as "joint-heirs (*synkleronoma*), a joint-body (*sysssoma*) and joint-sharers (*symmetocha*) with Israel in the promise, in Messiah Jesus, through the gospel."[94]

This language of "joint-ness" is especially significant Wright believes, since it not only "speaks of permanence, security, inclusion and practical responsibility," but also because it "evokes the pattern of relationships between God, Israel and their land within which the Israelites of old had found their security."[95]

Hence what Paul describes is nothing less than a full scale revolution to the extent that "through the cross of Christ, those [i.e., the Gentiles] [who] were *out* are now *in*" and "those [who] *were excluded* now *belong*."[96]

92. Ibid., 191.
93. Ibid.
94. Ibid., 192.
95. Ibid.
96. Ibid.

But whereas before the advent of Christ the primary locus of that security and inclusion was always positioned in Israel's land, Paul, says Wright, now boldly proclaims that "Christ himself *takes over the significance and the function* of the old land-kinship qualification."[97]

Accordingly "[t]o be *in Christ* just as to be *in the land*, denotes first, a status and a relationship that have been *given* by God; second, a position of inclusion and security in God's family; and third, a commitment to live worthily by fulfilling the practical responsibilities towards those who share the same relationship with you."[98]

This then, explains Wright, "is what is [finally] meant by the *typological* understanding of the significance of Israel's land. It simply means treating [Israel's] land as we do other great features and themes of the Old Testament, by relating it to the person and work of the Messiah, and through him to the nature of the community of those 'in Christ', messianic Israel."[99]

To be sure, there is certainly a strong exegetical basis to support Wright's claim that Paul's eschatological formula of being "in Christ" (ἐν Χριστῷ) carries with it a locative meaning that extends beyond the borders of territorial Israel.[100] However, notwithstanding that expanded spatial connotation, in what specific sense does being 'in Christ' "take over" both the ethical significance and function of Israel's land?

Such a question clearly seems to be in the front of Wright's mind as well. For as he asks in response to Paul's proceeding argumentation "[b]ut what has become of the *socio-economic* dimension of the land, which we found to be of such importance to Old Testament Israel? Has it just been transcended, spiritualized and forgotten?"[101]

That it has not is clearly attested to by the fact that Paul describes the "oneness of believers in Christ" not as a "mere, abstract, spiritual concept," but instead as a relationship that has "far-reaching practical implications in both the social *and* economic realms." [102]

Yet whereas before the Old Testament anchored Israel's socio-economic and political relationships within its land, Paul, says Wright, now situates them within the broader context of Christian "fellowship" or κοινωνία. For just as the "explicit purpose of the exodus was the enjoyment of the rich blessing of God in his 'good land," so now does Paul see that "the goal of

97. Ibid.
98. Ibid.
99. Ibid.
100. Ibid.
101. Ibid., 193.
102. Ibid., 194.

redemption through Christ is 'sincere love for your brothers' with all its practical implications."[103] Accordingly "[c]itizenship of the kingdom of God most certainly has a social and economic dimension." Nevertheless it is a dimension "that has transcended the land and kinship structure of the Old Testament" inasmuch as the "experience of *fellowship*—in its full rich, 'concrete' New Testament sense—fulfils analogous theological and ethical functions for the Christian as the possession of the *land* did for Old Testament Israelites."[104]

Thus constitutes three of the main ways Christian ethics has de-territorialized the kingdom of God. An analysis and comparison of them not only puts us in a position to recognize their similarities and differences, but also the symbiotic relationship they share with the de-territorializing tendencies of Third Quest historical Jesus scholarship. Furthermore, it also puts us in a position to understand one of the most forceful arguments against the kingdom's territoriality to be offered from both a historical and ethical perspective. I am speaking of course of John Howard Yoder's.

2.4 The Politics of Jesus: Nonviolent Enemy Love

In order to ascertain how and why Yoder reaches the conclusion that a diasporic ethic is determinative for the proper constitution of a Christian political identity, we must first begin with his scriptural appraisals of Jesus and the kingdom. That Yoder would choose to make Scripture his normative point of departure for developing a Christian political ethic is not to be unexpected as it is but the function of his "biblical realism"[105] as well as his correlative belief that Jesus and his eschatological vision of the kingdom are the primary if not the sole anchor upon which to ground a Christian political ethic.[106] Moreover it is also reflective of his anti-foundationalist

103. Ibid., 195.

104. Ibid.

105. By "biblical realism" I am referring to the school of biblical interpretation developed in part by Claude Tresmontant, Edmund Cerbonnier, Markus Barth, and others during the 1950s that posits that even amidst its literary, historical, and theological diversity the biblical canon nevertheless still possess a contiguous and coherent narrative. For further discussion on how Yoder's reading of Scripture is informed by this hermeneutical orientation, see Carter, *Politics of the Cross*, 63–65; and Nugent, *Politics of Yahweh*, 11–12. For examples of Yoder articulating a prescriptive ethical appropriation of Scripture in accordance with the principles of biblical realism, see his chapter "The Use of the Bible in Theology," in Johnston, ed., *Use of the Bible in Theology*, 103–20.

106. For instructive examples of Yoder's discussion on the normativity of Jesus for Christian ethics, see *Politics of Jesus*, 8–12, 97–109; Yoder, *Nevertheless*, 133–36; and Yoder, "How H. Richard Niebuhr Reasoned: A Critique of *Christ and Culture*," in Stassen

instinct to see Jesus' historical particularity as providing sufficient epistemological and methodological warrant for the universal applicability of his socio-political witness as opposed to having that witness wrung through the justifying machinery of some theoretical and abstract architectonic.[107]

With these convictions in view it is therefore not surprising to find Yoder deploying the same kind of hermeneutical strategy in their reading of the Gospels as that used by the Third Quest inasmuch as both seek to locate their scriptural reading of Jesus and the kingdom within the larger political and social orbit of a first-century Palestinian context while also seeking to preserve their Jewish inflection and content.

One of the main ways Yoder works to fulfill this strategy is by first juxtaposing and contrasting Jesus' own political posture of "revolutionary subordination" with the prevailing political philosophies of his day: i.e., the collaborationism of the Pharisees, the quiescence and separatism of the Essenes, and the violent militarism of the Zealots.[108] In doing so he strikes a note similar to that sounded by Borg in that both see all these parties as possessing and laboring toward the same essential goal, namely seeking liberation from Rome and effecting a restoration of Israel's national sovereignty.[109] Jesus proves himself to be no different in this regard, as his deliberate appropriation of the restorative trope of jubilee as well as his use of politically charged nomenclature like "gospel" (*euangelion*) and "kingdom" (*baselia*) show him to be "announcing the imminent implementation of a new regime whose marks would be that the rich would give to the poor, the captives would be freed, and [his] hearers would have a new mentality (*metanoia*), if they believe his news."[110]

---

et al., *Authentic Transformation*, 61–65.

107. See Yoder, *Priestly Kingdom*, 46–63. See also Yoder, "Walk and Word: The Alternatives to Methodologism," in Hauerwas et al, eds., *Theology without Foundations*.

108. Yoder, *Original Revolution*, 18–27.

109. Yoder, *Politics of Jesus*, 28–33.

110. Ibid., 32. For a sympathetic yet incisive critique of Yoder's Jubilee thesis, see Willard M. Swartley's essay "Smelting for Gold: Jesus and Jubilee in John H. Yoder's *Politics of Jesus*," in Ollenburger and Koontz, eds., *Mind Patient and Untamed*, 288–303. According to Swartley Yoder's particular reading of the Jubilee tradition into Jesus needs qualification for at least three reasons: (1) Jesus' invocation of Isa 61:1–2 in Luke 4:18–19 omits the line "he has sent me to bind the broken-hearted" and instead adds the line "to let the oppressed go free" from Isa 58:6. Hence while it possible that Jesus himself is responsible for this adaption Swartley thinks the more likely explanation is a Lukan redaction. (2) Swartley points to Ben Ollenburger's work comparing the Jubilee tradition in the Holiness and Deuteronomic codes, which notes that the Jubilee legislation in Lev 25 does cover liquidation of debts, while Deut 15 does address forgiveness of debts but contains no reference to the Jubilee. Thus even though the LXX uses the same Greek verb *aphesis* for "release" (*derôr*) of the land in Lev 25:11–13, "Jubilee"

Thus that Jesus possessed and acted upon an explicitly political objective is not a proposition that Yoder thinks worthy of further discussion. His decision to publicly thrust himself as a competing interlocutor into the highly contentious and serious debate over how best to restore Israel to its former national glory should, he maintains, put to rest any lingering suspicion that his was a purely spiritual mission unencumbered by worldly concerns. Instead the more pivotal question to be pursued and answered is what kind of politic did Jesus aspire to and practice, and here Yoder finds Jesus' own political approach to securing Israel's liberation and restoration to compare quite favorably to that of the Pharisees and Zealots save for two crucial distinctions.

For like the Pharisees Jesus shares an erstwhile conscientiousness about keeping every aspect of life under the moral authority and tutelage of the *torah*, even if such conscientiousness necessitated stark separation from those things and persons that imbrue. However, Jesus departs sharply from the Pharisaic program of astringent purity in that he actively engages, includes and reconciles with all those who, for various reasons, are deemed impure.

Similarly, like the Zealots Jesus is also gripped by an intense passion to win Israel its freedom and redemption and thus determined to counteract all those forces vigorously—both foreign and domestic—that keep Israel mired in subjugation. In fact the intensity of this passion is felt so acutely by Jesus that according to Yoder it constitutes a "real" and "genuine" temptation.[111] For on three separate occasions in his public ministry—his temptation by Satan in the desert, his provocative demonstration in the Temple, and his time of testing in the garden of Gethsemane—Jesus confronts the very distinct and real possibility of utilizing revolutionary violence as a means to further accomplish his liberative and restorative agenda.

And yet in each and every instance Jesus unequivocally and adamantly rejects the sword. More than that vigorously he radically instructs his disciples to pray for and love their enemies. That he does so, says Yoder, is again a clear demonstration that Jesus possesses a "readiness to associate with the impure,

---

(*yôbēl*) in Lev 25 and 27, and "debt-remission" (*šemit*) in Deut 15:2, 3, 9 "the difference in these Hebrew texts cautions against reading all aspects of *release* into Jubilee and into Jesus' words in Luke also" (290). (3) Since the stories immediately following Jesus' invocation of Isa 61 are about the inclusion of Gentiles, then it must be asked if "Luke really intend[s] to develop the Jubilee emphasis" (291). Despite these concerns, however, Swartley believes there is additional confirmatory evidence within Luke as well as Mark and Matthew to support aspects of Yoder's interpretation.

111. Yoder, *Original Revolution*, 21–22; cf. Yoder, *Politics of Jesus*, 42–48.

the sinner, the publican, the Roman."[112] But more than that, Jesus' disavowal of the sword is both a perceptive testament and stinging indictment about what is fundamentally wrong and self-defeating about all forms of political violence. For as Yoder states, it "is not the fact (which is historically demonstrable) that insurrectionary movements most often fail and thereby actually make worse the situation of the oppressed," which makes political violence untenable, nor is it "that successful insurrectionary movements most often are corrupted by the temptations of the very appeal to righteousness in the use of power which brought them victory."[113] Rather "[w]hat is wrong with the Zealot path for Jesus" is that it "still, by its subordination of persons (who may be killed if they are on the wrong side) to causes (which must triumph because they are right), preserves unbroken the self-righteousness of the mighty and denies the servanthood which God has chosen as His tool to remake the world."[114] Furthermore living as they did within and under the long shadow cast by the Exile, both Jesus and his contemporaries would be also keenly aware of how a call to take up arms betrayed a fundamental form of disbelief since Israel's prophets had repeatedly shown that "confidence in YHWH is an alternative to the self-determining use of Israel's own military resources in the defense of their existence as God's people."[115]

Hence as Yoder states in the context of explaining the political meaning of Jesus' crucifixion, "[h]ere at the cross is the man who loves his enemies, the man whose righteousness is greater than the Pharisees, who being rich becomes poor, who gives his robe to those who took his cloak, who prays for those who despitefully use him. The cross is not a detour or a hurdle to the kingdom, nor is it even the way to the kingdom; it *is* the kingdom come" (emphasis added).[116]

What is important to see here is not only how Yoder flags non-violence and enemy-love as being the most definitive ethical axioms to be culled from a political reading of Jesus and the kingdom, but also the way in which he describes these axioms as being coeval and indeed even *constitutive* of the kingdom of God itself—a perspective that upon closer examination is not altogether different from that espoused by Bryan above. Mysteriously dropped from sight, however is Yoder's original emphasis that the original political intent behind Jesus' announcement of the kingdom was not just a restoration of Israel's moral and political character but of the very nation itself.

112. Yoder, *Original Revolution*, 23.
113. Ibid., 23–24.
114. Ibid., 24.
115. Yoder, *Politics of Jesus*, 83.
116. Ibid., 51.

Yet this fluid interchangeability between Jesus' nonviolent and peaceable political witness and the kingdom's historical and ethical manifestation resonates throughout Yoder's thought, and so I would like to unpack it a bit further. I want to discern how it gives rise to his non-territorial reading of the kingdom and thus his diasporic ethic.

2.5 A Peaceable and Non-territorial Reign

For Yoder an appropriate, which is to say biblical, understanding of the political and ethical nature of the kingdom of God cannot be achieved apart from entering into the New Testament eschatological view that the current world sits astride two distinct and overlapping aeons.

As Yoder describes it, what distinguishes these aeons is not their chronology, since they coexist historically, but rather their fundamental orientation as "one points backward to human history outside of (before) Christ" with the other pointing "forward to the fullness of the kingdom of God, of which it is a foretaste."[117] At the point of their intersection stands Jesus whose historical incarnation marks the advent of the new aeon as well as the historical possibility of entering into and experiencing the kingdom of God even if only proleptically.

Given Yoder's language of "Christ" and "incarnation" one might infer that what endows the new aeon with its characteristic newness is perhaps the *communicado idiomatum* such that the metaphysical comingling of divine and human substances in the person of Jesus is itself the new historical site through which access to the kingdom is gained. However, for Yoder what is new about the aeon of the kingdom is not Jesus' ontology but rather his historical and political relationship vis-à-vis the Jewish expectation of Israel's national restoration. More specifically Yoder contends that what marks Jesus' vision of the kingdom as qualitatively new and thus distinct from the old aeon is not that it is any less political but rather that it fundamentally parts company with and soundly rejects the first-century Jewish hope and expectation of YHWH restoring Israel as a territorial nation. For whereas Jesus' contemporaries had understood YHWH's covenantal promise to Abraham to be a "vindication of their nationalism," Jesus reveals that "the universality of God's kingdom contradicts rather than confirms all particular solidarities and can be reached only by first forsaking the old aeon."[118]

Thus even though Jesus preached a gospel "expressed in terms borrowed from the realm of government and involving definite consequences

---

117. Yoder, *Priestly Kingdom*, 146.
118. Yoder, *Royal Priesthood*, 147.

for the social order," Yoder would have us see that what Jesus finally proclaimed was "the institution of a new kind of life, not of a new government." And in particular this is a life that is to be lived in conformity with Jesus' own example of nonviolent enemy love. Therefore in Yoder's eyes the eschatological reality of kingdom of God cannot be seen or experienced as anything other but the concrete embodiment of a political and ethical praxis of nonviolent enemy love since "[n]ationalism and pragmatism are both rejected in the life of the people of the new aeon, whose only purpose is love in the way of the cross and in the power of the resurrection."[119]

And yet even though this eschewal of territoriality and national solidarity in exchange for nonviolent enemy love makes Jesus' vision of the kingdom radically new from what his contemporaries conceived it to be, there is also sense of familiarity and continuity pervading it as well. For as Yoder states, what distinguishes the kingdom as a new political reality are not the non-territorial commitments to nonviolence and enemy love themselves, but rather that "these ideas became incarnate" in Jesus.[120] Where these ideas existed in a more embryonic and inchoate form Yoder suggests is within the tradition of Judaism itself. For instance, although ostensibly opposed to a political ethic of nonviolent enemy love, Yoder finds that a deeper reading of Israel's traditions and narratives of holy war are actually incipient of such an ethic insofar as their main subject is not the ethical permissibility of killing *per se* but rather "that even at the crucial point of the bare existence of Israel as a people, their survival could be entrusted to the care of Yahweh as their King, even if He told them to have no other kings. They did not need to trust their own institutional readiness or the solidarity of their royal house; Jahweh [sic] would provide."[121]

Hence Israel remains Israel not by developing the military resources necessary to preserve its national and territorial integrity but rather by placing its faith and trust in YHWH for protection. Yoder sees this theme being further developed by the prophets during the period of Israel's Assyrian and Babylonian captivity and culminating most potently and clearly in Jeremiah's injunction to his fellow exiles that they "seek the welfare of the city where I have sent you into exile, and pray to the Lord on its behalf, for in its welfare you will find your welfare" (Jer 29:7).

According to Yoder the ethical and political import we are to derive from this admonition is twofold. First, because it casts into serious doubt the legitimacy of Israel's own "Davidic Project," by which Yoder means Israel's

---

119. Ibid., 149.
120. Ibid.
121. Yoder, *Original Revolution*, 99.

constitution as a territorial state, it should therefore also call into question any political commitment centered and predicated upon a commitment to preserving territorial particularity. Second, it also shows that Israel's diaspora was not, as Yoder describes it, "a two-generation parenthesis, after which the Davidic and Solomonic project was supposed to take up again where it left off," but rather that "dispersion shall be the calling of the Jewish faith community."[122] And a fundamental component of what it means to see exile as a permanent political and ethical calling is to see that "since God is sovereign over history, there is no need . . . to seize (or subvert) political sovereignty in order for God's will to be done."[123]

What we are able to detect within the long arc of Israel's history, therefore, in Yoder's judgment, is a progressive movement away from seeing the kingdom of God as a territorial state towards an understanding that sees the kingdom as a diasporic mode of political existence. Once again, however, the trajectory of this movement should not be considered as a shift in "ethical codes"

> but rather in an increasingly precise definition of the nature of peoplehood. The identification of the people of Israel with the state of Israel was progressively loosened by all the events and prophecies of the Old Testament. It was loosened in a positive way by the development of an increasing vision for the concern of Yahweh for *all* people and by the promise of a time when *all* people peoples would come to Jerusalem to learn the law; it was loosened as well in a negative direction by the development of a concept of the faithful remnant, no longer assuming that Israel as a geographical and ethnic body would be usable for Jahweh's [sic] purposes.[124]

The ethical upshot of these changes accordingly lays the groundwork for why Yoder sees Jesus' own politics being defined by nonviolent enemy love and a concurrent rejection of a landed kingdom. For once "all men [sic] are seen as potential partakers of the covenant, then the outsider can no longer be perceived as less than human or as an object for sacrificing."[125] Furthermore, once "one's own national existence is no longer seen as a guarantee of Jahweh's [sic] favor, then to save this national existence by a holy war is no longer a purpose for which miracles would be expected."[126]

122. Yoder, *For the Nations*, 53, 52.
123. Ibid., 67.
124. Yoder, *Original Revolution*, 101.
125. Ibid.
126. Ibid.

Thus Jesus' political ethic of nonviolent enemy love may be new in the sense that it forswears a landed restoration of the kingdom of God, but it is hardly new in the sense of lacking Jewish precedent. For as Yoder states, "[i]t is rather the case that Jesus' impact in the first century added more and deeper authentically Jewish reasons, and reinforced and further validated the already expressed Jewish reasons for the already well established ethos of not being in charge and not considering any local state structure to be the primary bearer of the movement of history."[127] What makes Jesus politically normative then for Yoder is that his humanness and historicity give "warrant for the generalizability of his reconciliation." However, it is the "*nonterritorial particularity* of his Jewishness [that] defends us against selling out to *any* wider world's claim to be really wider, or to be self-validating."[128]

2.6 Conclusion

Throughout this chapter I have tried to demonstrate the various ways Christian ethics has de-territorialized the kingdom of God. In doing so I have sought to show how political and ethical interpretations of the kingdom bear more than a passing resemblance to the Third Quest's historical interpretation. For while both provide compelling and incisive arguments for why it is necessary to see both Jesus and the kingdom as irreducibly political in nature, and also make clear why Jesus' teaching and actions are inextricably tied to first-century Jewish eschatological expectations of Israel's restoration, both nevertheless view Israel's territoriality as being either inconsequential, or even more starkly, antithetical to a proper understanding and interpretation of Jesus' mission. As a result both make a territorial restoration of Israel and a landed conception of the kingdom of God either irrelevant or injurious to a reading of Jesus' historicity and ethics.

Yet ironically to make Israel's territoriality immaterial or even problematic to a political and ethical discussion of Jesus and the kingdom is unwittingly to re-inscribe some of the very same assumptions that have helped to rob them of their political and ethical purchase in the first place. For while it would indeed be a great mistake to suggest that the national and territorial restoration of Israel exhausts the entirety of what Jesus and his disciples conceived the kingdom to be, much less the political and ethical import we are able to draw from it, it is just as troublesome to claim that Israel's territoriality should have *no* historical or ethical bearing upon our reading of Jesus and the kingdom. Such a claim repeats the damage to Jewish authenticity that the

---

127. Yoder, *For the Nations*, 69.
128. Yoder, *Priestly Kingdom*, 62; emphasis added.

criterion of dissimilarity did; it blocks out the data that are most important for reconstructing a plausible historical and ethical re-presentation of Jesus and his mission in its Jewish context. It puts asunder the political and eschatological hopes of Israel's territorial restoration that were crucial in Jewish hopes. Thus it leaves us with a Jewish and political Jesus that is oddly alienated from a major component of his own historical, socio-political and theological context. It reduces Jesus' own normative political witness to a society without a location or a government. It seems utterly incapable and ill-equipped to engage the political and ethical dimensions of territorial governance aside from offering a posture of denunciation and rejection.

Moreover the move to discard Israel's territoriality as either irrelevant or injurious to a reading of Jesus and the kingdom is also to resurrect the haunting and menacing specter of supersessionism. As Scott Bader-Saye has stated, "if Christians are to worship and follow Israel's God, [then] they must not ignore or reject God's Israel."[129] Yet by choosing either to see Jesus subsume the kingdom of God into its people or else to re-locate it to an ethical praxis of nonviolent enemy love without a place moves Jesus toward Platonic idealism that ignores or rejects God's Israel.

A different kind of historical and ethical reading of Jesus and the kingdom needs to be offered. Such a reading should seek to build upon the fruitful historical and ethical insights already put forward by Davies, Borg, Sanders, Wright and Yoder, but it should also work to fill their lacunae and correct their misinterpretations. More specifically it would provide a historical account of Jesus and his mission that makes it possible to see why the eschatological restoration of *eretz* Israel was implied in his proclamation of the kingdom of God. Furthermore it would also explain why this landed vision of the kingdom is thus suggestive of a Christian political ethic of territorial governance that comports with Jesus' witness of peacemaking and nonviolent enemy love.

Before doing so however, we should first identify the origins and limn the contours of a perduring theological dynamic and problem that has been present in Christian thought and practice ever since the early second century CE—a problem that in many ways foregrounds and gives rise to the very de-territorialization of the kingdom that we have already observed. It is a problem that runs deeply within the grain of Christian thought and that has infected virtually every stage of Christian theological development over the last two millennia. Yet as is the case with most problems of this sort, it is a *specifically* theological problem. The tools and means of its rectification must be found within the Christian tradition itself.

---

129. Bader-Saye, *Church and Israel after Christendom*, 26.

3

The Ground(s) on Which We Stand: De-territorializing the Kingdom of God in the Christian Imagination and Its Implications for Contemporary Theology and Ethics

3.1 Introduction

THE TWO PREVIOUS CHAPTERS have outlined the various ways in which recent historical Jesus scholarship and Christian ethical discourse have de-territorialized Jesus' proclamation of the kingdom of God. In so doing, I have presented not only a basic taxonomy of the two, but also illuminated a conceptual interdependence. More specifically I have shown that just as a de-territorialization of the kingdom leads to a de-territorialized reading of Jesus' socio-political ethic, so too does a de-territorialization of Jesus' socio-political ethic result in a de-territorialized reading of the kingdom.

To be sure, there are compelling reasons—both historically and ethically—why these interpretations are in place and why both should be given due consideration in light of the formidable corpus of scholarship we have engaged thus far. Furthermore, when one considers the disastrous consequences of Christian theology being co-opted into colonial conquest and dispossession, the need for cultivating what Daniel Smith-Christopher has recently called a biblical theology of exile and diaspora becomes all the more apparent and incumbent. For if Jesus' proclamation of a universal kingdom of peace and justice is exemplary of anything then it most certainly speaks to the need of establishing "alternative corporeal, material, and social realities that refuse to accept the dominant mythologies and ideologies all around them."[1]

---

1. Smith-Christopher, *Biblical Theology of Exile*, 201.

Nevertheless, even while affirming the compelling reasons for interpreting Jesus' kingdom proclamation as entailing something beyond the territorial particularity of Israel and for rightly critiquing the dangers of Constantinianism, I also want to argue that there are equally compelling reasons for why an *exclusively* a-territorial interpretation of the kingdom should be, if not critically interrogated, then certainly juxtaposed with an interpretation that is explicitly territorial. For as I discussed in the previous chapter, one of the chief dangers implicit in this reading of the kingdom is that it ignores evidence within the gospels that strongly points towards Jesus' envisioning a territorial restoration of Israel. Thus to overlook or dismiss this evidence is to ironically re-iterate the very error that recent historical Jesus scholarship and Christian ethical discourse have both worked so assiduously and effectively to correct, namely painting a portrait of Jesus that is devoid of his first-century Jewish identity.

Moreover, I would go a step further and assert that the kingdom's complete de-territorialization poses significant theological and ethical problems as well. For not only does such an interpretation displace Israel's land—and thus transitively all other national territories—from the ambit of Christian political witness, but it also erodes, both figuratively and quite literally, the very theo-political ground(s) on which that witness itself stands. Stated more pointedly, it is my contention that a landless interpretation of Jesus' kingdom proclamation is no more theo-logically tenable than a docetic Christology for precisely the same reason the latter has been rejected as heterodox. That is because the insuperable materiality of Yahweh's covenant with Israel presupposes and demands that the full corporeality of both be maintained.

To see why this is so, requires us to engage in a more textured analysis of the theological and ethical problems that arise from a de-territorialized reading of the kingdom. But just as importantly, and perhaps even more so, it also requires us to engage in a fuller exploration of why a territorially restored Israel is incompatible neither with Jesus' kingdom vision nor with a correlative Christian political ethic of peace and justice. On the contrary, not only is a territorially restored kingdom integral to such concerns, but indeed also to the very integrity and coherence of the Christian tradition itself. Such then are the main foci of the rest of this project.

And yet as the old adage goes, it is impossible to know where one is going without first remembering from whence you came. In the same vein it is impossible for us to speak of where the Christian tradition can go vis-à-vis (re)territorializing its interpretation of Jesus and the kingdom of God without first remembering the extent to which a de-territorialized hermeneutic has endured. Indeed, as a closer reading of early patristic interpretation of the kingdom of God reveals below, such a hermeneutic has been at the core of the Christian tradition itself since its early inception.

3.2 On Hollowed Ground: The Ambivalent Territoriality of St. Justin Martyr's and St. Irenaeus's Interpretations of the Kingdom of God

As has already been demonstrated above, there is no paucity of scholarly opinion positing that Jesus himself is the figure most responsible for precipitating the kingdom's de-territorialization. Indeed, Peter W. L. Walker speaks for many when he states that

> the New Testament writers were well aware of this issue [i.e., the centrality of the land in both the patriarchal covenants and restorative eschatology] and that their distinctive views were a natural development of the direction Jesus himself in his ministry had given to the debate. In his role as a Jewish eschatological prophet, Jesus had announced the time when God was at work to fulfill his ancient promises of restoration from exile and of blessings to the nations, of the conquest of evil and the coming of the King; he had also in his own person embodied the coming of God's kingdom. In this new age, however, Israel would experience judgment, and former Jewish symbols of identity would come to be redefined as the gospel of the kingdom went to all nations. The divine purpose, in keeping with its original universal intention, now broke form from the confines of Jerusalem and the land towards the world.[2]

In the next two chapters I will show why it is problematic to ascribe such a direct causation to Jesus. Presently, however, even if troublesome Walker is certainly correct to trace the kingdom's de-territorialization to very early within the Christian tradition. Indeed such a judgment is quickly substantiated by a perusal of early patristic sources with two in particular being especially emblematic: St. Justin Martyr (100–165 CE) and St. Irenaeus of Lyons (?–202 CE). For it is within their writings that we begin to discern the initial contours of an inchoate a-territorial hermeneutic that eventually comes into full fruition in subsequent Christian theological reflection.

Before delving into the specifics of their kingdom interpretations, however, and more specifically the way they foreground its subsequent de-territorialization, it is first important to recall the theological crucible from

---

2. Peter L. Walker, "The Land and Jesus Himself," in Johnston and Walker, eds., *Land of Promise*, 115.

which those interpretations emerged. In particular, it is imperative to re-acquaint ourselves not only with Justin's and Irenaeus's *chiliastic* eschatology, but also the theological error with which they were most consistently and passionately consumed, namely the heresy of Gnosticism. For it is ultimately Justin's and Irenaeus's inability to let their critiques of the latter carry over and inform their appropriations of the former that lays the groundwork, so to speak, for the kingdom's de-territorialization.

3.2.1 *Chiliasm* and Gnosticism in St. Justin Martyr's and St. Irenaeus's Theology

Stated simply, *chiliasm* is an apocalyptic eschatology envisaging the establishment of a thousand-year global kingdom at Jesus' *parousia*. The term itself derives from the Greek word *chilias* (χιλιάς)—meaning "one thousand"—and is specifically referenced in Rev 20:1–6, which reads,

> Then I saw an angel coming down from heaven, holding in his hand the key to the bottomless pit and a great chain. He seized the dragon, that ancient serpent, who is the Devil and Satan, and bound him for a thousand [χιλιάς] years, and threw him into the pit, and locked and sealed it over him, so that he would deceive the nations no more, until the thousand [χιλιάς] years were ended. After that he must be let out for a little while. Then I saw thrones, and those seated on them were given authority to judge. I also saw the souls of those who had been beheaded for their testimony to Jesus and for the word of God. They had not worshipped the beast or its image and had not received its mark on their foreheads or their hands. They came to life and reigned with Christ for a thousand years. The rest of the dead did not come to life until the thousand [χιλιάς] years were ended. This is the first resurrection. Blessed and holy are those who share in the first resurrection. Over these the second death has no power, but they will be priests of God and of Christ, and they will reign with him for a thousand [χιλιάς] years.

Given its etymology and scriptural articulation, it is often assumed that *chiliasm*'s defining hallmark is the thousand-year reign of Christ. Such an assumption is complicated however, by a closer inspection of the patristic record. For as Robert L. Wilken perceptively notes in *The Land Called Holy: Palestine in Christian Thought and History*,[3] for both early *chiliastic* theologians in general and St. Justin and St. Irenaeus in particular, the main

---

3. Wilken, *The Land Called Holy*.

thrust of *chiliasm* is less "the idea of [Christ's] thousand-year reign" *per se*, and more "the belief that Christian hope is centered on a glorified Jerusalem that will come down from the heavens."[4] In other words for early Christianity the timing and duration of Jesus' millennial reign were of ancillary importance to its territorial location, that is Jerusalem and the land of Israel.

Furthermore as Wilken also observes, even though Justin's and Irenaeus's writings clearly demonstrate a familiarity with Revelation, and a *chiliastic* interpretation of its eschatology, the scriptural warrants they most often use to justify their own *chiliastic* visions are the "sayings of Jesus about the future of Jerusalem," the "writings of Paul" and most especially "passages from the prophets about the restoration of Jerusalem."[5] Revelation's *chiliasm* was therefore a confirmation and continuance of St. Justin's and St. Irenaeus's eschatology, not it source. Thus in contradistinction to later expressions of Christian eschatology that came to speak of the kingdom's eschatological consummation in increasing ethereal and 'otherworldly' terms, both Justin's and Irenaeus's interpretations remained firmly entrenched and grounded within (though not exclusively confined to) the gritty historical datum of territorial Israel.

Given this territorial orientation, which in this case is something of a tautology, it should therefore come as no surprise then to find a similar historical-material sensibility animating St. Justin's and St. Irenaeus's critiques of Gnosticism. We turn now to the helpful précis J. Kameron Carter provides in *Race: A Theological Account*,[6] which cogently encapsulates the crux of both, addressing first Carter's summation of Gnosticism or more precisely its syncretistic appropriation of Christianity, before moving to a consideration of his account of St. Irenaeus's response.

Although it would be facile to claim that disembodiment constitutes the whole of Gnosticism, there is no denying its centrality to a Gnostic cosmology nor the extent to which this aversion to embodiment features prominently in both St. Justin's and St. Irenaeus's anti-Gnostic polemics. Indeed as Carter observes, its ultimately this quest for disembodiment that renders Gnosticism, particularly in the eyes of Irenaeus, as fundamentally incompatible with orthodox Christianity, and this for two discrete albeit related reasons.

The first is how a Gnostic valorization of disembodiment established a de facto racialized human anthropology wherein a class of *pneumatic* or spirit people is set over and above those who either keep their carnal

---

4. Ibid., 56.
5. Ibid.
6. Carter, *Race: A Theological Account*.

passions in check by virtue of reason (i.e., the *psychics*), or most especially those who are slavishly subjected to their carnal passions (i.e., the *hylics*). What this racialized anthropology eventually gives rise to, Carter maintains, is a racialized biblical hermeneutic such that within a Gnostic reading of Scripture a "given interpretation would be situated either at the highest level of the Pleroma and then linked to the pneumatics, or at the middle level of the Kenoma and allocated to the psychics, or at the lowest level of the material Cosmos and tied to the fleshly hylics."[7] In so doing, Gnosticism actually served to reify a racialized human identity as opposed to its "transform[ation]" inasmuch as Gnostic exegesis failed to "reconstitute the identity of the scriptural reader" in light of the "scriptural witness to Jesus[.]"[8]

Second, the desire to extricate itself from the carnality of human existence also prompted a conjunctive "severing of [Gnostic] Christianity from its Jewish roots."[9] For once the Gnostics "were able to reimagine Christian identity in protoracial terms [that] supported the supremacy of the pneumatics (or Gnostics) over other [inferior] species of humankind" then, as Carter notes, there remained little reason why Christian identity should remain attached to "YHWH the Abrahamic God[.]"[10] Indeed, the Gnostic jettisoning of bodily flesh necessarily occasioned a concurrent denudation of historical and ethnic flesh inasmuch as both were viewed as material encumbrances to the acquisition of true knowledge or *gnosis*.

And so by "decoupling" itself from Judaism, Gnostic Christianity, writes Carter, "seized on the Pauline doctrine of election" not in order to affirm the permanence of YHWH's covenant with Israel (Rom 11), but instead "to rewrite it in Gnostic terms" such that "Paul's concern was not with YHWH's irrevocable promises to Israel as the people of his covenant" but instead with "the election of the true, pneumatic Christians—that is, the Gnostics."[11] And in particular the Gnostics took to reimagining themselves as "the 'new' Israel—the true church beyond Israel, the gathering of pneumatics who are an image of the nonmaterial 'Ecclesia' . . . of the Pleroma."[12]

This last point is crucially important as it will resurface again in a prominent way within our discussion of how Justin's and Irenaeus's interpretations of the kingdom prefigure its de-territorialization. For the present moment,

---

7. Ibid., 22.
8. Ibid., 21.
9. Ibid., 22.
10. Ibid.
11. Ibid.
12. Ibid.

however, let us now engage the specific reasons why St. Irenaeus finds this Gnostic predilection toward disembodiment fundamentally incompatible with the Christian narrative, both physiologically and historically.

First, in response to the degradation of material existence in general and human embodiment in particular, Irenaeus draws upon the christological doctrine of Christ's hypostatic union in order to reaffirm the intrinsic goodness of material creation. For as he argues in *Against Heresies*,

> in every respect, too, He [Jesus] is man, the formation of God; and thus He took up man into Himself, the invisible becoming visible, the incomprehensible becoming comprehensible, the impassible becoming, capable of suffering, and the Word becoming man, thus recapitulating all things in Himself. This was so that just as in super-celestial, spiritual and invisible things, the Word of God is supreme, so also in things visible and corporeal [the Word of God] might possess the supremacy, and, taking to Himself the preeminence, as well as constituting Himself Head of the Church, He might draw all things to Himself at the proper time.[13]

What is especially significant about this statement, as Carter notes, is Irenaeus's penetrating recognition of how Christ's "recapitulation of all things" bespeaks a "deep intimacy" between the whole of material creation and God even though there exists an implacable distinction between the two. More specifically, "this very intimacy is an intimacy ... that occurs inside the Father's love for the eternal Son who makes the Father visible even in the Son's materiality: that is, in his flesh in the economy of creation-redemption."[14] Read another way then, St. Irenaeus claims that "Christ's flesh" is nothing less than the material "site from which God as Creator mingles with creation yet maintains his distinction from creation."[15]

Accordingly, whereas a Gnostic soteriology was predicated upon a shuttering of material-historical existence, a Christian account of salvation, by contrast, proclaimed the exact opposite inasmuch as Jesus' incarnation as a member of the Holy Trinity testified to the reality that "there is no accessing of the supramaterial apart from its revelation, and thus mediation, in the materiality of creation and the flesh."[16] As such Christ's incarnation as a (hu)man not only refuted the Gnostic impugnation of bodily corporeality, but it also invalidated Gnosticism's racialized human hierarchy insofar as

13. Ibid., 24.
14. Ibid., 25.
15. Ibid.
16. Ibid.

Christ's enfleshment revealed that "Christ's flesh as Jewish, covenantal flesh" was a "social-political reality displayed across time and space into which the Gentiles are received in praise of the God of Israel."[17] Therefore to be "in Christ" was to be "liberated from the fiction of [racial] purity and thus every structure of dominance and slavery[.]"[18]

Second, that Jesus was incarnated not simply as a generic human being but more specifically as a Jew, also leads St. Irenaeus to affirm an inviolable linkage between Christianity and Judaism. Evidence of this affirmation is clearly discernible in *Against Heresies* in two ways, one indirect and negative and the other more direct and positive.

With respect to the former, when enumerating the litany of theological errors propagated by the Gnostic teacher Saturninus, St. Irenaeus states that "[h]e [Saturninus] says the God of the Jews is one of the Angels. On this account, because his [Jesus'] Father wished to destroy all the Principalities, Christ came to destroy the God of the Jews and to bring salvation to those who believed him."[19] Although more circuitous and inferential in nature than an explicit avowal of Christianity's continuity with Judaism, that Irenaeus castigates this teaching as erroneous nevertheless confirms his belief that orthodox Christian faith can no more legitimately obliterate the God of Israel than its own for the simple reason that the two are identical.

Regarding the latter Carter finds a more direct expression of the indissolubility between Christianity and Judaism within St. Irenaeus's account of Christ's recapitulation. For once again, what recapitulation describes, says Carter, is St. Irenaeus's notion that Jesus' body provides a "conspectus, a rhetorically potent and compacted reiteration, of the Law, that ratifies YHWH's covenant with Israel and analogically with creation as a whole."[20] Accordingly, just as Irenaeus holds that Christ's embodiment is exemplary of a deep congress between God and material creation, so also, says Carter, does he see Jesus' Jewishness illuminating a "deep unity between the Old and New Testaments[.]"[21] By doing so, Carter continues, "[St. Irenaeus] moves to overturn a key pillar of Gnostic theology and exegesis: namely, the inferiority of the God of Israel and the Old Testament Scriptures in which the story of this God in relationship to the people of Israel is told."[22]

17. Ibid., 30.
18. Ibid.
19. Irenaeus, *Against the Heresies*, 85.
20. Carte, *Race*, 26.
21. Ibid., 27.
22. Ibid., 26.

3.2.2 St. Justin Martyr's and St. Irenaeus's Interpretations of the Kingdom

Having now provided a thicker understanding of the theological milieu within which St. Justin and St. Irenaeus are working, we are now better equipped to understand their interpretations of the kingdom. In doing so, it is remarkable (though not altogether unexpected) to see how much their interpretations presuppose both these counter-Gnostic principles—that is an affirmation of material existence and the continuity between Christianity and Judaism. Indeed in some respects, their accounts of the kingdom are even more palpably territorial and Jerusalem-focused than those espoused by Jesus.

Consider, for example, the description of the kingdom St. Justin provides in *Dialogue with Trypho*.[23] When asked by his Jewish interlocutor, Trypho, whether he, as a Christian, "really believe[s] that this place Jerusalem shall be rebuilt, and do you actually expect that you Christians will one day congregate there to live joyfully with Christ, together with the patriarchs, the prophets, the saints of our race, or even those who become proselytes before your Christ arrived?" Justin responds as follows,

> If you have ever encountered any nominal Christians who do not admit of this doctrine, but dare to blaspheme the God of Abraham and the God of Isaac and Jacob by asserting that there is no resurrection of the dead, but that their souls are taken up to heaven at the very moment of their death, do not consider them to be real Christians; just as one, after careful examination, would not acknowledge as Jews the Sadducees or the similar sects of the Genistae, Meristae, Galileans, Hellenians and the Pharisees (please take no offence if I say everything that I think), but would realize that they are Jews and children of Abraham in name only, paying lip service to God, while their heart, as God himself declared, is far from him.
>
> Whereas I, and all other wholeheartedly orthodox Christians, feel certain that there will be a resurrection of the flesh, followed by a thousand years in the rebuilt, embellished, and enlarged city of Jerusalem, as was announced by the prophets Ezekiel, Isaiah and others.[24]

Taken as a whole, this response is truly remarkable both for its depth and complexity. Nevertheless there are three aspects that are especially

---

23. Justin Martyr, *Dialogue with Trypho*.
24. Ibid., 267.

significant and therefore deserving of further elaboration. The first is Justin's rather begrudging concession at the beginning of his statement that there exists a group of so-called "nominal Christians" who reject the coincidence of the kingdom's full eschatological consummation with a physically restored Jerusalem. Of course it would be overly speculative to presume that these "nominal Christians" were in fact Gnostics given that Justin offers no further clue about their identity other than their purported disbelief in a bodily resurrection. Nevertheless, even if not Gnostic by name, the spirit (if not the letter) of their beliefs certainly seems to comport with a Gnostic penchant toward disembodiment, which is why Justin ultimately rejects their authenticity as "real Christians."

Second, notice the theological symmetry with which Justin views the bodily resurrection of the dead and the territorial restoration of the kingdom. It is as though the two are inextricable inasmuch as a human soul cannot be fully resurrected apart from a human body any more than can a resurrected body fully indwell the kingdom of God apart from its being (re)placed in a territorially restored Jerusalem. Indeed in Justin's theological purview both events are predicated upon the fully restored materiality of the other.

Finally, there is Justin's rather jolting insistence that denial of a territorially restored kingdom is tantamount to committing an act of blasphemy. And why is this so? Precisely because such a kingdom is foretold by "the prophets Ezekiel, Isaiah and others." In other words it is not to the teachings of Jesus that Justin appeals when verifying this promise's authenticity and theological credence, but instead the tradition of Israel's prophetic witness. Thus not only does Justin establish the canonicity of the Hebrew Scriptures, but he also re-affirms Christianity's unbreakable continuity with Judaism inasmuch as he and all other "orthodox Christians" worship the "God of Jacob."

This is not to assert, however, that Justin views Jesus as simply another Jewish prophet. Nor does he think Jesus wholly disinterested in the kingdom's territorial restoration. Instead, much like St. Irenaeus, St. Justin views Jesus as in some sense repeating yet also bringing into fuller completion the prophetic promises of the kingdom's eschatological restoration. And so as he also writes in *Dialogue with Trypho*,

> And just as [Joshua], not Moses, conducted the people into the Holy Land and distributed it by lot among those who entered, so also will Jesus the Christ gather together the dispersed people and distribute the good land to each, though not in the same manner. For Joshua gave them an inheritance for a time only,

since he was not Christ our God, nor the Son of God; but Jesus, after the holy resurrection, will give us an inheritance for eternity... After his coming the Father will, through [Jesus], renew heaven and earth. This is he who is to shine in Jerusalem as an eternal light.[25]

Notice again that it is not the physical nature of the land that differs between Christ's act of re-allocation and Joshua's but its duration. The former is taken to be permanent and eternal while the former is considered temporary. Nevertheless despite the difference in chronology, St. Justin is still fully convinced that Christ's restoration of the kingdom entails nothing less than a physical return to and redistribution of Israel's land.

Not surprisingly, one finds a comparable dynamic of repetition and completion within St. Irenaeus's interpretation of the kingdom as well. For once again, it is within the hermeneutical frame of Christ's recapitulation that St. Irenaeus situates his views. He begins the discussion by first noting that insofar as Christ's recapitulation encompasses all things, it most certainly redounds to Yahweh's original covenant with Abraham and therefore, *inter alia*, to Yahweh's promise that Abraham and his descendants would inherit the land of Canaan. For as St. Irenaeus states, the "promise to Abraham... remains firm."[26]

With the advent of Christ, however, or rather Christ's eschatological advent, St. Irenaeus sees the scope of Israel's original land covenant being expanded to include not only diaspora Jews, but all Gentile believers as well. This is confirmed, St. Irenaeus maintains, by Jesus' words in Matt 26:27–29 when he tells his disciples, "Drink of it, all of you; for this is my blood of the new covenant, which is poured out for many for the forgiveness of sins. I tell you I shall not drink again of this fruit of the vine until that day when I drink it new with you in my father's kingdom." The meaning of this verse, as St. Irenaeus interprets it, is that "when Christ speaks of drinking the fruit of the vine in the kingdom he is speaking of the inheritance of the land that he will renew and restore."[27] In other words, for St. Irenaeus the main import of Jesus' words is not that they prefigure a Eucharistic theology of sacramental elements, but rather their attestation that fulfillment of Yahweh's promise to Abraham cannot be achieved "outside the flesh" of either the body or the land. And lest one succumb to a Gnostic spiritualization of these territorial references to the kingdom, St. Irenaeus sternly issues the following exegetical admonishment: "If some are tempted to allegorize passages of this kind

---

25. Justin Martyr, *Dialogue with Trypho*, 322.
26. St. Irenaeus, *Against the Heresies*, 100.
27. Ibid., 101.

they will not be found consistent with the texts and will be refuted by the meaning of the words themselves."[28]

We have thus observed how St. Justin's and St. Irenaeus's interpretations of the kingdom remain firmly entrenched within a Palestinian territorial locale. Furthermore, we have also seen how this entrenchment is directly tied to and a direct function of their respective commitments to preserve the materiality of creation and the inseparability between Christianity and Judaism. And yet even as both these findings remain indisputable, there is one facet of their interpretation that nevertheless begins to dislodge the kingdom from its territorial moorings.

Ironically enough, this facet turns out to be a repetition, or a recapitulation if you will, of a Gnostic error both inveighed against so ardently. For recall from above that both Justin and Irenaeus are extremely critical of the Gnostic belief that the pneumatics, by virtue of their incorporeality, will supplant carnal Israel as YHWH's chosen covenantal community. In their eyes this act of covenantal (dis)-placement not only violates the permanence and integrity of Israel's election, but also the bodily integrity of Christ inasmuch as he remains Israel's messiah. It is quite disorienting then, both literally and figuratively, to find instances of St. Justin and St. Irenaeus indulging in a kind of rhetoric that very nearly duplicates this trope of covenantal replacement.

Consider, for example, the relationship St. Justin sees existing between Gentile Christians and the Abrahamic and Mosaic covenants vis-à-vis the coming of Christ. His first move is to once again re-establish the continued theological legitimacy of these covenants as well as their complementarity with Christianity. For as he states,

> Trypho, there will never be, nor has there ever been from eternity, any other God except him who created and formed this universe. Furthermore, we do not claim that our God is different than yours, for he is the God who, with a strong hand and outstretched arm, led your forefathers out of the land of Egypt. Nor have we placed our trust in any other (for, indeed, there is no other), but only in him whom you also have trusted, the God of Abraham and of Isaac and of Jacob.[29]

"But," he continues with a caveat that portends significant departure, "our hope is not through Moses or through the Law, otherwise our customs would be the same as yours."[30] On the contrary in Justin's estimation not

28. Ibid.
29. Ibid.
30. Justin Martyr, *Dialogue with Trypho*, 163.

only is the "law promulgated at Horeb ... already obsolete" since it "was intended for you Jews only, whereas the law of which I speak [that is Christ's new covenant] is simply for all men," but it is also nullified insofar as "a later law in opposition to an older law abrogates the older" then "so, too does a later covenant void an earlier one."[31] In other words not only does Justin view Christ's covenant as being *sui generis*, but prohibitively superior to Mosaic covenant as well.

That being the case, Justin therefore comes to the rather ominous conclusion that "[w]e," that is Gentile Christians, "have been led to God through this crucified Christ, and *we are the true spiritual Israel*, and the descendants of Judah, Jacob, Isaac, and Abraham, who, though uncircumcised, was approved and blessed by God to his faith and was called the father of many nations."[32] Thus in one fell swoop, Justin has gone from resolutely affirming Christianity's inescapable dependency on Israel to a position where not only is that dependency now called into serious question, but in fact considered retrograde inasmuch as the Gentile Christian community has now come to be the "true spiritual Israel." Inexplicably then, carnal and historical dependence has suddenly given way to spiritual independence.

The tone of this independence takes on an even sharper and more punitive edge with St. Justin's imprecatory assessment of continued Jewish disbelief in Jesus' lordship. For what this stubborn and persistent intransigence is finally causative of, says St. Justin, is a dramatic decision by Yahweh to re-place carnal Israel with the Church. As he writes,

> For you [Jews] are neither wise nor understanding, but sly and treacherous; wise only for evil actions, but utterly unfitted to know the hidden will of God, or the trustworthy covenant of the Lord, or to find everlasting covenants. For this reason he [YHWH] says, "I will raise up to Israel and Judah a seed of men and a seed of beasts." And through Isaiah he speaks of another Israel: "On that day shall Israel be third among the Assyrians and the Egyptians, blessed in the land which the Lord of Hosts blessed, saying: Blessed shall my people be who are in Egypt, and who are among the Assyrians, and my inheritance Israel." Since God blesses and calls this people [Gentile Christians] Israel, and announces aloud that it is his inheritance, why do you not feel compunction both for fooling yourselves by imagining that you alone are the people of Israel, and for cursing the people whom God has blessed? Indeed when he spoke to Jerusalem and its surrounding communities, he said, "And I will beget men upon

---

31. Ibid., 164.
32. Ibid.

you, my people Israel, and they shall inherit you, and you shall be their inheritance, and you shall no more be bereaved by them of children."[33]

Absent here is any sense of the historical and material continuity that previously permeated Justin's discussions of the kingdom. On the contrary here is a symbolic appropriation of Isaiah and Ezekiel guided by a quasi-Gnostic principle that they contain "hidden" knowledge that the Jews by virtue of their rebellious insubordination to Jesus are too spiritually obtuse and addled to perceive. Were it not so then they would be humbled and enlightened enough to see that not only are they no longer YHWH's true Israel, but instead, in Justin's words, a "seed of beasts."

Of course, such a provocative and defamatory claim elicits no small measure of incredulity and indignation from St. Justin's Jewish interlocutor, Trypho. "Do you mean to say," he asks of St. Justin, "that you [i.e. Gentile Christians] are Israel and that God says all this about you?"[34] And lest St. Justin's previous statement allow any equivocation to remain, he doubles down with emphatic boldness:

> If you have ears to hear it, in Isaiah, God, speaking of Christ in parable, calls him Jacob and Israel. This is what he says: "Jacob is my servant, I will uphold him; Israel is my elect. I will put my spirit upon him and he shall bring forth judgment to the Gentiles. He shall neither strive nor cry, nor shall any one hear his voice in the streets. The bruised reed he shall not break, and smoking flax he shall not quench, but he shall bring forth judgment unto truth. He shall shine, and shall not be broken, till he set judgment in the earth; and in his name shall the Gentile trust." Therefore, as your whole people was called after that one Jacob, surnamed Israel, so we who obey the precepts of Christ, are, through Christ who begot us to God, *both called and in reality are, Jacob and Israel and Judah and Joseph and David and true children of God.*[35]

A similar dynamic of continuity and replacement is also echoed within St. Irenaeus's interpretation of the kingdom. For instance, when commenting on the provenance of the Hebrew and Christian canons, St. Irenaeus states that "[Jesus] did not teach that he who brought forth the old was one, and he that brought the new, another; but that they were one and the same."[36]

33. Ibid., 339.
34. Ibid.
35. Ibid., 339–40; emphasis added.
36. Irenaeus, *Against the Heresies*, 118.

Indeed so integral is the connection between the two testaments that the modifiers "old" and "new" should not be construed to mean that they share "nothing in common between themselves, and are of an opposite nature, and mutually repugnant," but rather that they are "of the same substance [*homousious*]" and merely differ in number and size; such as water from water and light from light and grace from grace."[37] Thus not only does St. Irenaeus affirm the theological equivalency of the Jewish and Christian Scriptures, but the theological inseparability of Christianity and Judaism as well inasmuch as they both worship the same divine author. "But one and the same householder produced both covenants," says St. Irenaeus, "the Word of God, our Lord Jesus Christ, who spake with both Abraham and Moses, and who has restored us anew to liberty, and has multiplied that grace which is from Himself."[38]

Nevertheless, even while declaring their theological unity, St. Irenaeus, like St. Justin, introduces an interpretive element that starts to chip away at the legitimacy of both the Jewish Scriptures and the nation of Israel and therefore begins to cast both in a subservient and inferior light. For even though "the natural precepts" of the Scriptures are "common to us [Gentile Christians] and to them [the Jews]," says St. Irenaeus, "they [the Jews] had in them indeed the beginning and origin; but in us [Gentile Christians] they have received growth and completion."[39] Upon closer scrutiny then, the difference between the "Old" and "New" Testaments turns out to be one not just of quantity as Irenaeus had earlier maintained, but of quality as well inasmuch the latter's "greatness" connotes not just a sense of enlarged proportionality, but theological superiority also. For as Irenaeus writes, the New Testament is in fact "[g]reater" than the Old to the extent that the former is "legislation which has been given in order to liberty" while the latter was issued "in order to bondage[.]"[40]

In what sense, however, does Irenaeus believe the New Testament and thus Christianity to be more liberative than the Old Testament and Judaism? An answer is forthcoming when he explains that the "law," by which Irenaeus means the Old Testament, "since it was laid down for those in bondage, used to instruct the soul by means of those *corporeal objects* which were of an external nature, drawing it, as by a bond, to obey its commandments, that man might learn to serve God."[41] The "Word" by contrast, which

37. Ibid.
38. Ibid.
39. Ibid.
40. Ibid.
41. Ibid., 119.

refers to Christ and Christianity "sets free the soul, and taught that through it the body should be willingly purified."[42] Thus just as Justin argues that Gentile Christians are the "true spiritual Israel" by virtue of the fact that they have shed the Judaistic encumbrances historicity and carnality, so too does Irenaeus claim that Christianity is greater than Judaism insofar as it "sets the soul free" from the latter's "corporeal objects."

Furthermore, not only is the New Testament greater than the Old in terms of its extending a larger swath of pneumatic liberty to the individual human souls, but it is also greater in terms of expanding the kingdom's geographic scope since it has been "diffused, not throughout one nation [only], but over the whole world."[43] More specifically, not only has the kingdom been expanded to encompass the whole earth, but the Church, by virtue of being a universal (catholic) community, has now arrogated to itself the locative status of being the sole proprietorship of Yahweh's blessing. For as Irenaeus states "in Christ every blessing [is summed up], and therefore the latter people [Gentile Christians] has snatched away the blessings of the former [the Jews] from the Father, just as Jacob took away the blessing of this Esau."[44] Once again then St. Irenaeus's words communicate a stance in which not only has the Church re-placed Israel as the geographic site of covenantal blessing, but it has done so as a direct act of punitive retribution against the latter's corporeal intransigence.

We have come to see then how St. Justin's and St. Irenaeus's interpretations of the kingdom, and indeed Judaism itself, are marked by a deep-seated ambivalence. For as Paula Fredriksen notes, on the one hand both are thoroughly Jewish "to the degree that they insisted that Christ had had a fleshly body, that he had indeed descended from the house of David, and that the entirety of the Septuagint, understood correctly, actually referred to Christ and his church."[45] Furthermore, because neither thought creation "itself was evil," both insisted it was just as essential to envision the kingdom's eschatological restoration as "a thousand-year-long Sabbath in a renewed and resplendent Jerusalem" as it was to envision a bodily resurrection.[46] Indeed in their minds, to attenuate or deny the corporeality of either was tantamount to compromising the integrity of both. In this regard then, both Justin and Irenaeus were unequivocally anti-Gnostic.

42. Ibid.
43. Ibid.
44. Ibid.
45. Fredriksen, "Birth of Christianity," 25.
46. Ibid.

At the same time, however, both continued to view Jewish obduracy toward Christ as symptomatic of a larger congenital defect, namely a Jewish insistence to read both the Scriptures and the kingdom "in a carnal way" such that both were "interpret[ed] literally rather than allegorically."[47] Accordingly, while St. Justin's and St. Irenaeus's *chiliastic* eschatology prescribed a territorial interpretation of the kingdom, their quasi-Gnostic reading of Yahweh's covenants with Israel, in which it became increasingly normative to regard them as "spiritual" in nature rather than "carnal," ultimately interjected a theological and material fissure between not only Christianity and Judaism, but also the kingdom and territorial Israel as well. And it is precisely by recognizing this theological and material cleavage that we more fully observe and appreciate how St. Justin's and St. Irenaeus's critiques of Gnosticism fail to carry over and inform their *chiliasm*. For in their eyes God's kingdom had always been and would always remain landed; indeed the validity and authority of Israel's prophetic witness, the irrevocability of YHWH's covenant with Israel, and Christ's very own incarnation as a Jewish man demanded that it be so; nevertheless this landedness, by virtue of Christ's "greater" revelation no longer had to be anchored to or confined by the particularity of Israel's territoriality. On the contrary, in their judgment the kingdom was going to, and indeed to a great extent already had been, re-placed, both theologically and territorially, by the catholic Christian community known as the Church.

Here then are some illustrative examples of how early prominent Christian theologians began to de-territorialize the kingdom of God. Many more could be presented all to the essentially the same effect. Nevertheless even this partial sampling is sufficient to prove a critical point: when it comes to assessing the kingdom's territoriality, the history of Christian theological reflection has been marked by a profound ambivalence. At best such reflection has affirmed the kingdom's generic territoriality albeit in a manner that effectively negates any sense of historical or material continuity with *eretz Israel*. At worse not only has such reflection actively excised the very idea of territoriality from the kingdom, but also punitively excoriated such a notion as an anchoritic lapse into a reprobate form of Judaism.

And yet despite the fact that Christian theological reflection has oscillated somewhere between these two nullifying poles, a crucial question still remains lingering: are these in fact the only possible responses that Christianity permits? In other words, are there any elements within the Christian theological and ethical imagination that not only render these responses problematic but also provide a constructive basis from which to articulate

---

47. Ibid., 26.

a positive territorial interpretation of the kingdom? I believe the answer to both these questions is an unequivocal "yes" and will thus use the remainder of this chapter to explain why.

3.3 Theological Implications of a De-territorialized Kingdom

The following is a set of theological considerations that make a de-territorialized interpretation of the kingdom problematic to the Christian theological imagination. In brief these difficulties are covenantal and supersessionist in nature. Let us address each in turn.

3.3.1 Covenantal

One of the most significant harms to result from a de-territorialized reading of the kingdom is the way such an interpretation enervates Yahweh's enduring covenant with Israel. This is so in two ways.

First, as Tommy Givens has perceptively noted, such a reading tends to impugn and thus effectively excise a whole segment of people from Israel's covenant on account of their steadfast fidelity to preserving and restoring Israel's territoriality. For by asserting that the essence of Jewish identity since the exile has been a diasporic turn toward non-territoriality, Yoder and those sympathetic to his project often identify those who remain committed to Israel's territoriality as somehow being "unfaithful" and thus "not a part of the people of God, or at the very least, as unrepresentative of the people of God."[48] Such a position, however, betrays a fundamental misapprehension of the irrevocable and non-voluntarist nature of Yahweh's covenant to the extent that it fails to see that Yahweh constitutes a people not according to the vagaries of "human faithfulness to the exclusion of unfaithfulness," but instead by "faithfully holding human faithfulness and unfaithfulness together with forgiveness[.]"[49] Accordingly, "[t]o be chosen by the God of Israel is not," as Givens explains, "in the first place, to get that God right, whether ethically, doctrinally, or otherwise, although ethics and doctrine do matter given that some ethical and doctrinal ways of being that people have proven difficult to sustain over generations."[50] On the contrary, "[t]o be chosen by the God of Israel is to have been seized in *time and space*

---

48. Givens, "Election of Israel," 82.
49. Ibid., 85.
50. Ibid., 87.

by God as among those God claims as already God's own by covenant, and so to have been compelled by God to live in response to that claim, to find that name of that God on the lips, even if is to curse him."[51]

Thus suppose for the moment, for the sake of argument, that Israel's landedness is one of the more challenging if not the most difficult ways, both doctrinally and ethically, for its people to maintain covenant fidelity to Yahweh. Even this difficulty with all of its attendant pitfalls, temptations, and impediments is not so vexing and inscrutable as to breach or even exceed the gratuitous capaciousness of Yahweh's commitment to Israel precisely because it is Yahweh who has elected Israel to be Israel in a particular time and *place*. Hence to view the kingdom as de-territorialized is not only to deny the place of election in Israel's covenant, but also to ignore the election of its very place. For as Peter Ochs explains,

> One cannot have it both ways: if revelation is continual, then it refers to the specific places in which it is embodied, which means that there is no way to speak of revelation in general, independently of where and when, or to identify the words of revelation with clear-and-distinct concepts or principles that apply to all places at all times. Clarity is a local and landed temporal thing. The alternative is to claim the power to read revelation as a direct source of articulable, universal claims-but then, to refer to revelation as only as a once-and-for-always event whose character is not disclosed locally and, in that sense, not embodied or landed. As I understand them, both Second Temple and rabbinic Judaisms take the route less clear: revelation is landed, but landedness is not a clear concept or principle that we can understand in general apart from the particulars of life in some place and time.[52]

And this leads to the second way a de-territorialized interpretation of the kingdom is covenantally deleterious and that is the fact that the scope of Yahweh's election of Israel is confined neither to just a single person nor to a group of persons but instead encompasses an entire nation. For as Wyschogrod has written, with respect to Israel "the relationship that started with Abraham, the individual, soon become a relationship with a nation that became an elect nation."[53] Accordingly "[t]he promise of salvation is thus not held out to man as an individual but as a member of this nation."[54]

---

51. Ibid.; emphasis mine.
52. Ochs, *Free Church and Israel's Covenant*, 40.
53. Wyschogrod, *Body of Faith*, 68.
54. Ibid.

To think therefore of the kingdom as de-territorialized, that is to think of it as purely an ethical praxis, or an ecclesial community or a transcendent realm untethered to any land in general or Israel's in particular, is to inevitably invite a retrenchment of that promise. It is, as Wyschrogod notes, to believe that "the individual can be lifted out his nation and brought into relation with God[.]"[55] Yet to save a person individually and "leave the national order unredeemed is to truncate man and then to believe that this remnant of a human being is the object of salvation."[56] By contrast by electing the nation of Israel, Yahweh not only sanctifies Israel's national order, but also "confirms the national order of all peoples and expresses his love for the individual in his national setting and for the nations in their corporate personalities."[57] Paradoxically then to deny the territorial particularity of Israel's kingdom is to deny the universal sweep and scope of its covenant.

3.3.2 Supersessionist

In his seminal work titled *The God of Israel and Christian Theology*, Kendall Soulen argues that Christian systematic theology has been plagued by three distinct expressions of supersessionism, or the notion that "because the Jews refused to receive Jesus as Messiah, they were cursed by God, are no longer in covenant with God, and that the church alone is the 'true Israel' or the 'spiritual Israel.'"[58]

The first of these is what Soulen refers to as *economic supersessionism*. It is so called, Soulen explains, because in maintaining that the "written law of Moses is replaced by the spiritual law of Christ, circumcision by baptism, natural descent by faith as criterion of membership in the people of God, and so forth[,]" carnal Israel "*becomes obsolete*" and therefore, "the ultimate obsolescence of carnal Israel is [considered] an essential feature of God's one overarching economy of redemption for the world."[59]

The second expression of supersessionism that Soulen identifies is called *punitive supersessionism* and it is punitive insofar as it believes that "[b]ecause the Jews obstinately reject God's action in Christ, God in turn angrily rejects and punishes the Jews."[60]

---

55. Ibid.
56. Ibid.
57. Ibid.
58. Soulen, *God of Israel and Christian Theology*, 3.
59. Ibid., 29.
60. Ibid., 30.

Finally there is what Soulen describes as *structural supersessionism*. Structural supersessionism consists of the idea that the Old Testament or Hebrew Bible is rendered *"largely indecisive for shaping conclusions about how God's purposes engage creation in universal and enduring ways."*[61] It is a particular feature and artifact of what Soulen terms the "standard canonical narrative" or Christian theology's hermeneutical predilection for reading and organizing biblical Scriptures around four epochal events or episodes, namely, creation, fall, redemption, and consummation. The effect of reading the canon through this interpretive grid is, as Soulen asserts, twofold: "First, the foreground portrays God's engagement with human creation in cosmic and universal terms. Christ figures in the story as the incarnation of the eternal Logos, humankind appears as descendants of the first parents and as possessors of a common nature and so on."[62]

Second, however, this foreground "completely neglects the Hebrew Scriptures, with the exception of Gen 1–3! The story tells how God engaged Adam and Eve as Consummator and how God's initial consummating plan was almost immediately disrupted by the fall. The foreground story then leaps immediately to the Apostolic Witness interpreted as God's deliverance of humankind from the fall through Jesus Christ."[63] "So conceived," Soulen continues, "God's purposes as Consummator and Redeemer engage human creation in a manner that simply outflank the greater part of the Hebrew Scriptures, and, above all, their witness to God's history with the people of Israel."[64]

Consequently, there are two major theological lacunae the standard canonical narrative and its structural superssessionism promulgate. One is the disappearance of national Israel. For as Soulen explains by affirming "God's passionate and enduring engagement with creation" at the expense of "God's equally passionate and enduring engagement with the people Israel," the standard canonical narrative "provides a framework in which it appears evident that the God of Israel's abiding commitment to creation goes not by the way of Israel of the flesh but by way of the Israel of the spirit."[65] As a result, "[b]ecause God's enduring purposes engage humankind as spirit, Israel's flesh can drop out."[66]

---

61. Ibid., 31.
62. Ibid.
63. Ibid.
64. Ibid., 32.
65. Ibid., 55.
66. Ibid.

The other is a loss of any kind of substantive theological consideration of national existence, whether it be Israel's or another nation's. For with the "loss of orientation toward the Hebrew Scriptures and the history of Israel" comes "a more general loss of orientation toward such 'middle range' dimensions of human life as public history, economics, politics, and so on, all of which are of central concern to the Hebrew Scriptures."[67]

That this is so is somewhat ironic since, as Soulen points out, the primary impetus behind the standard canonical was a "repudiation of Gnosticism."[68] More specifically the aim of the standard canonical narrative is to reject Gnosticism "at the level of ontology" by affirming that "God's abiding commitment to creation passes through the flesh of the people Israel in the Old Covenant and ultimately lodges with irrevocable finality in the one Jewish man, Jesus of Nazareth."[69] Nevertheless, as we saw in St. Justin and St. Irenaeus above, by eliding the theological significance of national Israel, the standard canonical narrative actually perpetuates a form of Gnosticism insofar as it "drives an *historical* wedge between the gospel and the God of Israel *by collapsing God's covenant with Israel into the economy of redemption in its prefigurative form*" and thus "misinterprets redemption in Christ as deliverance from God's history with Israel and the nations."[70]

In light of this discussion, I would like to suggest that the kingdom's de-territorialization is a corollary of structural supersessionism. This is so in at least two ways. First, by stripping the kingdom of its territoriality in general and Israel's in particular, a de-territorialized hermeneutic is structurally closed-off from not only the carnality of Israel's people but their territoriality as well. And yet as we have discovered from our discussion above, there are compelling reasons, both textually and ethically, why the carnality of Israel's people is inextricably linked to its territoriality. To deny the latter then is drive a further historical wedge between the gospel and the God of Israel. Second, to de-territorialize the kingdom is to assert that territorial Israel has no theological import or bearing on Christ's redemption and thus the "middle range" dimensions of public and political life.

---

67. Ibid., 50.
68. Ibid., 110.
69. Ibid.
70. Ibid.

3.4 Ethical Implications of a De-territorialized Kingdom

To grasp why a de-territorialized interpretation of the kingdom is ethically problematic for a Christian theological perspective, it will be helpful to briefly review Nancey Murphy's and James McClendon's respective arguments concerning the importance of human embodiment to Christian moral reflection. To some extent we have traversed this terrain already in our discussion of St. Justin's and St. Irenaeus's critiques of Gnosticism above and the theological importance both pay to corporeality. Even so, Murphy's and McClendon's projects add some fresh insights into this matter that can help us further illuminate and deepen the already perspicacious observations brought to bear by Justin and Irenaeus. Let us begin with Murphy's perspective first.

In her seminal volume *Bodies and Souls, or Spirited Bodies?*,[71] Murphy tackles a question that has long been both the focus and bane of Christian theology, namely, the debate over whether human beings are comprised of a material body and a non-material soul, or whether we exist as purely physical beings. In response to this perennial metaphysical and anthropological conundrum, Murphy puts forward the novel proposal of *non-reductive physicalism* or the idea that even though human beings exist as soul-less material beings, our biological and cultural complexity nevertheless imparts us with a capacity for moral reasoning discernment that far exceeds our basic materiality. The moral human self, in other words, is both coincident with yet vastly more than the sum of its constitutive physical parts. Or as Murphy explains it, where as "[r]eductive physicalism says that human beings are physical organisms, and nothing but that, and in addition—and this is the reductionistic part—*everything* about us can be explained in naturalistic terms," nonreductive physicalism, on the other hand, "grants that we are biological organisms, but emphasizes that our neurobiological complexity and the history of cultural development have together resulted in the capacity for genuine moral reasoning."[72]

Once again limits of time and space prevent us from exploring the profound ontological, epistemological and philosophical repercussions this innovative proposal yields. We will be content, therefore, to limit ourselves to its ethical implications.

The first of these is how non-reductive physicalism accounts for the source of human morality. For as Murphy notes, the fields of evolutionary

---

71. Murphy, *Bodies and Souls, or Spirited Bodies?*
72. Ibid., 121.

biology and evolutionary psychology, both of which are predisposed to reductive physicalism, have long made the claim that human morality is simply an accretion of human genetic programming. That is since "[e]volution favors whatever is good for the survival of one's genes," then "human morality can be seen, also, as a product of genetics."[73] Or to state it another way, human biology is moral destiny.

There are, however, two fundamental problems with this account of human morality from a Christian perspective. The first is that such a view fails to provide a satisfactory explanation for the linkage between moral action and motivation and specifically human action and divine command. "That is," explains Murphy, "morality for Christians and for those in other monotheistic traditions is, at its heart, obedience."[74] More specifically, a Christian chooses to act according to a certain set of moral precepts "because it is obligatory, and it is obligatory because it fits with God's purposes for human life."[75] Accordingly the motivation for heeding the Christian injunction to sacrifice one's self for the welfare of the other is, as Murphy states, "as different as it could possibly be from doing it because it is genetically programmed."[76]

Furthermore a Christian account of human morality is not only distinguished by divine motivation, but also by the content of its morality as well. And once again the commitment to self-sacrifice for the other is instructive in illustrating this difference. For as Murphy asserts the "other" for whom Christians are regularly enjoined to sacrifice themselves is often the stranger, and "most particularly, the enemy."[77] By contrast, the "sociobiologists' account [of morality] depends on similarity of genes in the group for which one sacrifices; that is they must be family, kin."[78] In sum then evolutionary biology and psychology may provide an important window into the "how" of human morality, but they are ultimately ill-equipped to explain its "why." "Only a worldview that addresses [these] ultimate issues," Murphy contends, "can answer this question."[79]

Yet it is not just an overarching account of ultimate reality that Christianity provides. It also supplies a specific moral character and set of attendant moral practices as well. In particular Murphy notes that in contrast

73. Ibid., 119.
74. Ibid.
75. Ibid., 120.
76. Ibid.
77. Ibid.
78. Ibid.
79. Ibid.

to the atomism of a Cartesian perspective, which presents "an overly cognitivist account of human nature in general and of morality in particular," recent Christian ethical reflection has come to refocus its attention on the importance of developing moral character and particularly the idea that "the emphasis is not on the rules and principles one ought to follow, but rather on the kind of person one ought to be."[80]

One of the reasons this shift toward the development of moral character is important, says Murphy, is because it further underscores the importance of human embodiment. For just as it is impossible to separate a sense of memory from physicality, so too, maintains Murhpy, "are character and physical criteria" inseparable insofar as "moral perception may be hypothesized to depend on the downward efficacy of high-level evaluative processes in reshaping lower-level cognitive process—and these changes, too are recorded in the tuning of neural nets."[81] In other words, just as one can no more become a skilled three-point shooter apart from engaging in the disciplined practice of shooting a basketball, so also does a person only become a skilled moral agent by physically embodying the moral virtues that are commensurate with a Christian moral character. Accordingly ethical theories that fail to account for this inescapable relationship between physical embodiment and moral virtues will be "incomplete and most likely misleading if not balanced by recognition of the drives, needs and capacities of the *embodied* self."[82]

Moreover, our existence as Christian moral agent not only depends on our physically embodying certain moral virtues, but it also depends on our physically embodying those moral virtues in relation to embodied others as well. For as opposed to thinking that the moral self "can be constructed by assuming either that all relations are external (logical atomism) or that all are internal (absolute idealism)," it is better, Murphy maintains, "to recognize that there are some of each."[83] As such it is therefore clear "that a great deal of what lasts in the post-resurrection kingdom must be those relationships within the body of Christ that now makes us the people we are."[84]

What all of this means then, as James McClendon aptly explains, is that when it comes to the enterprise of moral reflection "Christians do not live two lives, one life as Christians and another as bodily selves and parts

---

80. Ibid., 137.
81. Ibid., 139.
82. Ibid.
83. Ibid.
84. Ibid.

of the organic universe."[85] Rather, "[o]ur Christian life *is* our life as organic constituents of the crust of the planet."[86] As such, Christian morality has always been, always is, and always will be even after the eschaton inextricably embodied. This is not to say however, that embodiment itself is inherently virtuous. To be sure, as McClendon points out via the apostle Paul, human embodiment is often the source of and occasion for indulging in the vices of our 'lower natures.' Moreover there is enough "fallenness and rebellion and ruin" present in the world to confirm that "the world is not Christian."[87] Even so, the "lower nature" of which Paul speaks is not, as McClendon states, "our embodied selfhood, but a false image of that selfhood, a disguise we must repeatedly penetrate and discard."[88] Furthermore, "the eyes through which we Christians see the world are redeemed eyes; it is through these eyes that we must be trained to look if we would see without double or narrow vision."[89] Hence Jesus' own embodiment through incarnation "encourages us to seek the way of Christ in a life truly organic, truly God's; fully created; fully Christ's."[90]

Thus as Murphy's and McClendon's arguments make clear, while human embodiment is not, in and of itself, sufficient to the task of Christian ethical reflection it is most certainly and undeniably necessary. Furthermore not only is embodiment necessary to the task of Christian ethical reflection, it is absolutely essential. And yet as both their arguments seem to intimate and at times obliquely acknowledge, a Christian moral agent exists not only as an embodied moral self in relation to other embodied moral selves, but also an embodied moral self placed within a particular territorial locale. Indeed if one grants the premise that Christian morality is always and necessarily embodied by virtue of the fact that both Christ and Christians are always and necessarily embodied, and deduces from this claim that embodiment is itself a Christian ethical modality, then one must extrapolate and apply this same logic to the reality of territoriality as well and admit that it too is a Christian ethical modality insofar as both Christians and their embodied moral practices are always territorially placed.

This latter point is communicated quite perceptively by Michael R. Curry in his discussion of the "normativity of place." For as Curry observes,

---

85. McClendon, *Ethics*, 95.
86. Ibid.
87. Ibid., 96.
88. Ibid., 95–96.
89. Ibid., 96.
90. Ibid.

places themselves, the basic sites of human activities, are intrinsically normative. We live in a world in which value is not a post hoc add-on, an after-effect or after thought, something to be rejected by self-assured academics. Rather, the value that exists in the world is there right from the outset ... We are at home in the bedroom and in New Jersey, or at work and in an office in California, or in an airplane seat and in the United States in first class. And it is because different activities and objects and ideas "fit" within different places that we are inexorably faced with moral dilemmas. Those moral dilemmas are geographical dilemmas.

And so, the inquiry into the nature of places can shed light on the ways in which the everyday activities by which we make and maintain places involve appeal to ethical and normative concepts usually seen as the provenance of philosophers; at the same time, it can suggest to philosophers what are in the end geographical sources to many of the ethical dilemmas that we face.[91]

Hence to be a Christian moral agent is to be both embodied *and* territorialized. Moreover it is to be an embodied and territorialized self in relation to "other" selves, whether that "other" inhabits the same territorial space as the self or another territorial locale. With that being the case, it must therefore be asked what happens to Christian ethical reflection when the modality of human embodiment is disaggregated from its territoriality? Or to ask the same question in a slightly different inflection, what happens when Jesus' kingdom proclamation is taken to be normative for human socio-political embodiment but considered inconsequential or even nullifying to its territorial placement?

Ironically such a move can best be described as constituting not just another iteration of so-called "neo-Constantianism," but Constantianism *par excellence*. This is so in two ways. First, recall from our discussion above that not only did Eusebius' imperial interpretation of the kingdom effect a political transference from the *ekklesia* to the *imperium*, but it also prompted a correlative territorial transference as well namely from Jerusalem to Rome. Such transferences would not have been possible let alone conceivable, however, were it not for Justin's, Irenaeus's and Origen's previous arguments for removing the kingdom from its original territorial setting and re-placing its theo-political locus within either the Christian Church or a transcendent heavenly realm. In other words early Christian arguments for the kingdom's de-territorialization gave license to and indeed ultimately

---

91. Curry, "'Hereness' and the Normativity of Place," 96.

encouraged subsequent Christian theologians to not only separate the politic of the kingdom from the body of Christ, but also to separate the concrete witness of Jesus' social-political embodiment from the kingdom. Both separations could not have obtained, however, without there first being a theo-political separation of the kingdom of God from *eretz Israel*. Thus what made the Constantinian conflation between kingdom and empire possible was not just the erasure of the distinction between Church and world, but also the early Church's own original erasure of the distinction between itself and territorial Israel.

To leverage, therefore, Jesus' kingdom ethic as constituting either a diasporic alternative to or replacement of Constantinianism is not only to once again ignore the ethical significance of territoriality, but also to paradoxically perpetuate the very error such a political ethic is said to correct.

This leads then to the second way a de-territorialized kingdom is ethically problematic. For suppose that Jesus' kingdom pronouncement and ethic are in fact exclusively a-territorial and thus inapplicable or even antithetical to the political pursuit of territorial governance; what other distinctively normative Christian sources can the Christian community avail itself to in order to fill the resulting void?

Consequently to deny the territoriality of the kingdom is to deprive Christian ethical reflection of the very normative sources it needs to be politically normative. And without access and use of such sources not only does such a Christian political ethic run the risk of becoming something less than Christian and political, but it also loses its capacity to speak and demonstrate an alternative politic of territorial governance to a watching and waiting world. For as Gerald Schlabach explains,

> Even as peace churches argue that the Constantinian way of "living in the land" has been wrong, however, they must eventually take on the challenges of living not only faithful critique, but of faithful settling, faithful institution-building, and faithful management of community life ... If the only alternative that peace churches, free churches, and other reform movements in Christianity have to offer is a perpetual starting over with primitive forms of face-to-face community, then they are admitting that they really have no idea how to live long in the land that God has given them. And they should not be surprised if mainstream "Constantinian" Christians dismiss their witness as little more than an effort to avoid the most basic problem of Christian social ethics.[92]

---

92. Schlabach, "Deuteronomic or Constantinian," 464.

3.5 Conclusion

I have thus sketched some of the more significant theological and ethical problems that arise out of a reading of Jesus and the kingdom that is exclusively a-territorial. By the same token I have also demonstrated why the Christian theological imagination is not only hospitable to but indeed predicated upon the landedness of our existence. This is especially the case when we consider the territorial reality of our existence in general and Israel's covenantal existence in particular. However, while these are important and indeed necessary to recognize the theological and ethical significance of territoriality, and thus to the tasks of forging a Christian ethic of territorial governance, they are ultimately not sufficient. What is also needed, and perhaps most so if it is to be a *specifically* Christian ethic of territorial governance, is a persuasive explanation of how Jesus' kingdom announcement itself envisioned and instituted such an ethic. This then is the subject and task of the next two chapters.

4

A Restoration of Land and a Restoration of Justice Governance: Restoration Eschatologies in Prophetic Texts and Late Second Temple Literature

4.1. Introduction

IN THE PREVIOUS CHAPTERS I have indicated—sometimes obliquely and other times more explicitly—that there exists a compelling body of evidence within the gospels that not only calls a landless interpretation of Jesus' kingdom pronouncement into question but also the theological assumptions from which it proceeds. Indeed not only do I believe a restoration of Israel's land to be an indispensible component of Jesus' kingdom vision, but so too do I think it integral to the very integrity and intelligibility of the Christian tradition itself.

In making these claims the time has thus arrived to move beyond the safe and comfortable redoubt of intimation to the more pain-staking and arduous task of formal demonstration. It is now time I stop simply critiquing the various problems I find besetting a de-territorialized interpretation of Jesus' kingdom proclamation and instead start explaining why and how such deficiencies can and should be overcome.

Notwithstanding their judgments that Jesus in some way disconnects the kingdom of God from the land of Israel, Davies, Borg, and Wright are nevertheless convinced that Jesus' conception of the kingdom was informed and shaped by a first-century Jewish restoration eschatology. More specifically, all agree that the restorative eschatology underpinning his proclamation of the kingdom of God is largely reflective of the restorative eschatological schema that is found in both the prophetic literature of the Hebrew Bible and Late Second Temple Jewish literature.

If that is in fact the case, and Davies, Borg, Wright along with the whole of Third Quest scholarship have certainly made a convincing case that it is, then it therefore stands to reason that one should be able to discern recognizable connections between the visions of Israel's eschatological restoration as articulated in prophetic and Late Second Temple Jewish literature and Jesus' own kingdom proclamation in the Gospels. Furthermore, and specifically with reference to Israel's land, it also stands to reason that if one is able to detect substantive continuity between Jesus' kingdom logia in the Gospels and eschatological images of Israel's territorial restoration in prophetic and Late Second Temple literature then it is plausible to deduce that Jesus also had the restoration of Israel's land in mind. The key then in order to mount a successful counterargument for why Jesus' kingdom proclamation entails the territorial restoration of Israel and is therefore evocative of a Christian ethic of territorial governance will be to find those points of textual continuity where there is significant theological and ethical overlap between the restoration of Israel as it is conceived by Jesus and as it is conceived by prophetic and Late Second Temple Jewish perspectives.

Toward fulfilling those objectives I will structure this chapter as follows. In the sections to follow I will explore in both greater depth and detail how Israel's land features in the restorative eschatologies of Jeremiah and Isaiah as well as in the extracanonical book of *Jubilees* and *Psalms of Solomon*. In particular, I will pay specific attention to how these texts not only discuss an inseparable relationship between Israel's restoration and its land but also the inseparability between the restoration of land and an ethical commitment to rule over and govern its land in a just and peaceful manner. In so doing we will not only ascertain a better comprehension of how these texts envision the territorial and ethical contours of Israel's restoration, but we will also be well prepared to compare and contrast them with Jesus' own vision of restoration in the next chapter.

4.2 נַחֲלָה: Jeremiah's Theological and Ethical Symbiosis between Yahweh, Israel, and the Land

Before exploring Jeremiah's account of Judah's restoration laid out in chapters 29–33, it is first important to understand the reciprocating relationship between Yahweh, Israel and the land that is posited at the outset of the book. As Norman Habel has astutely observed the term that best captures and explicates this symbiosis is Jeremiah's repeated use of the word נַחֲלָה (naḥalah).

Throughout most of the Hebrew Bible as well as in Jeremiah, נַחֲלָה typically refers to an inheritance, and more precisely to the inheritance of a plot of land that is apportioned by Yahweh to either Israel as a whole or to individual clans or families within its tribal system (Exod 23:30; 32:13; Deut 19:14; Num 35:8). This is the meaning employed in both Jer 2:7 and 17:4, for instance, wherein Jeremiah describes the land both as Yahweh's נַחֲלָה and Judah's נַחֲלָה respectively. However, the term can possess other meanings as well. On some occasions נַחֲלָה refers to a prized or cherished possession. Thus in Jer 10:16, for example, it is the people of Judah itself, apart from their land that is recognized as Yahweh's נַחֲלָה.

What this polysemy denotes then, according to Habel, is a perichoretic-like relationship between Yahweh, Israel and the land. For on one level the land is "YHWH's own personal נַחֲלָה and abode, vineyard and plot."[1] Yet the land is not Yahweh's exclusive domain alone but Israel's as well since "Israel is brought to this rich home of YHWH, not to be a slave, a household servant, or a poor peasant[,]" but rather "as a bride, a favorite child, and a choice vine."[2] Thus in Jeremiah's prophetic imaginary "[l]and, god, and people [are] united [together] in a privileged intimacy."[3]

Furthermore Jeremiah's use of נַחֲלָה evinces a distinctive religio-ethical posture as well. This is indicated in Jer 2:7 when Yahweh rails against the people of Judah for "defiling my land" and making "my inheritance [נַחֲלָה] an abomination." According to Jeremiah there are two principal sources of the land's corruption. The first is Judah's idolatrous worship of Baal (Jer 2:23). Using language that is graphic in its sexual explicitness Jer 3:1–10 likens Judah's veneration of Baal to the carousing of a promiscuous spouse committing multiple acts of adultery against its betrothed—an infidelity so shocking and repugnant that it results in Judah's expulsion from the land (Jer 16:13).

Yet it is not just a lack of cultic propriety that fouls the land and incurs Yahweh's wrath, but Judah's moral decadence as well. Indeed Yahweh is especially incensed at Judah's habitual (mal)treatment of those whose social and economic standing is most tenuous and therefore the most susceptible to oppression and exploitation, namely the poor, the widow, the orphan and the alien.

---

1. Habel, *Land Is Mine*, 76.
2. Ibid.
3. Ibid., 79.

This sentiment clearly underlies the harsh language of Jer 5:20–31 wherein Yahweh declares, "For scoundrels are found among my people; they take over the goods of others. Like fowlers they set a trap; they catch human beings. Like a cage full of birds, their houses are full of treachery; therefore they have become great and rich, they have grown fat and sleek. They know no limits in deeds of wickedness; they do not judge with justice the cause of the orphans, to make it prosper, they do not defend the rights of the needy" (5:26–29).

What this passage clearly reveals is that Judah's oppression is neither incidental nor sporadic. On the contrary, it is systematic and deliberate. It has thus become, in the words of Brueggemann, a "society of rapacious exploitation, supported and legitimated by institutional structures."[4] And the penalty for this repeated malfeasance is the same that is meted out for Judah's idolatrous worship of Baal: eviction from the land (7:15).

Thus two important points emerge from this brief exposition of נַחֲלָה's meaning(s). First, it confirms the land plays an essential role in defining the covenantal relationship between Israel and Yahweh. To be sure this essentiality does not preclude making a distinction between the people and the land since both are affirmed as Yahweh's נַחֲלָה. Nevertheless the identity of one נַחֲלָה is so tightly connected to the other that it is impossible for Jeremiah to conceive of Judah's existence without either. And herein may lie one of the book's most significant theological insights. As far as Jeremiah is concerned neither a people without homeland nor a homeland without a people fully qualifies as Yahweh's נַחֲלָה and neither therefore fully qualifies as Israel.[5]

Second, it also shows that Israel is tasked with a distinct set of cultic and moral responsibilities regarding its habitation of the land. In particular the kind of fidelity Israel is required to display in properly worshiping Yahweh within the land is the same kind of fidelity it must execute in securing justice for those who dwell upon it, especially the poor, the widow, the orphan and the alien. Compromising the integrity of one of these responsibilities invariably affects the integrity of the other and results not only in the land's degradation but also in eventual banishment from it as well. Thus from the very beginning Jeremiah sees Israel's land possessing a deep theological and ethical significance—a significance that is made all the more palpable in his subsequent visions of Judah's restoration.

---

4. Brueggemann, *Commentary on Jeremiah*, 68.

5. This raises an indispensable point raised by Frankel in *The Land of Canaan and the Destiny of Israel* that "communal life in the land of Israel is a necessary though insufficient of Israel's ideal mode of religious existence" (71).

4.2.1 Jeremiah 29–34: A Return to the Land and a Return to Justice

In keeping with the book's opening theological and ethical symbiosis, the vision of Judah's restoration in Jer 29–33 is an extended discourse on how the pursuit of justice requires a return to the land and return to the land requires the pursuit of justice.

However, this vision begins with what is perhaps one of the most inauspicious and non-sequitur preambles in the whole of the biblical canon. Indeed Jer 29:5–6 seems to put the whole project of Judah's restoration into serious doubt if not outright disrepute. For instead of calling the exiles to prepare for a return to Jerusalem, Yahweh instead instructs them to "[b]uild houses and live in them; plant gardens and eat what they produce; Take wives and have sons and daughters; take wives for your sons, and give your daughters in marriage that they may bear sons and daughters; multiply there and do not decrease."

It is difficult to appreciate just how disorienting—both figuratively and literally—these imperatives would have sounded until one examines their language and subtext more closely. That is because the otherwise quotidian activities of building, living, planting, eating, taking and giving were considered more than just the necessary prerequisites of a functioning domestic life. On the contrary they were normally reserved for Israel's life within its own covenanted land.

To suddenly be told then that these same activities were to be performed not only within the confines of a foreign land but within the land that was directly responsible for Judah's exile in the first place would have suggested a theological possibility heretofore thought unfathomable: that Babylon had somehow inexplicably replaced Israel as the territorial site of Yahweh's covenant!

And the verse immediately following does very little to dispel that notion or assuage its angst. For after instructing the exiles to make Babylon their new home, Yahweh then further admonishes them to "seek the welfare [שָׁלוֹם] of the city where I have sent you into exile, and pray to the Lord on its behalf, for in its welfare [שָׁלוֹם] you will find your welfare [29:7] "[שָׁלוֹם]).

Once again a closer inspection of language and subtext is in order to comprehend just how groundbreaking this admonition is. While not immediately obvious, the invocation of שָׁלוֹם would have surely conjured up remembrances of Jerusalem. And it would have done so not simply because the exiles were prone to episodes of wistfulness or atavism, but because the name "Jerusalem" itself literally means foundation or place of holistic flourishing.[6] Indeed Jerusalem and the Temple in particular was considered to be the place where Yahweh was thought to dwell most intimately and proximately with Israel.

Thus to be commanded to seek the שָׁלוֹם of Babylon would have once again indicated that a radical inversion was occurring. For no longer was Judah's שָׁלוֹם now contingent upon its placement in Jerusalem but instead "the well-being of Judah is [now] dependent upon and derivative from that of Babylon."[7] And yet as confounding and disconcerting as these pronouncements may have been, they also bear the mark of a sober political pragmatism. For at that moment it was perfectly even if painfully obvious to Jeremiah that a return to Jerusalem was neither imminent nor feasible. These exiles, therefore, had no other recourse but see Babylon as "God's chosen habitat."[8]

Nevertheless it would be a mistake to read these instructions as merely counseling acclimation to the hard realities of exile. Indeed what they also impart, states Brueggemann, "is a large missional responsibility."[9] More specifically, they "preven[t] the exilic community from withdrawing into its own safe sectarian existence, and gives it work to do and responsibility for the larger community." In short then Yahweh is exhorting these exiles to make Babylon their new נַחֲלָה.

Were this entirely the case then it would surely mark a truly radical break and reconfiguration of the previously existing relationship between Yahweh, Israel and the land. Nevertheless the radicalism of this improbable and unnerving prospect is itself radically qualified by the fact that Yahweh's message to the exiles does not conclude with verse 7 much less with chapter 29. Indeed one need only read three verses further to find Yahweh making the following pronouncement:

> For thus says the Lord: Only when Babylon's seventy years are completed will I visit you, and I will fulfill to you my promise and bring you back to this place. For surely I know the plans I

---

6. The etymology of Jerusalem is somewhat contested. There is unanimity that the second part of the name—שָׁלֵם—is a cognate of שָׁלוֹם, a word that is normally rendered as "peace" but in fact connotes a much more comprehensive and dynamic sense of holistic flourishing. The first part of the name is a bit more opaque to decipher. The BGDB states that it is a derivative of יָסוֹד, which means foundation or a cornerstone. According to the Midrash, however, the first part of the name is a combination of YHWH יִרְאֶה meaning "God will see to it," which is the name Abraham gives to the place where attempted to sacrifice his son Isaac.

7. Brueggemann, *Commentary on Jeremiah*, 257.

8. Ibid.

9. Ibid., 257–58.

have for you, says the Lord, plans for your welfare [שָׁלוֹם] and not for harm, to give you a future with hope. Then when you call upon me and come and pray to me, I will hear you. When you search for me, you will find me; if you seek me with all your heart, I will let you find me, says the Lord, and I will restore your fortunes and gather you from all the nations and places where I have driven you, says the Lord, and I will bring you back to the places from which I sent you into exile.[10]

Prior to this proclamation the hope of returning to Jerusalem not only seemed futile but illusory. Indeed every indication pointed to the scandalous yet unavoidable conclusion that Babylon had replaced Jerusalem as Judah's place of שָׁלוֹם. But then, like a rubber band quickly snapping back into place after being stretched just to its breaking point, Yahweh pivots and unequivocally affirms that exile in Babylon is neither an open-ended affair nor a permanent condition. Yes, the Jewish exiles are to make Babylon their home. And yes, they are even to seek its שָׁלוֹם. But only for an appointed time. For once that period has concluded Yahweh then promise to gather these exiles out of Babylon, return them to the land of Jerusalem, and restore their fortunes.

And this same pattern of being gathered up, returning to Jerusalem, and having fortunes restored is repeated throughout Jer 30–31. To wit, in Jer 30:3 Yahweh declares that "I will restore the fortunes of my people Israel and Judah, says the Lord, and I will bring them back to the land that I gave to their ancestors and they shall take possession of it." As Brueggemann notes there is a deep connection between the phrase "restoring the fortunes of my people" and "bring[ing] them back to the land." For the first "means to give back to the covenant people the life, destiny and well-being that belongs to its identity as Yahweh's people."[11] Nevertheless it lacks specificity. What the second phrase does therefore is "mak[e] concrete the programmatic theme of reversal" by showing that the "end of exile" is directly tied to "restoration

---

10. For all the attention, sophistication, and nuance Yoder brings to his interpretation of Jer 29:7 it is incredible how he entirely ignores this continuation of Yahweh's message to the Jewish exiles. Then again, perhaps it is not. For as Ochs perceptively observes in *The Free Church and Israel's Covenant*, "I must assume that Yoder was purposeful in the way he extended only one of Jeremiah's letters (and one of his chapters out of 52) into a type of a much larger diasporic Judaism. I think it is a powerful typological and figural reading. My objection is that he promoted typology in the name of a kind of historical science" (18).

11. Brueggemann, *Commentary of Jeremiah*, 272.

to the land."[12] The promise of restoration to the land, in other words, "gives materiality to biblical faith."[13]

Also in Jer 31:4–6 Yahweh proclaims, "[a]gain I will build you and you shall be built, O virgin Israel. Again you shall take your tambourines, and go forth dance of merrymakers. Again you shall plant vineyards on the mountains of Samaria; the planters shall plant and enjoy the fruit." Here there is a recapitulation of the directives encountered above in Jer 29:5–6 of planting and building. However, the word "again" connotes something both different and familiar about their location. For whereas before the exiles were instructed to plant and build within Babylon, now they are to plant and build within Israel. Hence the "again" signifies the full "restoration of urban life and of agriculture, this is, all aspects of the community" will take place within the land.[14] And how is this possible? Because as Jer 31:8 states Yahweh will bring the exiles "back from the land of the north, and gather them from the farthest parts of the earth, among them the blind and the lame, those with child and those in labor together, a great company, they shall return here."

This restorative vision finally culminates in the account of Jeremiah's purchase of a plot of land from his cousin Hanamel in chapter 32. This is instructive for three significant reasons. First, it recalls the importance of the נַחֲלָה and the theological relationship between Yahweh, Israel and the land. Read on a more practical and immediate level, Jeremiah's purchase is compliant with the *torah* requirements delineated in Lev 25:25–28, which specify that a kinsman (גֹּאֵל) redeem (גָּאַל) a familial plot of land (נַחֲלָה) lest it be sold and lost. In Jeremiah's particular situation however, the loss of his נַחֲלָה is neither a function of financial mismanagement on the part of Hanamel, nor is it due to the cyclical vicissitudes of an agrarian economy. Instead it is because his family's land will be seized and commandeered by the Babylonians. Thus by exercising his "right of redemption" Jeremiah is powerfully and concretely acting "to keep a family inheritance of land intact, just when circumstances made such an investment seemingly foolish."[15]

Second, on a more symbolic and prophetic level the import and scope of this transaction exceed the parameters of Jeremiah's own נַחֲלָה. This is indicated in verse 15 when Yahweh declares that "[h]ouses and fields and vineyards shall again be bought in this land." As Brueggemann notes, the triad of houses, fields and vineyards acts as a synecdoche for the essential

12. Ibid.
13. Ibid.
14. Ibid.
15. Ibid., 301.

elements of Israel's economic life.¹⁶ Thus when Jeremiah assures his audience that they will again (עוֹד) buy and sell these basic economic staples, two messages are being simultaneously conveyed. The first is that there will indeed be a major disruption and even a temporary cessation of Judah's normal economic life on account of its exile. The second message, however, is just as clear. As Brueggemann notes, "'[b]ought again' means the economy will resume and regain its health."¹⁷ Thus Judah is once again promised that it will be gathered up, returned to the land, and have its fortunes restored. Accordingly, this act of redemption far outstrips the territorial borders of Jeremiah's own נַחֲלָה. Indeed, in keeping with the term's polysemy, it serves as a broader theological paradigm for how the redemption of "this piece of land is a symbol of all the land of Canaan as YHWH's *naḥalah*[.]"¹⁸

Finally, it is important to recognize the degree to which this act compares and contrasts with the Jubilee. As John Sietze Bergsma observes, despite the obvious similarities between Jeremiah purchasing his נַחֲלָה and the stipulations of land redemption spelled out in Lev 25, there are nevertheless important differences between the two and thus compelling reasons why this account should not be read as an actual implementation of the Jubilee. One of these is that Lev 25:8–55 states that a familial נַחֲלָה should automatically revert to the original owner in the Jubilee year without any form of monetary exchange and/or compensation. Another is that "Anathoth was a Levitical town, and Jeremiah and his family were almost certainly Levites."¹⁹ As such, not only would have Jeremiah's נַחֲלָה been excluded from the Jubilee regulations, but even more significantly as a Levite Jeremiah would not even have been eligible to own a plot of land in the first place. Thus as Bergsma concludes, "regardless of what is occurring in Jeremiah 32, it is not strictly in accord with Leviticus 25."²⁰

Nonetheless, these differences notwithstanding, there is still one significant way in which Jeremiah's purchase mimics the Jubilee and that is the how the "concept of redemption (*ge'ullah*) and the figure of the redeemer (*go'el*) are applied typologically to the anticipated return of exile."²¹ In other words, just as Jeremiah acts as Hanamel's גֹּאֵל to redeem his family's plot of land, so too does he believe that Yahweh will decisively act as Israel's גֹּאֵל by redeeming its land. There is a sense then in which this narrative has

16. Ibid., 302.
17. Ibid.
18. Habel, *Land Is Mine*, 90.
19. Bergsma, *Jubilee from Leviticus to Qumran*, 159.
20. Ibid.
21. Ibid., 160.

come full circle and returned to the book's opening reflection on the נַחֲלָה. For as Habel argues, "According to this narrative account, Jeremiah stays behind in Canaan because his ideology also embraces the stubborn vision that beyond the pollution, beyond the purging, and beyond the exile, there will be redemption, a restoration of the land-god-people relationship of the idealized past. The land will be redeemed, God's people will returned home, and YHWH will again plant the people in YWHW's own *naḥalah*."[22]

Furthermore, aside from assuring the restoration of Judah's land, this Jubilee act of redemption also posits the restoration of a just system of government and set of ordinances by which that land is to be ruled. This is indicated both in Jer 33:12–15 and Jer 34:8–22.

Jeremiah 33:12–13 uses the metaphor of a desolate and hostile wasteland being restored to a bucolic place of plentitude to once again indicate that Judah will be restored. However, in verse 13 Yahweh is specific that this restoration will occur under the aegis of an appointed agent, his shepherd. And who might this appointed shepherd be? An answer is provided in verse 15 when Yahweh declares that "I will cause a righteous Branch to spring up for David." As Brueggemann observes, the introduction of the Davidic dynasty at this point is "peculiar and unexpected" since "for the larger casting of the Jeremiah tradition regards the dynasty as the main problem (cf. 22:13–18, 24–30), and does not characteristically envision a David-shaped future."[23]

Nevertheless, its inclusion is also significant in that it shows that "God's good inclination toward the dynasty and family belongs to Israel's central stock of promises" and that "one will arise in the dynasty who will do what kings are supposed to do," namely, "execute justice and righteousness in the land."[24] Thus there is both a harkening back and looking forward associated with this future Davidic ruler. With respect to the former, he is to perform the political duties that are expected of all kings. However, he is also to undertake an endeavor that is qualitatively new and unprecedented, mainly "the assurance that royal Israel will act in ways that make new life possible" and that "a new social reality is authorized."[25]

And what are the contours of this newly authorized social reality and life that the future Davidic king is to implement upon Judah's restoration? Jeremiah 34:8–22 helps fill in the gaps. Ostensibly this narrative records King Zedekiah's decision to free all the slaves within Judah and the

---

22. Habel, *Land Is Mine*, 91.
23. Brueggemann, *Commentary on Jeremiah*, 318.
24. Ibid.
25. Ibid.

subsequent rejection of that decision by the populace. Yet as Brueggemann states, the contrast in governance—both in style and substance—provides a powerful and poignant "'case study' in fidelity and infidelity."[26]

Jeremiah does not explicitly state what prompts King Zedekiah to issue his manumission, but most interpreters attribute it to an observance of the שְׁמִטָּה or the *torah* practice of releasing debt slaves every six years and cancelling their debts that is prescribed in Exod 21:1–12 and Deut 15. There is good reason to see this as being the case since 34:10 twice uses the verb שָׁמַע to indicate that the people of Judah heard and initially obeyed King Zedekiah's order.[27] However, despite the congruity between King Zedekiah's order and the legislation of Exod 21 and Deut 15, there are important differences between these ordinances as well. For example, unlike Exod 21, King Zedekiah's release includes both male *and* female slaves.[28] Furthermore, in contrast to Deut 15, which bases the timing of release upon when a person became enslaved, King Zedekiah's release "is universally simultaneous[.]"[29]

These deviations thus lead Bergsma to conclude that "the covenant of emancipation instigated by Zedekiah does not, in fact, aim to fulfill any specific law of the Torah to the letter, but rather is an *ad hoc* enactment meant to fulfill the spirit of all of them[.]"[30] In fact, as Bergsma notes, in keeping with its plenary and synthetic perspective there is also a good deal of overlap between King Zedekiah's decree and the law of debt and slave release found in the Jubilee legislation of Lev 25. In particular the phrase "proclaiming liberty" (דְּרוֹר קָרָא) that appears in Jer 34:8, 15, and 17 is found in only two other places in the whole of the Hebrew Bible: Lev 25:10 and Isa 61:1. In and of itself this data point does not prove that King Zedekiah was proclaiming and enacting a year of Jubilee. What it does do, however, as Berger suggests, is "make it reasonable to suppose that it does"—a supposition that is further strengthened by the recognition that "the only universal, simultaneous release of persons in bondage in the biblical legal corpa is Leviticus 25."[31] Thus whether or not King Zedekiah's release was in fact a Jubilee proclamation is somewhat of a moot question since the practical effect of both was the same: "to eradicate the practice of Israelites (=Judeans) enslaving one another."[32]

---

26. Ibid., 325.
27. Ibid., 326.
28. Bergsma, *Jubilee from Leviticus to Qumran*, 161.
29. Ibid.
30. Ibid., 162.
31. Ibid., 164.
32. Ibid., 165.

Accordingly, the moral and theological upshot of this passage is clear and in keeping with Jeremiah's theme of restoration. As Brueggemann notes it conveys with unmistakable clarity that the "practice of torah and the implementation of the commandment of release would generate safety and well-being for the city. Reneging on the covenant and consequently practicing economic exploitation evoke the invasion of Babylon."[33] Once again then Israel's restoration presupposes an inseparable connection between the land and the practice of justice.

4.3 Israel's Restoration in Isa 56–61: A Landed, Particular Universalism

The prophetic oracles of Israel's restoration in Isa 56–61 provide some of the most well-known and oft-cited passages among Christian interpreters. Indeed there are many who suppose these traditions form the very backbone if not the whole skeletal structure of Jesus' kingdom vision, and for good reason. For as several scholars have recently pointed out, the uncanny parallels between Jesus' kingdom logia and Isaiah's narrative, both in terms of their shared themes and specific language, are so numerous and obvious that it is now considered virtually certain that Jesus drew upon an Isaiah tradition.[34]

Yet perhaps one of the most compelling convergences between Jesus' and Isaiah's restorative eschatologies is the palpable emphasis on universalism that echoes throughout. Sean Fryne, for instance, has argued that Jesus' parables of a final eschatological banquet in which all people, including presumably Gentiles, are invited to partake in the kingdom of God (Matt 22:1–14; Luke 14:16–24) is specifically rooted in none other than Isaiah's eschatological vision of Israel being a "light to the nations" (Isa 49:6).[35] In fact this sense of universalism reverberates so strongly and pervasively throughout Isaiah that some wonder whether it constitutes a decisive shift in how Israel's national election and restoration were to be (re)conceived, namely

---

33. Ibid., 330.

34. See, for example, Chilton, *Pure Kingdom*; Freyne, *Jesus, a Jewish Galilean*; and Stassen and Gushee, *Kingdom Ethics*.

35. It is important to note that in Matthew's version the only guests who are allowed to remain at the banquet are those who are suitably attired and properly behaved. Thus it could be that Matthew thinks that only Gentiles who are analogous to righteous Jews are worthy of entrance into the kingdom.

A Restoration of Land and a Restoration of Justice Governance 133

away from the idea of Israel being restored as a particular landed nation and instead it being restored as a permanent missionary community.[36]

Thus, as was the case with our examination of Israel's restoration in Jer 29–33, the initial divine pronouncements that mark Israel's restoration in Isa 56–61 leave Israel's landed existence if not in doubt, then at least in serious reconsideration.

Isaiah 56 begins with a familiar invitation and one we already explored well in our discussion of Jer 29–33: a call to practice justice (vv. 1–2). And verses 9–12 reprise the similar and related predicament of Israel's rulers failing to practice justice and how this failure invites not only their own perversion, but also the ultimate destruction of Israel by its foreign enemies. In this respect then Isaiah's restoration vision possesses a similar moral temperament as Jeremiah's insofar as a commitment to practice justice is prominently featured.

Where Isaiah's vision of restoration begins to depart from Jeremiah's, however, and quite radically, is found in the intervening verses sandwiched between these two passages. For as it reads,

> Do not let the foreigner joined to the Lord say, "The Lord will surely separate me from his people; and do not let the eunuch say "I am just a dry tree." For thus says the Lord: To the eunuchs who keep my sabbaths, who choose the things that please me and hold fast my covenant, I will give, in my house and within my walls, a monument and a name better than sons and daughters; I will give them an everlasting name that shall not be cut off. And the foreigners who join themselves to the Lord, to minister to him, to love the name of the Lord, and to be his servants, all who keep the sabbath, and do not profane it and hold fast to my covenant—these I will bring to my holy mountain, and make them joyful in my house of prayer; their burnt offerings and their sacrifices will be accepted on my altar; for my house shall be called a house of prayer for all peoples. Thus says the Lord God, who gathers the outcasts of Israel, I will gather others to them beside those already gathered. (56:3–8)

That this is a restorative pronouncement is clearly indicated in verse 8 when Yahweh declares that Israel's "outcasts" will be "gathered" up. The Hebrew word used for "outcasts"—נִדְחֵי—is a derivative of the verb דָּחָה, which means to push or thrust out. Thus as was the case in Jeremiah, it refers to exiled Jews who were literally pushed out of the land on account of their failure to practice justice. Yet despite this dereliction and subsequent

---

36. See, for instance, Lindblom, *Servant Songs in Deutero-Isaiah*, esp. 52–54, 70–73.

expulsion these same outcasts will nevertheless be "gathered"—מְקַבֵּץ—by Yahweh and returned to the land.

However, it is not Israel's outcasts alone that will be gathered up and returned to the land but "others" as well. In this instance the "others" being gathered up most certainly refers to the figure of the "foreigner" or Gentile and "eunuch" mentioned in verses 3–7. That such persons are considered distinct and separate from Israel's own covenanted community is confirmed not only by their identification as "foreign"— הַנֵּכָר‎—but also by the fact that they are described as choosing to "join" (הַנִּלְוָה) themselves to Yahweh as opposed to being chosen.

And what is the means through which this improbable enjoinment of gentiles to Yahweh takes place? Incredibly it is through a demonstration of covenantal faithfulness. More specifically these gentiles choose the "things" that are "pleasing" (חָפַצְתִּי) to Yahweh, namely the "keeping" of Yahweh's sabbaths (אֶת שַׁבְּתֹתַי יִשְׁמְרֵהוּ) in verses 4 and 6. Surely the irony of this eschatological vision would have been acutely felt by Isaiah's exilic audience as it indicates that despite not being original members of the covenant, these foreigners are nevertheless described as holding a high reverence and commitment to preserving the integrity of Yahweh's covenanted land. Such a portrait of faithful and committed obedience to Yahweh's justice by supposed interlopers would have made Israel's fecklessness and injustice by contrast all the more stark and convicting.

And yet by virtue of holding fast to Yahweh's sabbaths, and thus the integrity of Israel's land, interlopers are precisely what these foreign gentiles are not. For as verse 7 states not only will they accompany the Jewish exiles on their return to Israel to once again worship Yahweh on the "holy mountain" (הַר קָדְשִׁי), but even more significantly they will be allowed to enter into the Temple and offer sacrifices on its altar on account of Yahweh's declaration that "my house" (בֵּיתִי) will be called a house "for all peoples" (הָעַמִּים לְכֹל).

This extraordinary vision of a universal inclusion being woven into Israel's restoration harkens back to a similar vision put forward in Isa 49 where Israel's restoration becomes a centripetal catalyst for the drawing in of gentile nations. In fact, 49:6 makes it clear that Yahweh considers Israel's restoration in and of itself to be "too light [נָקֵל] a thing." Instead the ultimate eschatological dénouement is for Israel to become a "light to the nations" (גּוֹיִם לְאוֹר) so that Yahweh's salvation (יְשׁוּעָתִי) might reach "the end of the earth" (הָאָרֶץ קְצֵה).

Thus while Israel's restoration, and more specifically a restoration of its land, certainly plays an important role in these prophetic oracles, in some ways it also seems to serve as a backdrop, albeit an essential one, to the unfolding of an even more important and dramatic event: the universal inclusion and salvation of gentile nations. Indeed, there is a sense in which a theological and ethical commitment to faithfully executing Yawheh's *torah*, a commitment that is even open to the הַנֵּכָר and the גּוֹיִם, "is basically unbound by issues of territory."[37] As such the "national-territorial aspect of" Israel's identity "is here" both "paradoxically . . . affirmed" and yet "superseded at the same time."[38]

At this point then we are left in a situation that is comparable to the one found in Jer 29:5–7. For just as the divine injunctions to build houses, plant crops, and take and marry wives within Babylon ultimately suggested that Yahweh had replaced Israel's land with a new נַחֲלָה, so too does Isaiah's emphases on covenantal fidelity and the universal inclusion and salvation of gentiles seem to subordinate and even relegate Israel's land to the status of ancillary footnote in the grander scheme of its restoration.

However, as was the case in Jer 29–33, there is more to Isaiah's narrative of restoration that returns the theological and ethical focus both to the uniqueness and indispensability of Israel's land. After once again excoriating and rebuking Israel's people for their habitual idolatry in Isa 57:1–13, and then again promising to "build" (סֹלּוּ) them back up, "heal"(וְאֶרְפָּאֵהוּ) them, "restore comfort"(נִחֻמִים וַאֲשַׁלֵּם) to them, as well as bring them "peace" (שָׁלוֹם)in 57:14–19, Yahweh then shifts to a discussion of what constitutes improper and proper forms of worship in chapter 58. Thus as was the case in Jeremiah, there is here a recognition that the land's corruption and eventual redemption are ultimately tied to a demonstration of covenant faithfulness in both its cultic and socio-political dimensions.

Isaiah 58:1–5 describes a situation where there is a putative and ostentatious observance of Yahweh's "justice"(צְדָקָה) and "just judgments" (צֶדֶק־מִשְׁפְּטֵי) by Israel's people through a meticulous practice of fasting (צָמְנוּ). The problem with this demonstration, however, lies neither with the practice of fasting itself, nor with the punctilious manner in which it is observed. Instead, as Bergsma notes, the problem "lies in the fact that the people have observed ceremonial aspects of the law (fasting) without practicing its requirements concerning social justice[.]"[39] In particular, in the midst of their sanctimony Israel's people selfishly served their "own interests"(חֵפֶץ) by "oppress[ing] all your workers" (תִּנְגֹּשׂוּ עַצְבֵיכֶם), "quarreling" (לָרִיב) and "strik[ing] with a wicked fist" (רֶשַׁע בְּאֶגְרֹף וּלְהַכּוֹת). As a result of this moral hypocrisy Yahweh is unresponsive to their supplications.

---

37. Frankel, *Land of Canaan*, 71.
38. Ibid., 75.
39. Bergsma, *Jubilee from Leviticus to Qumran*, 194.

In order to remedy this situation Yahweh goes on to prescribe a form of fasting in 58:6–7 that not only comports with the ceremonial needs of humbleness and physical mortification, but that also "loose[s] the bonds of injustice"(פַּתֵּחַ חַרְצֻבּוֹת רֶשַׁע), "[undoes] the thongs of the yoke" (מוֹטָה אֲגֻדּוֹת הַתֵּר), "let[s] the oppressed go free" (וְכָל־חֲפֻשִׁים רְצוּצִים), and finally feeds and houses those members of Israel's community who are homeless and destitute. In other words Yahweh enjoins the people of Israel to once again honor and observe his Sabbath (v. 13). Then and only then, according to 58:12, 14, will their land, or the "נַחֲלָה of Jacob," be restored and their formerly demolished and decrepit buildings be "rebuilt" (וּבָנוּ).

Three aspects of this passage resonate strongly with Jeremiah. First, like Jeremiah, Isaiah envisions Israel's restoration to occur squarely within the land. Even more specifically, Isaiah claims that Yahweh will return the Jewish exiles to the territory that comprises Jacob's inheritance or נַחֲלָה of land. Thus whereas in Isaiah 56 the specificity of Israel's land seemed to fade into the background, now it reasserts itself into the foreground in indisputable fashion.

Second, the strong emphasis on the importance of practicing justice shows that Isaiah sees the same reciprocating relationship between cultic and social purity as does Jeremiah. Absent just treatment of not only the land itself but also those who dwell upon it, especially the poor and disenfranchised, Israel's worship not only rings hollow. It makes a mockery of Yahweh and his covenant.

Finally, as Bergsma has also observed, like Jer 32–33, Isa 58 contains a number of references to the jubilee. For instance, Bergsma notes that the discussion of what Yahweh considers to be improper and proper forms of fasting in 58:3–6 is significant since the only "fast actually *commanded* in the Torah is the Day of Atonement (Lev 23:26–32), on which the jubilee was proclaimed."[40] Similarly, the "acceptable day" (לַיהוָה רָצוֹן) of fasting mentioned in 58:5 has strong parallels with the jubilee being known as an "acceptable year."[41] What is perhaps the strongest connection to the jubilee, however, is the series of ethical commandments enumerated in 58:6–7 and 9–10. As Bergsma states the "freeing of debt-slaves, the protest against the abuse of workers, and the sharing of food and shelter with the needy, especially the needy kinsman can all be found reflected in the jubilee legislation."[42] In fact no other assemblage of biblical commandments corresponds as closely to the jubilee as do these passages. Accordingly, "the

---

40. Ibid., 195.
41. Ibid., 196.
42. Ibid.

prophet leaves no doubt that he wishes his audience to attend to the very real matters of social and cultic justice—that is, just toward mankind [*sic*] (e.g. humane treatment of the poor) and God (proper observation of the Sabbath)—*now*, in the present."[43]

Each of these connections are in turn reiterated and further intensified in Isa 60–61. Regarding the uniqueness, specificity, and essentiality of Israel's land to its restoration, Isa 60:3 at first strikes a similar tone as 56:6–7 by stating that "[gentile] nations [גּוֹיִם] shall come to your light and kings to the brightness of your dawn."

However, whereas in Isa 56 the גּוֹיִם are described as joining themselves to Yahweh and thus possessing an equal opportunity to return to the land and even enter into the Temple as that provided to the Jewish exiles, 60:4–10 depicts an entirely different scene. To begin with verse 4 indicates that those who are being "gathered together" (נִקְבְּצוּ) by Yahweh are not the גּוֹיִם or the "foreigner" (הַנֵּכָר), but instead "your sons"(בָּנֶיךָ) and "your daughters" (וּבְנֹתַיִךְ) from "far away"(מֵרָחוֹק). In other words, the population that Yahweh is most concerned with gathering up and returning to the land are Jewish exiles.

This is not to say, however, that the gentiles are excluded from this vision of an eschatological re-gathering of the exiles within the land. Indeed, they are included albeit in a manner that looks completely different than that presented in Isa 56. For instead of being depicted as coequals with the people of Israel, now the "foreigners" (נֵכָר) are described as rebuilding the shattered walls of Jerusalem and "serving" (יְשָׁרְתוּנֶךְ) the exiles.[44] This same theme of gentile subservience to the restored people of Israel is repeated in 60:14 and in 61:5. What is to be made of this sudden and abrupt change of gentile status? First, it is important to note that this shift does not in any way abrogate or nullify the proceeding vision of universal inclusion of gentiles at least as it pertains to the practicing of Yahweh's *torah*. Those gentiles who choose to join themselves to Yahweh by observing the stipulations of the Sabbath and practicing the dictates of justice are still to be included in the ambit of Yahweh's salvation. What these verses do signify, however, is that the particularity of Yahweh's covenant with Israel and thus the particularity of its covenanted land still retain their integrity and uniqueness within the universal scope of Yahweh's salvation.

Indeed this point is made rather explicitly in Isa 60:21 when Yahweh informs the exiled Jews that "Your people shall be righteous and they shall

---

43. Ibid.

44. The NRSV renders יְשָׁרְתוּנֶךְ as "ministering." However, the root of the verb is שָׁרַת whose primary meaning according to the *BDB* is to serve.

possess the land forever. They are the shoot I planted, the work of my hands so that I might be glorified." Here Yahweh unequivocally reaffirms that the people of Israel alone are his chosen possession. No other nation, including even a nation of faithful gentiles who faithfully adhere to Yahweh's justice, can replace the people of Israel any more than can another nation replace Israel's land.

When viewed from this perspective, the subservience of the gentiles that accompanies Israel's restoration in Isa 60–61 not only keeps the particularity and uniqueness of Israel's land intact, but conversely it also preserves the particularity and uniqueness of the gentile people and their lands. Yes, the gentiles will come to Israel to rebuild its ruins. And yes, they will do so not as co-equals but as servants (Isa 60:14). But in order to do so, they must first depart from their own lands (Isa 60:3). In other words there is a presumption within these verses that after the gentiles have helped the people of Israel rebuild its nation they will ultimately return to their own homelands—a presumption that also seems to lie behind Isa 2:1–4. They will do so, however, without being empty-handed. For like Isa 2:1–4, Isa 60:3 indicates that the nations coming to and eventually departing a restored Israel will do so in the aura of "your light" (לְאוֹרֵךְ).

And what is the nature of this light? As is often the case with biblical imagery an object or phenomenon can have more than one meaning simultaneously. For instance as we saw with נַחֲלָה above the word can either mean the inheritance of a familial plot of land or it can refer to the people of Israel as whole. And in some instance it can even mean both.

A similar kind of dynamic is also at work with the symbol of light. On the one hand, Isa 60:19–20 states that upon the completion of Israel's eschatological restoration, the cosmos itself will be so fundamentally transformed that Israel will no longer need to rely upon the sun and moon to provide its light because "the Lord will be your everlasting light [עוֹלָם לְאוֹר], and your God will be your glory." Thus Yahweh himself will be the light that suffuses Israel.

However, Isa 61:3 indicates that there is another source of Israel's light or glory as well. In particular the text states that "they will be called oaks of justice [הַצֶּדֶק אֵילֵי], the planting [מַטָּע] of the Lord, to display his glory [לְהִתְפָּאֵר]." What is indicated here is that the people of Israel will themselves also be a source of Yahweh's glory or light. More specifically, the people of Israel will display and reflect Yahweh's light not simply by virtue of their personhood alone, but because they are oaks of justice (הַצֶּדֶק אֵילֵי) that are firmly planted (מַטָּע). The metaphor of an oak tree firmly rooted in the ground accomplishes two important tasks. First, it conveys the sturdiness and integrity with which the people of Israel are to take and practice their commitment to justice. This commitment is no mere sapling, but a thick, robust tree. Thus Israel's commitment to practicing justice should also be thick and robust. Second, "the planting of the Lord" (יְהוָה מַטָּע) can be interpreted in two ways. It can reiterate Israel's identity as Yahweh's chosen people, but it can also reiterate the fact that as Yahweh's chosen people, Israel should always be firmly rooted and anchored in its land.

In fact when these two images are combined, a reciprocating relationship between Israel's justice and its land comes into view. It is a thick commitment and practice of justice that allows Israel to be firmly re-planted within its land, and it is by virtue of being re-planted within the land that Israel's commitment to practicing justice will be firmly re-established. And it is ultimately both of these elements, that is a commitment to practice justice in order to be firmly re-planted within the land and a commitment to be firmly re-planted within the land in order to practice justice, which allows a restored Israel to become a source of Yahweh's light.

Indeed this same view is evident in Isa 61:4–11. After being called "oaks of justice" and the "planting of the Lord" in verse 3, the text then describes how the people of Israel "will build up the ancient ruins," "raise up the former devastations," and "repair the ruined cities[.]" The succession of the verbs "build up" (וּבָנוּ), "raise up"(יְקוֹמֵמוּ) and "repair" (וְחִדְּשׁוּ) all clearly demonstrate that Isaiah envisions Israel's restoration to be synonymous with a wholesale project of societal and economic refurbishment. And such a project would be impossible to implement apart from being firmly re-entrenched within the land.

In fact verse 7 states that the exiles returning to Israel "shall receive a double portion; everlasting joy shall be theirs." On its face the "double portion" (מִשְׁנֶה) that these returning exiles are due to receive would seem to be "everlasting joy"(עוֹלָם שִׂמְחַת). However, this is not what the Hebrew text states. Strangely, the NRSV omits the prepositional phrase בְּאַרְצָם, which means "in their land." Thus a more literal translation of this verse would read something more along the lines of "Therefore *in their land* (emphasis added) they shall possess a double portion; everlasting joy shall be theirs." In other words, the verse makes it clear that the receipt of a double portion of "everlasting joy" is directly dependent upon and connected to the antecedent of the exiles returning to and being reestablished within the land. Without receipt of the latter, receipt of the former is neither complete nor possible.

Yet receipt of its land and the commensurate renewal of its political, social and economic life encompasses neither the full scope of Israel's restoration, nor its full import. For as verses 8–9 state, the restoration of Israel's land becomes both the stage and platform for it to recommit itself to the theological/ethical practice that is most coveted and "loved" (אָהֵב) by Yahweh: "justice" (מִשְׁפָּט). And it is precisely by re-committing themselves to the practice of justice within the land that the "descendants" (זֶרַע) of the exiles "shall be known among the nations" (בַּגּוֹיִם וְנוֹדַע) and be acknowledged as a people "whom the Lord has blessed" (יְהוָה בֵּרַךְ).

Verse 10 puts an even finer point on this integral relationship between the restoration of Israel's land, its commitment to justice, and the broader witness this commitment has to surrounding nations by employing the horticultural analogy of a blossoming garden. For just as "the land (כָּאָרֶץ) brings forth its shoots, and as a garden causes what is sown in it to spring up," the text states, so too will Yahweh make all the nations stand and take notice of Israel through the practice of "justice [צְדָקָה] and praise." We thus end where Isa 56 began, with the inclusion of the nations within Israel's restoration. However, this universal inclusion does not come at the expense of or even as a substitute to the restoration of Israel's particular land, but rather as a direct result of it. Israel is indeed restored for the inclusion and ultimately the salvation of all the nations, but only because Israel is first restored as its own nation.

And this brings us to the third and final connection that Isa 60–61 shares with Jer 29–33 and that is the rise of a messianic figure and the recapitulation of the Jubilee. Both elements are clearly in view in Isa 61:1–3. There is spirited and continuous debate over whom Yahweh anoints (מָשַׁח) with the spirit (רוּחַ) in verse 1. As Bergsma notes the most popular theories are that this is either Isaiah himself, one of his descendants, or perhaps even the "servant" figure that is previously identified in Isa 42.[45] In fact, given the symmetry between Isa 61:1 and Isa 42:1, Bergsma thinks this last option is the most likely.[46]

Whatever the identity of this mysterious servant, however, it is clear that by virtue of being anointed he is to be recognized as some kind of a royal figure. After all, although there are memorable examples of both prophets and priests being anointed in the Hebrew Bible (e.g., 1 Kgs 19:16; Exod 28:41; 29:7; 40:13–15; Num 32:25), the ceremony was most commonly associated with the coronation of Israel's kings.[47] Thus as Bergsma concludes, there "are good reasons to view this speaker—the 'servant'—as a royal figure."[48]

---

45. Bergsma, *Jubilee from Leviticus to Qumran*, 199.

46. Ibid., 200.

47. See, for example, 1 Sam 9:16; 10:1; 16:3; 2 Sam 2:7; 5:17; 19:10; 1 Kgs 1:34; 5:1; 19:15; 2 Kgs 9:3, 6, 12.

48. Bergsma, *Jubilee from Leviticus to Qumran*, 200.

Yet it is not just his anointing that suggests a royal status, but also the fact that this servant is charged with discharging the kingly duties of "proclaiming liberty to the captives" (לִשְׁבוּיִם֙ דְּרוֹר לִקְרֹא) and "binding up the broken-hearted" (לְנִשְׁבְּרֵי־לֵב). As Moshe Weinfeld has observed it was a common practice amongst Near Eastern monarchs throughout the Neo-Assyrian period to regularly issue proclamations of "liberty."[49] This "liberty" or liberation entailed a number of different political and socio-economic elements, but most often they resulted in "the freeing of slaves and debtors for their debts, pardon of prisoners and rebels (*amnestia*), the release of captives and the return of exiles to their homeland, annulment of taxes, the restoration of estates to families, and the division of the land to the needy."[50]

Accordingly "while the idea of anointing does bear overtones of prophetic and priestly status as well," it is ultimately this call to proclaim "liberty" and to "bind up" that for Bergsma decisively cements the "royal office" of this Isaianic servant.[51] More specifically, states Weinfeld, "he is a servant upon whom God, his king, places his spirit *to establish justice in the land . . . and free those who are imprisoned* (Isa. 42:1–7)."[52]

However, despite the parallels between the kind of political and socio-economic liberation the messianic servant-king proclaims and grants in Isa 61:1–3 and that that is proclaimed and granted by the monarchs in the ancient Near East there is, as Weinfeld notes, a qualitative difference distinguishing the two. For whereas "the granting of freedom and the restoration of individual rights is interpreted" within Egypt, Mesopotamia, and Greece, "as the return of the individual to God" such that it is "literally understood as service of the gods in their temple," in Isaiah by contrast, "servitude to God is expressed in submission to the Divine will *and* to His religious and ethical commandments[.]"[53]

In other words the kind of liberation that Isaiah envisions this messianic servant proclaiming and enacting is not just the freedom of Israel to worship Yahweh within its land apart from the oppression and subjugation of foreign domination, but also the freedom of Israel to practice Yahweh's ethical commandments within the land. And this brings us to the strong linkages that Isa 61:1–3 shares with the Jubilee.

As mentioned above, the phrases "proclaiming liberty to the captives" and "binding up the broken-hearted" were commonly associated with a

---

49. Weinfeld, *Social Justice in Ancient Israel*, 12.
50. Ibid., 15.
51. Bergsma, *Jubilee from Leviticus to Qumran*, 200.
52. Weinfeld, *Social Justice in Ancient Israel*, 12–13; emphasis added.
53. Ibid., 16; emphasis added.

royal figure in the Ancient Near East. However, as Bergsma states, these phrases are also "freighted with connotations of the jubilee year[.]"[54] In particular, the connection with the Jubilee is confirmed by the following phrase in Isa 61:2—"to proclaim a year of the Lord's favor" (לַיהוָה רָצוֹן שְׁנַת־ לִקְרֹא)—"the best biblical analogy for which," according to Bergsma, "is the year of the jubilee."[55] This strong connection to the Jubilee may be somewhat muddled, however, by the following phrase "and the day of vengeance of our God" (לֵאלֹהֵינוּ נָקָם וְיוֹם) since it indicates that time periods "year" and "day" are "being used figuratively and not literally."[56] However, this juxtaposition actually serves to underscore the connection to the Jubilee since "the jubilee was a *year* proclaimed on a day (Lev. 25:9–10)."[57]

In a similar vein, the juxtaposition of "liberty" and "favor" with "vengeance" can also cast doubt on a Jubilee connection since Lev 25 does not include any specific reference to vengeance. However, as Bergsma also points out, Lev 25 does mention and spell out a specific role for the "kinsman redeemer" or גֹּאֵל as does Num 35:9–34, which does prescribe acts of vengeance. Thus while neither Yahweh nor the messianic servant is ever specifically identified as a גֹּאֵל in Isa 61:1–3, "he is so identified in immediately adjacent passages (Isa 60:16; 62:12) and in passages that have clear intertextual relationships with Isaiah 61 (49:7–13; 52:7–10)."[58] Thus the upshot is that "the dispensing of "favor" to his people and the enacting of "vengeance" on their enemies are flipsides of the Lord's role as [גֹּאֵל]."[59]

What Isa 61:1–3 ultimately presents then in Bergsma's judgment is perhaps the first "*messianic* re-interpretation of the jubilee" insofar as Isaiah does not issue a call "for a return to the actual law codes of ancient Israel," but instead he "foresees the coming-one would assume in the near future-of one endowed with the Spirit of the Lord who will personally execute the kind of socio-economic restoration envisioned, to a certain extent, in the ancient jubilee institution."[60]

Thus in reading and comparing the respective visions of Israel's eschatological restoration put forward in Jer 29–34 and Isa 56–61 we begin to see a similar theological and ethical pattern emerge. First, both posit that there is an intimate and symbiotic relationship between Yahweh, Israel and

---

54. Bergsma, *Jubilee from Leviticus to Qumran*, 201.

55. Ibid.

56. Ibid.

57. Ibid.

58. Ibid.

59. Ibid., 201–2.

60. Ibid., 202.

the land. Accordingly, both speak of Israel's restoration as being inseparable from a physical return to the land from exile and the re-establishment of a flourishing socio-economic life within the land. Second, in conjunction with the theological relationship between Yahweh, Israel and the land, both prophets also assume there to be a deep and abiding connection between possession of land and the practice of justice. More specifically, both Jeremiah and Isaiah assume that Yahweh restores Israel to the land in order to fully embody and practice the dictates of מִשְׁפָּט and צְדָקָה. However, both also assume that it is the full embodiment and practice of מִשְׁפָּט and צְדָקָה, especially as it is encapsulated in the Jubilee tradition, that allows Israel to not only be firmly re-entrenched with the land, but also to serve as an ethical witness to other lands. Finally, both also identify the rise of a messianic figure who will not only herald the restoration of Israel to its land, but who will also take an active role in re-establishing its commitment to practicing justice within it.

With this prophetic pattern of eschatological restoration in view, I would now like to turn our attention to how Israel's restoration was conceived in late Second Temple Jewish literature in order to discern how these same theological and ethical elements are repeated and/or modified.

4.4 Israel's Restoration in Late Second Temple Jewish Literature

4.4.1 The Book of *Jubilees*

Written sometime between 160 and 150 BCE in Palestine, the book of *Jubilees* is, as Brant Pitre states, an "'expansionistic paraphrase' of the books of Genesis and Exodus up until the revelation at Mount Sinai."[61] As such the book essentially recounts, often times verbatim, the biblical narratives of Gen 1 through Exod 12, although as Doron Mendels notes it also contains a number of significant departures. Indeed, the author of *Jubilee* re-reads and re-interprets these biblical narratives in light of his own historical and socio-political context—a context in which "Eretz Israel... was still, around 125–130 [BCE], largely in the hands of other [Gentile] peoples."[62]

In particular although the author of *Jubilees* is "conscious of the outward aspect, namely the 'grand debate' with the Greek eastern world about the origins of peoples, culture, etc., he is mainly preoccupied with the inward aspect[,]" that is, he is "less concerned with fending off Hellenism, and

---

61. Pitre, *Jesus, the Tribulation, and the End*, 65.
62. Mendels, *Land of Israel*, 59.

more interested in addressing his fellow Jews."[63] As such one of the major foci of the book is to ask and answer the questions of "what borders the Jewish state is to have, what is to be its political authority, and what exactly should be done with the foreigners settled upon the Land."[64]

In terms of its basic plot, *Jubilees* recounts the archetypal story of the creation, rise, fall, punishment, and finally the restoration of Israel by Yahweh. Accordingly, three of the book's major themes are an identification of Israel's apostasy, an explanation of how this apostasy corrupts and defiles Israel's land, which thus hastens a period of great tribulation and exile, and then ultimately an eschatological vision of how Israel will be restored to its land. Thus it contains several elements common to late Second Temple Jewish literature such as accounts of war, plagues, sickness, and foreign captivity.

"What is distinctive about the book of *Jubilees*, however," states Pitre, "is the explicit link that is drawn between the tribulation and an evil generation that has despised the covenant and forgotten the festal calendar[.]"[65] A particularly salient example of this link can be found in *Jub.* 23:18–23, which reads,

> Behold the land will be corrupted on account of all their deeds, and there will be no seed of the vine, and there will be no oil because their works are entirely faithless. And all of them will be destroyed together: beast, cattle, birds, and all of the fish of the sea on account of the sons of man. Some of these will strive with others, youths with old men and old men with youths, the poor with the rich, the lowly with the great and the beggar with the judge concerning the Law and the Covenant because they have forgotten the commandments and covenant and festivals and months and sabbaths and jubilees and all of the judgments. And they will stand up with bow and swords and war in order to return to "the way," but they will not be returned until much blood is shed upon the earth by each (group). And those who escape will not be turned back from their evils to the way of righteousness because they will lift themselves up for deceit and wealth so that one shall take everything of his neighbor; and they will pronounce the great name but not in truth and righteousness. And they will pollute the holy of holies with their pollution and with the corruption of their contamination.

---

63. Ibid.
64. Ibid.
65. Pitre, *Jesus, the Tribulation, and the End*, 67.

> And a great punishment shall befall the deeds of this generation from the Lord, and He will give them over to the sword and to judgment and to captivity, and to be plundered and devoured. And He will wake up against them the sinners of the Gentiles, who have neither mercy or compassion, and who shall respect the person of none, neither old or young, nor any one, for they are more wicked and strong to do evil than all the children of men. And they shall use violence against Israel and transgressions against Jacob. And much blood will be shed upon the earth. And there shall be none to gather and none to bury.

As was the case with Jeremiah and Isaiah, this passage clearly shows that the author of *Jubilees* sees both an intimate and reciprocating relationship between the quality of Israel's worship and the possession of its land and thus how defilement of one inevitably attenuates the integrity of the other. In particular *Jubilees* recognizes that the failure of Israel's political leadership and populace to properly observe the covenantal stipulations of the Jubilee and the Sabbath—both of which provide justice to both the land itself as well as those who dwell upon it, especially the poor and marginalized—is directly tied to its stark displays of socio-economic oppression. Thus the rot of Israel's cultic and social corruption is so pervasive and pungent that it contaminates not only its worship but also the very land on which that worship is illegitimately offered. Hence the punishment of this cultic and social malfeasance is the same that is foreseen by Jeremiah and Isaiah: first physical desecration of Israel's land and then ultimate expulsion and exile from it at the hands of Israel's foreign enemies.

However, as is also true with Jeremiah and Isaiah, while *Jubilees* does see despoliation of Israel's land and expulsion from it as punishments for its cultic and social apostasy, it does not see exile as a permanent theological and political state. For almost immediately after the somber vision of desecration, banishment, and subjugation described in the passage above, one then reads the following:

> And in those days the children shall begin to study the laws. And to seek the commandments. And to return to the path of justice. And the days shall begin to grow many and increase amongst those children of men till their days draw nigh to one thousand years. And to a greater number of years than (before) was the number of days. And there shall be no old man nor one who is not satisfied with his days. For all shall be (as) children and youths. And all their days they shall complete and live in peace and joy. And there shall be no Satan nor any evil destroyer; For all their days shall be days of blessing and healing. And

at that time the Lord will heal His servants. And they shall rise up and see great peace. And drive out their adversaries. And the just shall see and be thankful. And rejoice with joy forever and ever. And shall see all their judgments and all their curses on their enemies. And their bones shall rest in the earth. And their spirits shall have much joy. And they shall know that it is the Lord who executes judgment. And shows mercy to hundreds and thousands and to all that love Him. (*Jub.* 23:26–31)

Thus juxtaposed against the proceeding pronouncements of punishment and exile is a sweeping eschatological vision of Israel's restoration, a restoration that includes not only the replenishment of Israel's people, but also the restoration of their national independence and territorial sovereignty. And the means through which both aspects of this restoration occurs is once again none other than a return by Israel's people to "study the laws," "seek the commandments," and "return to the path of justice" (v. 26). In this respect then *Jubilee*'s vision of Israel's eschatological restoration is slightly different than that presented in both Jeremiah and Isaiah insofar as it is not the rise of a messianic figure that precipitates the end of exile, "but rather the emergence of a righteous remnant[.]"[66]

Furthermore, while *Jub.* 26:29–30 leaves little doubt that Israel's restoration is considered to be conterminous with the re-conquering of its land and the driving out of foreign adversaries, Mendels observes how *Jubilees* nevertheless also makes an effort to establish "a new pattern of relationship with some of the [foreign] people of the Land[.]"[67] Indeed, as he states, "*Jubilees* on the whole no longer repeats the familiar biblical *topoi* expressing hatred of all the peoples living in the Land of Israel, but introduces a different view of the matter."[68] Instead, it "wishes to reshape and redefine these relations so as to reach the conceptual *modus vivendi* with the peoples of the Land."[69]

This sense of a restored Israel seeking to develop a coexistent, even if at times subjugating, rapprochement with foreign peoples cohabitating their land is especially evident in *Jub.* 34 and 37–38. *Jubilees* 34:1–9 retells the story of Jacob and his household waging a retaliatory battle against the Amorites after the latter had "surrounded thy sons and plundered their herds" (v. 5). It appears to be based on Gen 48:22 when Jacob tells Joseph, "I now give to you one portion that I took from the hand of the Amorites with

---

66. Pitre, *Jesus, the Tribulation, and the End of Exile*, 68.
67. Mendels, *Land of Israel*, 66.
68. Ibid., 67.
69. Ibid., 81–82.

my sword and my bow." However, there is a minor albeit crucial difference between the Genesis account and that presented in *Jubilees*. For whereas the Genesis version concludes with Jacob simply defeating and conquering the Amorites and thus repossessing the land, in *Jub.* 34:9 Jacob is also described as "making peace" with Amorites even while making them his servants.

A similar narrative plays out in *Jub.* 37–38. These two chapters tell the story of Jacob and his descendants waging war against Esau and his descendants the Edomites. Once again Jacob and his forces prove to be victorious and once again their victory secures control over the land. However, in *Jub.* 38:11 Jacob's sons are said to inquire of him whether they "make peace" with the defeated Edomites or instead "slay them." In response to this query Jacob responds in 38:12 that they are indeed to make peace with the Edomites while also placing them into servitude.

Thus while these narratives certainly reinforce the notion that Israel's restoration necessarily entails the repossession and re-control of its land they also, as Mendel states, "focu[s] on the foreign peoples with whom the Jews had clashed with in the struggle for their historical rights of the Land, and [are] even willing to accept some of them."[70] In other words what we find in *Jubilees* is a conception of Israel's restoration that is not unlike what we discovered in Isa 56–61. Both unequivocally maintain the uniqueness and sovereignty of Israel's territorial integrity. However, both also foresee a situation in which the restoration of Israel's land redounds in some beneficial way to the Gentiles. In Isa 56–61 that benefit takes the form of receiving the blessing of Yahweh's *torah* and being included amongst his people. In *Jubilees* the idea of Gentile inclusion is not present, but there is nevertheless a sense in which Israel's territorial restoration reshapes its relationship with Gentile nations in such a way that it makes peaceful coexistent relationships within the land possible.

4.4.2 *Psalms of Solomon*

Written as a short collection of eighteen psalms attributed to King Solomon, the eponymously named *Psalms of Solomon* is thought to have been composed approximately in 63 BCE, shortly after Pompey's conquest of Jerusalem.[71] Thus in terms of its historical context, *Psalms of Solomon* shares a similar socio-political sensibility as *Jubilees* insofar as it is written in a context where Jewish autonomy and political sovereignty are becoming increasingly circumscribed. Furthermore, also like the book of *Jubilees*, *Psalms of*

70. Ibid., 82.
71. Pitre, *Jesus, the Tribulation, and the End*, 79.

Solomon is intently interested in first identifying the cultic and social causes of Israel's corruption and how this corruption invites wrathful punishment from Yahweh at the hands of an oppressive foreign ruler.

With regard to identifying the source of Israel's corruption *Psalms of Solomon* once again points to the familiar transgressions of failure to properly follow and obey Yahweh's law (2:3, 12), as well as the commission of societal injustice (4:9–13). In the wake of such wickedness, Yahweh is once again seen as punishing Israel by setting loose a foreign ruler who attacks and invades Jerusalem and exiles its inhabitants (2:1, 29; 8:22–26).

However, unlike *Jubilees* but like Jeremiah and Isaiah, *Psalms of Solomon* also identifies a messianic figure that plays a prominent role in both bringing and implementing Israel's restoration. This figure is clearly described in chapters 17–18. Chapter 17 of *Psalms of Solomon* begins with an acclamation of Yahweh's universally sovereign kingship and kingdom as well as a reaffirmation of David's royal status (17:1–4). This is then followed by a critical skewering of a corrupt Jewish leadership in 17:5–6 as well as the rise of a harrowing "lawless" foreign ruler who "laid waste to the land so that no one could inhabit it" and who "destroyed young and old and their children together" (17:11).The effect of juxtaposing these two modes of political leadership, the former being divinely appointed and just while the latter being historically contingent and oppressive, is twofold.

First, it reminds the author's audience that despite the current circumstances of Israel's political oppression and exile, Yahweh's kingdom is still ultimately sovereign. Second, in light of the evils perpetrated by both a corrupt Jewish leadership and a foreign ruler, it also underscores the need for Israel to return to a political ruler in the mold of a King David. Indeed this sentiment is clearly expressed in 17:21, which reads, "See, O Lord, and raise up for them their king, the son of David, at that time which you choose, O God, to rule over your servant, Israel."

After securing the need for *Yahweh* to raise up and establish a Davidic messianic political leader, *Psalms of Solomon* then proceeds to describe in great and inspiring detail the instrumental role he will have in effecting Israel's restoration:

> And he [the Messiah] will gather a holy people whom he will lead in righteousness, and he shall judge the tribes of the people that has been sanctified by the Lord, his God. And he shall not allow injustice to lodge in their midst any longer, nor shall there dwell with them any person who knows evil; for he shall know them, that all are their God's sons. And he shall distribute them according to their tribes upon the land, and no resident alien and alien shall sojourn among them any longer. He shall judge

people and nations in the wisdom of his righteousness. And he shall have the peoples of the nations to be subject to him under his yoke, and he shall glorify the Lord in the mark of all the earth, and he shall purify Jerusalem in holiness as it was in the beginning so that nations may come from the end of the earth to see his glory, bringing as first her sons who are exhausted, and to see the glory of the Lord with which God has glorified her. And he shall be a righteous king, taught by God, over them, and there shall be no injustice in his days in their midst, for all shall be holy and their king anointed of the Lord. (17:26–32)

Thus according to this passage there are six main tasks this Davidic messiah carries out that comprise Israel's restoration. These are (1) re-gathering exiled members of Israel's twelve tribes back to the land, (2) executing just judgments between and over the reconstituted tribes, (3) re-distributing Israel's land according to the original tribal allotments, (4) expelling both Gentiles and sinners from the land, (5) subjugating the nations, and (6) cleansing both Jerusalem and the Temple. In looking at these tasks there are two things that stand out that are worth commenting upon further.

First, as Michael E. Fuller has noted, there are a number of substantive parallels between this Davidic messiah and the Davidic messiah that is described in Isa 11:1–4. Among these are the notion that both messiahs are undergirded by "strength," "wisdom," and "righteousness" by Yahweh (*Pss. Sol.* 17:22–23; cf. Isa 11:2) and that both messiahs eradicate the unrighteous nations "with an iron rod" (*Pss. Sol.* 17:24; cf. Isa 11:4) and "the word of his mouth" (*Pss. Sol.* 17:24; Isa 11:4). Thus, by drawing on Isa 11 to inform his understanding of the Davidic messiah the writer of *Psalms of Solomon* "underscore[s] the point that the Davidic king's anointing is to be understood not only in terms of divine authority to defeat Israel's enemies, but as one guided by the wisdom of the Spirit to administer God's rule over Israel and the world[.]"[72]

Second, as Fuller also observes, it is also important to see how *Psalms of Solomon* divides Israel's restoration into two main stages. The first is when the Davidic messiah re-gathers Jewish exiles back to the land and reassembles them according to their tribal membership (17:26–29). It is only after this first stage of Israel's restoration is completed that the Davidic messiah then initiates a wider return of Jewish exiles from the broader Diaspora (17:31). What this division and sequencing suggests then, according to Fuller, is that the author of *Psalms of Solomon* held the first stage of Israel's restoration—i.e., the re-establishment of the twelve tribes

---

72. Fuller, *Restoration of Israel*, 166–67.

within the land—to be the most important. In fact, it suggests that "*Israel's first stage of re-gathering pertains to the 'return' of a Jewish group, possibly already within the Land.*"[73] That this is so is further underscored by the fact that "while the messiah gathers those who have been recently driven from Jerusalem, he does not gather those who [are] carried off to Rome (17:12) or those Jews actually liv[ing] among the nations."[74] On the contrary, just as in Isa 55 "the messiah stays put within the borders of Palestine, while the nations return the Diaspora Jews[.]"[75] Thus even though certain features of the division and sequencing of Israel's restoration in *Psalms of Solomon* may be idiosyncratic, the themes and overall pattern that emerge are quite similar to that found in *Jubilees* and Jeremiah and Isaiah before it. In the main all of these texts envision Israel's eschatological restoration as taking place within the land and all also envision it entailing a recommitment to the practices of justice.

4.5 Conclusion

Our review of Jeremiah, Isaiah, the book of *Jubilees*, and *Psalms of Solomon* has revealed that when it comes to Israel's eschatological restoration, it more appropriate to speak of a variety of different eschatological restorations. Indeed each text articulates a unique eschatological vision as to how and when Israel will be restored, through or by whom, and how this restoration will redound to either the salvation, punishment, and sometimes the punishment and salvation of the Gentiles.

Despite these variances, however, it also clear that all these texts see the restoration of Israel's territorial integrity and sovereignty as being an essential feature. Furthermore, all also see an integral relationship between the restoration of Israel's land, and the simultaneous restoration of an ethical and political commitment to rule over that land justly in accordance with the precepts of the Sabbath (שַׁבָּת) and the Jubilee (יוֹבֵל). In fact all see the restoration of Israel's land and the just governance of that land as coterminous.

It is with those relationships in mind that I would now like to turn to Jesus' own pronouncement of Israel's restoration in the Gospels via the proclamation of the kingdom in order to juxtapose his conception of Israel's restoration with those enunciated in Jeremiah, Isaiah, the book of *Jubilees*, and *Psalms of Solomon*. In so doing, it will become

---

73. Ibid., 168.
74. Ibid.
75. Ibid.

clear that Jesus is also working in the same eschatological paradigm of Israel's territorial restoration and the concurrent restoration of a just ethic of territorial governance.

5

Jesus and the Kingdom: A Restoration of the Land and a Restoration of Just Governance for Israel and the Nations

5.1 Introduction

As demonstrated in the survey above, the conception of Israel's eschatological restoration as it was envisioned in both prophetic and late Second Temple Jewish literature is both a complex and diverse affair. Indeed there is no single motif or trope (aside from restoration itself, of course) that adequately encompasses or explains this event in all its richness.

Nevertheless, despite this diversity, we still managed to discern a familiar constellation of theological and ethical themes whose orbit repeatedly revolved around Israel's land. More precisely our examination of Jeremiah, Isaiah, the book of *Jubilees*, and *Psalms of Solomon* showed that one of the more central patterns to emerge in Israel's restorative schema was Yahweh acting decisively, sometimes directly and sometimes in concert with a messianic figure, to gather up Jewish exiles from both the Assyrian and Babylonian Diasporas and physically return them to an Israel whose territorial sovereignty and integrity had been unequivocally reconstituted. In some instances this process of landed reconstitution entailed the harsh punishment and subjugation of the Gentile nations. In other instances, however, this process occasioned not only these nations' salvation through a miraculous and gratuitous incorporation into Israel's covenant but also a corresponding socio-political commission to learn of Yaweh's *torah* and re-enact its dictates of justice within the confines and institutions of their own native lands.

Furthermore, for Israel itself, the restoration of its land coincided with the re-emergence of an earlier governance structure wherein the נַחֲלָה of the land would be re-apportioned and ruled over in accordance with the נְחָלָה of a twelve-tribe system. And alongside this system of territorial re-distribution and governance would be a recommitment to once again embody the economic and social obligations of Yawheh's מִשְׁפָּט and צְדָקָה as they were inscribed in both the *torah* and the Jubilee.

It is with these themes and this pattern in mind that I would now like us to re-read and re-interpret Jesus' proclamation of the kingdom of God within the Gospels. For in doing so it will begin to become clear that not only did Jesus share the same theological conviction that the kingdom's eschatological manifestation would coincide with Israel's territorial restoration, but also the idea that this landed restoration would occasion both a recommitment to a politics of justice within Israel and a commissioning of this same kind of politics within the Gentile nations. As such it therefore becomes possible to read Jesus' kingdom ethic not as one that diminishes or even rejects Israel's territoriality for the sake of justice, but rather one that embraces justice for the sake of all lands.

Despite numerous assessments to the contrary, when it comes to finding evidence within the Gospels that substantiate this landed interpretation of both Jesus' kingdom proclamation and ethic there is certainly no shortage to draw from.[1] Unfortunately, neither time nor space allows for an exhaustive overview. In lieu of a more comprehensive examination I would therefore like us to concentrate our attention on four pericopes: (1) Jesus' beatitude of blessing the meek in Matt 5:5; (2) the Lord's prayer in Matt 6:9-13 || Luke 11:1-4; (3) Jesus' public reading of Isa 61:1-2 in Luke 4:18-19; and (4) the *Palingenesia* in Matt 8:11-12 || Luke 13:28-29. Lest the selection of these pericopes seem random and arbitrary I have opted to engage them for two reasons. First, all of these pericopes, both individually and collectively, contain either some portion or several parts of the restorative themes we identified in Jeremiah, Isaiah, *Jubilees*, and *Psalms of Solomon*. Taken together then, they present a compelling case for why it is not only plausible but necessary to read Jesus' kingdom proclamation and ethic through a territorial lens. Second, some of these very same pericopes have been marshaled as evidence by others in favor of a de-terriorialized reading of Jesus' kingdom proclamation. Thus to show how these pericopes have been misread makes the case for a territorial reading of the kingdom and its ethic all the stronger.

---

1. See Allison's extensive catalogue in *Constructing Jesus*, esp. 164-203.

5.2 Matthew 5:5—Jesus' Beatitude of Blessing the Meek

This well-known verse appears third in the list of nine so-called "Beatitudes" that begin Jesus' Sermon on the Mount—the single largest block of his teaching in the whole of the New Testament and one in which the kingdom of God features prominently. As such both it and the other Beatitudes are not to be interpreted as "wisdom teachings" or the articulation of impossibly attainable "high ideals," but rather as *"prophetic teachings"* that emphasize "God's presence, God's active deliverance, God's giving us a share in that deliverance and so blessedness and joy"—a point that is substantiated by their strong overlap and continuity with Isa 61.[2] Thus as Stassen and Gushee note, in uttering these prophetic Beatitudes, Jesus is "pointing to the reality of God's coming reign[.]"[3]

The New Revised Standard Version renders Matt 5:5 as "Blessed are the meek, for they will inherit the earth," which in Greek appears as μακάριοι οἱ πραεῖς ὅτι αὐτοὶ κληρονομήσουσιν τὴν γῆν. As W. D. Davies observes, there is no parallel of this verse in Jesus' Sermon on the Plain in Luke 6:17–49.[4] We already encountered some of the arguments for why this verse should not be read as Jesus affirming a territorial conception of the kingdom above in chapter two but it will be worth our while to briefly reengage them here so as to re-familiarize ourselves with their basic contours. Though Davies is at first dubious of the authenticity of the saying since he contends there are a variety of factors that suggest it is a Christian interpolation,[5] we might ask whether the more important and difficult question is "what did he mean?" even if it can be shown that this verse legitimately originated from Jesus.[6]

Part of the problem in answering this question, as Davies himself acknowledges, is that it is difficult if not impossible to "disengage the verse, in its Matthaean context, from the territorial promise of the Old Testament and Judaism."[7] One important reason this is so is because of the strong parallels Matt 5:5 shares with Ps 37:11, which reads, "But the meek shall inherit the land, and delight themselves in abundant prosperity." Davies concedes that this particular verse as well as the whole of Ps 37 has an unmistakable messianic and "this wordly connotation" since "dwelling in the land is as-

---

2. Stassen and Gushee, *Kingdom Ethics*, 34–35.
3. Ibid., 37.
4. Davies, *Gospel and the Land*, 359.
5. Ibid., 359–61.
6. So also ibid., 361.
7. Ibid., 362.

sociated with security (v. 3, 9), with permanence (vv. 10–11, 18, 29), and abundant prosperity (v. 11), with the Day of the Lord (v. 13), with Divine blessing (v. 22)."[8] Hence "[t]here is an unmistakable eschatological dimension to the possession of the land in Matthew 5:5 as to all of the beatitudes."[9]

Nevertheless, despite accepting the fact that Jesus may well be referring to "inheriting, not the earth, but the land of Israel, in a transformed world, in the Messianic Age or the Age to Come" Davies still contends that it is more appropriate to see Jesus as speaking of "inheriting the land" as being "synonymous with entering the Kingdom and that this Kingdom transcends all geographic dimensions and is spiritualized." [10] And why is this so? "[B]ecause," Davies states somewhat tautologically, "we have previously recognized in Judaism itself, as elsewhere in the New Testament, the notion of 'entering the land' has been spiritualized."[11]

Gary M. Burge offers a similar kind of argument in *Jesus and the Land*.[12] Like Davies, Burge acknowledges the strong parallels between Matt 5:5 and Ps 37:11 but puts an even sharper point on their connection. While the Greek word γῆ can take a variety of meanings in the New Testament including "soil (Matt. 13:5), a region ('land of Judea,' Matt. 2:6), the earth itself (Matt. 5:18, 35), or the inhabited world (Luke 21:25)," it can also "refer to the land of Israel (Luke 4:25)."[13] What makes it likely that both Jesus and his audience would have understood this reference to the γῆ to mean "not the entire *earth*" but rather "to the land of Promise, the Holy Land" comes from the fact that he "refers to these recipients as *inheritors* of this land."[14] As Burge notes, the Greek word for "inherit"—κληρονομέω—"was commonly used to refer to the assignment of land in the Old Testament promises."[15] Hence Jesus' combination of "land" and "inheritance" in Matt 5:5 has a clear and unambiguous meaning: "this is the *land of inheritance*, the Land of Promise."[16] Furthermore, beyond the explicit territorial connotation, there is also a clear socio-political upshot to this message as well. For as Burge explains,

8. Ibid.
9. Ibid.
10. Ibid.
11. Ibid.
12. Burge, *Jesus and the Land*.
13. Ibid., 34.
14. Ibid.
15. Ibid.
16. Ibid.

In a world where the powerful were ready to make bold political and military claims on the land; where the strong assumed that they had the right, thanks to their position or privilege, to take what is theirs, Jesus appears as "the re-arranger of the Land." Meekness leads to inheritance—the strident will walk away empty-handed. The great reversal keenly felt throughout Jesus' ministry—*the last will be first!*—has now been applied to the land, this land of inheritance, the land of Judah, no doubt the most precious commodity fought for in Jesus' day.[17]

And yet like Davies despite adducing a persuasive body evidence indicating why a territorial reading of Matt 5:5 is not only likely but probable, Burge is quick to hedge his bets. For in responding to the consequent question of does the proceeding "mean that Jesus here offered a territorial promise to his followers," Burge pivots 180 degrees and states that this "is not likely."[18] And this is because "Jesus and his followers reinterpreted the promises that came to those in his kingdom."[19] More specifically, Jesus held that "[t]heir kingdom [was] in heaven (Matt. 5:30, 10), they shall see God (5:8), and their rewards will be counted in heaven (5:12)."[20]

Finally, we have Stassen and Gushee's ethical interpretation of this verse. Once again both see a clear and direct connection between Jesus' words and Ps 37:11 and therefore conclude that the latter is the basis of Jesus' saying. However, in addition to Ps 37:11, Stassen and Gushee also think it likely Jesus has Isa 61:1 in view since the Hebrew word for "meek"—עָנָו—appears in both texts. A deeper exegesis of this word shows it possessing a much deeper meaning than merely "meek." Indeed עָנָו is used to denote those persons who have been oppressed by injustice and more specifically the injustice of being dispossessed of their land. Thus Stassen and Gushee conclude that when Jesus invokes the "meek"—πραεῖς (from the root πραΰς)—he has in mind not simply those who are diffident and unassuming but rather those who are "*surrendered to God, and socially and economically powerless.*"[21]

Furthermore, the authors note that עָנָו (πραΰς) has other connotations as well. More specifically they note that πραΰς "always points to peacefulness and peacemaking" and point to Zech 9:9 as an illustrative example in that it depicts a messianic figure who is "humble [עָנִי] and mounted on a donkey"

17. Ibid., 35.
18. Ibid.
19. Ibid.
20. Ibid.
21. Stassen and Gushee, *Kingdom Ethics*, 40.

and who will "banish the chariot from Ephraim, the war-horse from Jerusalem; the warrior's bow will be banished, and he will proclaim peace to the nations. His rule will extend from sea to sea, from the river to the ends of the earth."[22] Thus when these two aspects of עָנָו's meaning are brought together we see that Jesus is telling his disciples that *"blessed are those who are surrendered to God, who is the God of peace."*[23]

Yet nowhere in this otherwise thoughtful analysis is there any corresponding discussion of how the "meek" are assured by Jesus that they will inherit the land let alone how their commitment to peacemaking and peaceableness is integrally connected to this inheritance. The closest that Stassen and Gushee get is their approving quotation of Hans Weder's comment that Jesus' commitment to peace "'rightly lies [at] the heart of his differentiation from the Zealots, from the violence-using battlers for the reign of God. Blessed [are] the nonviolent. They will inherit the world.'"[24] Thus while there is a fleeting recognition that the "meek" and the "land" are connected, the disproportionate emphasis on the ethical character of the former is so complete that the latter is relegated to a generic category if not swallowed up and subsumed altogether.

Here then are three representative examples of how his beatitude has been interpreted so as to de-territorialize Jesus' kingdom vision and ethic. However, I would argue there are good reasons for why this beatitude actually confirms rather than shutters the kingdom's territoriality. And ironically, some of these reasons are alluded to by Davies, Burge, and Stassen and Gushee.

Let us first address the question of whether the "land" (γῆ) mentioned in Matt 5:5 in fact refers to the actual physical land of Israel. That it likely does is indicated in the first beatitude, "Blessed are the poor in spirit, for theirs is the kingdom of heaven" (Matt 5:3).

As Sean Freyne has discussed, the qualification of the "poor" (πτωχοί) by the addition "in spirit" (τῷ πνεύματι) has led many to conclude that this "is a deliberate spiritualizing of a more radical statement preserved by Luke's 'blessed are the poor,' and thus provides a hermeneutical key for how the rest of the beatitudes should be interpreted," namely, as spiritualized transcendent ideals and not as concrete moral and socio-political instruction.[25] However, there are several reasons why this "spiritualized" line of interpretation of both the "poor" as well as the "land" is not appropriate.

22. Ibid., 40–41.
23. Ibid., 41.
24. Ibid.
25. Freyne, *Galilee, Jesus and the Gospels*, 72.

First, it is important to remember the restive socio-economic and political climate in which Jesus uttered this specific pronouncement as well as his larger proclamation of the kingdom of God in general. As we previously discussed in depth in chapter one above, the context of Jesus' public ministry was one in which there was both increasing Jewish resentment toward Roman imperial subjugation as well as a growing internal dissatisfaction with an economic system of pronounced inequality. With respect to the latter, Freyne argues that it is important to recognize that the prevailing socio-economic class in first-century Galilee were Jewish poor farmers and peasants who held and worked small plots of land.[26] On the other end of the spectrum was a minority of wealthy landowners who possessed large estates.

And it was the latter who were continually exploiting the former for their own economic benefit through a perverse distortion and (mis)application of the very *toranic* prescriptions that were suppose to preserve some modicum of economic parity. For as Richard Horsley explains the situation in first-century Palestine was such that the "process of increasing indebtedness under the pressures for tithes and tributes led to the growth of the large landed estates of the Herodian families and of the priestly aristocracy who were probably themselves often the creditors."[27] In other words, more and more Jewish peasants were having to taking out loans in order to survive, which meant more and more were pledging their meager plots of land as a form of collateral. However, the sabbatical laws of debt remission codified in the *torah* were supposed to address and remedy this structural imbalance by cancelling these land debts and returning the plot to its original owner at the end of every seventh year.

Of course this meant that these wealthy creditors were then reluctant to offer loans in the years immediately prior to the Sabbatical for fear that they would then lose their "capital."[28] So to work around this dilemma these creditors thus created a legal instrument known as the *prosbul*, "which enabled the creditor to avoid the literal requirement of the sabbatical cancellation of debts."[29] Thus while the implementation of the *prosbul* may have meant that loans were "more easily obtainable," it also meant that "once peasant families fell into the whirlpool of indebtedness, they now had no sabbatical protection to aid their recovery."[30] Thus as Horsley concludes, the impoverished peasant Jewish farmers of Palestine were faced with a

26. Ibid., 159.
27. Horsely, *Jesus and the Spiral of Violence*, 31.
28. Ibid.
29. Ibid.
30. Ibid.

reality wherein the "structural violence rode roughshod right over the very traditional mechanisms designed originally to prevent the development of structurally based injustices."[31]

In light of this harsh and unjust economic reality, it therefore needs to be asked whether both Jesus and his audience, several of whom were these poor peasant farmers, would have heard and understood the phrase "poor in spirit" (πτωχοὶ τῷ πνεύματι) as taking on a purely spiritual connotation. Freyne makes a compelling argument for why this is not the case. Far from "spiritualizing" the poverty of the "poor" and making it an internal existential state, the phrase τῷ πνεύματι is meant to serve as an "affirmation of blessedness for those who are not just poor, but who have taken that condition to their very heart, by not allowing themselves to be deceived by the attraction of wealth, instead trusting their lives totally to the heavenly Father ([Matt]5:25–34)."[32] Thus, "in Matthew's view, the poor who are really poor, that is in their very spirit, are a challenge to those who live their lives on assumptions such as those expressed in the injunction of [Matt] 6:19f., namely storing up wealth in terms of money or fine clothing (cf. 11:8)."[33] In other words, the phrase τῷ πνεύματι intensifies the materiality and concreteness of meaning of the "poor," which therefore means that subsequent beatitudes should be read in the same kind of material frame, including inheriting the land of Israel.

Even so, what is one to make of Matthew's idiosyncratic preference for using the expression "kingdom of heaven" (βασιλεία τῶν οὐρανῶν) as opposed to the more common phrase "kingdom of God" (βασιλεία τοῦ θεοῦ)? Once again, there has been a strong tendency amongst several interpreters to see this invocation of "heaven" (οὐρανός) as being an indication that Jesus views the kingdom as transcending conventional geographic boundaries, let alone the specificity of Israel's land. However, there are solid exegetical reasons why this assumption is questionable. For as Jonathan Pennington convincingly argues in his work *Heaven and Earth in the Gospel of Matthew*,

> Both the source genitive and attributive genitive understandings of ἡ βασιλεία τοῦ οὐρανοῦ retain some sense of territory and space. As a source genitive, the kingdom is one which comes *from heaven* and whose origin is *in heaven*. As an attributive genitive, the kingdom is one that is characterized as having a heavenly nature, referring to the realm of heaven in distinction to the earth ... The addition of τῶν οὐρανῶν to βασιλεία

31. Ibid.
32. Ibid.
33. Ibid.

in Matthew makes it inevitable that some sense of spatial understanding of the kingdom is communicated: understanding ἡ βασιλεία τῶν οὐρανῶν as meaning only the rule or reign of God in a non-spatial sense fails to account for the importance of Matthew's ascription of the τῶν οὐρανῶν.[34]

Thus Matthew uses the phrase 'kingdom of heaven' not to suggest that the kingdom is somehow non-spatial or a-territorial, but rather to "emphasize that God's kingdom is not like earthly kingdoms, stands over against them, and will eschatologically replace them (on earth)."[35]

Consequently neither the "poor in spirit" nor the "kingdom of heaven" phrases of Matt 5:3 undermine a territorial reading of Jesus' kingdom vision. On the contrary, when read appropriately, they confirm it. And further confirmation is provided when one considers the close proximity of Matt 5:3 to Matt 5:5. As Dale Allison notes, the "poor" (πτωχοὶ) in 5:3 is virtually synonymous in meaning with the "meek" (πραεῖς) in 5:5 since the LXX regularly uses both to translate the Hebrew word we encountered above to describe those who were destitute on account of being disposed of the inheritance of their land: עָנָו.[36] Thus it is significant, Allison explains, that verse 5 so closely follows verse 3 since it "suggests that v. 5 was formulated precisely in order to explicate v. 3" insofar as it is "natural to regard 'theirs is the kingdom of heaven' and 'they will inherit the earth [or "the land"]' as saying much the same thing, or at least to suppose that 'the promise of the earth makes clear that the kingdom of heaven includes a this-worldly earth.'"[37]

And since there is a consensus even among those who do not subscribe to a territorial reading of Jesus' kingdom vision in Matt 5:5 that Jesus is nevertheless drawing upon Ps 37:11, which has Israel's specific land in view, the proceeding discussion makes it all the more likely that Jesus is not simply assuring his audience that those who have been territorially displaced will receive a generic plot, but that they will re-receive their specific familial נַחֲלָה. In other words Matt 5:5, in concert with Matt 5:3, confirms that Jesus, like Jeremiah, Isaiah, the book of *Jubilees*, and *Psalms of Solomon*, views the kingdom of God (or heaven) and its restoration as inextricable from a restoration of Israel's land to those who have been alienated from it.[38]

---

34. Pennington, *Heaven and Earth*, 296.

35. Ibid., 321.

36. Allison, *Constructing Jesus*, 183.

37. Ibid.

38. Indeed the early Christian community thought as much, as indicated in the *Didache*. To wit *Did.* 3:7 states, "Be meek, since the meek, will inherit the land" (ἴσθι δὲ

Yet it is not just a restoration of Israel's land that Jesus pronounces in this kingdom vision, but the restoration of an ethical vision for how that restored land is to be governed as well. Here again it is instructive to re-examine the content of Ps 37 albeit more intensely and substantively than discussed above. In terms of purpose and structure, Ps 37 is recognized as a wisdom psalm. As such it is written in a didactic style with the intent of conveying knowledge and wisdom to the reader as it has been gleaned from the author's own personal observations and experience. It is also written as an acrostic, meaning that the initial character of each alternate verse is arranged in accordance with the sequence of the Hebrew alphabet.

Although the psalm initially reads like a continuous succession of proverbs, C. J. A. Vos has argued that upon closer inspection it is actually possible to distinguish three "locutionary acts"—i.e., vv. 1–11, vv. 12–26, and vv. 27–40.[39] One of the theological and ethical dynamics that reoccurs throughout Ps 37 is the intersection between three related themes, namely, the contrast between the "wicked" (רָשָׁע) and the "righteous" (צַדִּיק), between doing "good" (טוֹב) and departing from "evil" (רָע), and between "trusting in the Lord" (בֵּיהוָה בְּטַח) and "fretting" (תִּתְחַר). Indeed, in the eyes of the psalmist, it is precisely by doing good and trusting in Yahweh while refraining from evil and anxious fretting that the righteous are separated from the wicked.

However, the first two verses also makes it clear that while doing good and remaining steadfast are what makes one righteous in the eyes of Yahweh, neither acts as a guarantor of material blessing nor do they serve as an inoculation against suffering. In fact, these verses make it evident that at the present time at least, the wicked are prospering in spite of and perhaps *even because* of their evil-doing and fretting. Conversely those who are presently doing good and trusting in Yahweh are the עָנָו—that is the poor and dispossessed. Nevertheless, despite their present circumstances of injustice, there is also an eschatological assurance that Yawheh will ultimately punish the wicked and vindicate the righteous. Consequently, the latter are enjoined

---

πραΰς, ἐπεὶ οἱ πραεῖς κληρονομήσουσιν τὴν γῆν). Aside from the similarities in phrasing and verbiage, one has to wonder why, if Jesus intended his audience to understand the inheritance of the "land" (γῆ) as being strictly spiritual and non-territorial in character, then why does a more materialistic understanding of the land remain extant in subsequent early Christian teaching? As with our discussion with Justin and Iraneaus it would seem the reason is because the early Christian community, following Jesus, understood him as referring to the physical land of Israel.

39. Vos, "Hermeneutical-Homiletic Reading," 576.

to endure and persevere. In this regard then Ps 37 is Job-like insofar as it "postulates an individual and efficacious retribution."⁴⁰

We already noted above how in verse 11 *Yahweh* promises that the "meek" (עָנָו) will "inherit the land" (אֶרֶץ יִירְשׁוּ־) and that this forms the basis of Jesus' similar pronouncement in Matt 5:5. However, this is not the only instance in Ps 37 where there is a divine assurance given that the land will be (re)inherited. Such a promise is also made in verses 9, 22, 29 and 34. In each case, the Hebrew verb "inherit" (יָרַשׁ) appears in the future tense meaning that those who currently do good and trust in Yahweh are not in possession of their land.

And why is this so? A number of reasons are offered and most have to do with immoral conduct. The "wicked" (רָשָׁע) launch plots against the "righteous" (לַצַּדִּיק) (v. 12); they use armaments to oppress the "needy" (וְאֶבְיוֹן) and kill the "upright" (יִשְׁרֵי־) (v. 14); there is famine throughout the land (v. 19); the wicked exploit the poor by reneging on repaying their loans (v. 21); and finally, the wicked conspire to kill the righteous (v. 32).

With the exception of verse 9, all the other impediments to inheriting the land are directly attributable to the malfeasance, deceit, and violence of the "wicked." In other words, the reason the poor and the righteous of Israel cannot rightfully re-inherit their land back is because the wicked are acting in direct defiance of Yahweh's *torah*. And more specifically, as Mark Vander Hart observes, "Psalm 37 makes it clear that the sabbatical and especially the jubilee commandments were not being observed by members of the Israelite covenant community."⁴¹ Thus we observe a similar kind of theological and ethical dynamic that was on display in Jeremiah, Isaiah, *Jubilees*, *Psalms of Solomon*: alienation and dispossession of the land is both a cause and effect of injustice.

However, the obverse of that dynamic is also on display as well. For while the poor are repeatedly promised they will re-inherit the land in due time, they are also told that repossession of the land is not, in and of itself, a sufficient restorative dénouement. Instead, repossession of the land must be coupled with a robust recommitment to once again "do good" (v. 3) execute justice (v. 29), and follow *torah* (v. 34). Indeed, as verse 3 states, it is only by doing the latter that makes repossession of the former possible—so much so that the psalmist exhorts the landless poor to practice justice and follow Yahweh's *torah* even despite their landlessness. Thus the string of present imperatives included in verses 5–8—"trust" (וּבְטַח), "commit" (גּוֹל), "be still" (דּוֹם), "wait patiently" (וְהִתְחוֹלֵל), and even "refrain from anger" (מֵאַף)

---

40. Ibid.
41. Vander Hart, "Possessing the Land," 148.

הֶ֫רֶף) and "forsake wrath" (חֵמָה וַעֲזֹב)—are all issued independent of the inheritance of the land. Yet this does not mean inheritance of the land is unimportant or that following these ethical commandments is somehow unrelated to it. On the contrary it is precisely because the land is so important that the landless are counseled to maintain their integrity less they become like the wicked and allow their greed, violence and oppression to create an irreparable fissure between possessing the land and practicing justice. Once again then the land requires justice, but justice also requires the land.

With this theological and ethical relationship that Ps 37 posits between justice and the land in view, we are now able to see how Jesus' kingdom pronouncement in Matt 5:5, and indeed the whole of Matt 5–7, is similarly evocative of not just a generic restored socio-political ethic, but a restored ethic of territorial governance. First, there is the similarity in structure. For just as Ps 37 follows an eschatological assurance to the poor and dispossessed that they will re-inherit their land (37:3) with a series of ethical imperatives on how they are to do good, be just and patiently and peacefully await *Yahweh's* vindication in the midst of their landlessness (Ps 37:4–8), so too does Jesus follow his eschatological promise that the poor and landless of his context will re-inherit their land (Matt 5:5) with an extended discourse on how they are to live and act in anticipation of the kingdom's full manifestation (Matt 5:21–48). Thus like the psalmist, Jesus links the restoration of Israel's land with specific ethical and political practices that are necessary to rule over that land justly. Second, the nature of the ethical and political practices that Jesus prescribes is also instructive. Above we discussed how the imperatives included in Ps 37:4–8 are in the present tense. In other words the psalmist fully expects and commands his audience to do justice and wait peaceably for *Yahweh's* eschatological vindication here and now—even in the face of oppression and landlessness. There is to be then an ethical continuity between how the psalmist's audience is to behave and act in the present—without their land—and how they are to behave and act once they have re-inherited the land. Similarly as Stassen and Gushee insightfully observe, the ethical commandments that Jesus issues in Matt 5:21–48 are not a series of idealistic hard teachings that are impossible to implement this side of the kingdom's full eschatological manifestation, but instead are concrete, practical "transforming initiatives"—the intent is of which are to diagnose and counteract vicious cycles of violence and revengeful retaliation.[42] Thus like Ps 37, as well as Jeremiah, Isaiah, *Jubilees*, and *Psalms of Solomon*, in proclaiming an eschatological assurance of the restoration of Israel's land, Jesus is not counseling his audience to adopt

---

42. Stassen and Gushee, *Kingdom Ethics*, 135.

"mere inner attitudes, vague intentions, or moral convictions only[.]"[43] Instead he is calling them to "regular practices to be engaged in," and more specifically ethical practices that provide "deliverance from vicious cycles of anger and insult."[44] In other words, Jesus sees a restoration of the kingdom's land and its ethics as inextricable.

Furthermore, it is not only the structure of Jesus' paraenesis in Matt 5 that is indicative of restoration of Israel's land but its content as well. Recall from above that the audience Jesus is addressing is composed of the "meek" (πραεῖς) and the "poor" (πτωχοί)—that is, those who have been dispossessed of their land both through the economic exploitation of fellow Jews and through expropriation by the Romans. Indeed, it was this dispossession that made first-century Palestine such a restive and volatile political climate— a climate that had no shortage of Jewish nationalist groups willing to use violence in order to retake and reinstate Jewish sovereignty over the land.[45] On the one hand, Jesus' affirmation of an eschatological re-inheritance of the land in Matt 5:5 shows he is sympathetic with that cause. However, like Ps 37 and especially like Isaiah and *Psalms of Solomon* Jesus nevertheless abjures the use of violence to re-take possession of the land. Instead, he is continually encouraging his followers to patiently trust in and await *Yahweh's* power and vindication (Matt 6:25–34) and not to take matters into their own hands. This does not mean, as Richard Fuller states, that Jesus is telling his followers that "Israel must accept her enemies—whether Roman or Jewish—for all time, with no hope of change."[46] On the contrary Jesus is assuring his audience that Israel's "vindication [is] to be reserved for God; thus Israel's task is to await his intervention."[47] Thus Jesus' claims that "the true members of Israel will submit to the messiah's ethical and religious code of conduct and receive the baptism of the Spirit, thus demonstrating in part, what is anticipated in the future."[48] Or to state it a different way, Jesus is telling his landless followers that there is to be no ethical separation between how the land is to be governed once it is re-inherited and the means through which that re-inheritance is to occur. There is no other way to a territorially restored Israel than an ethically restored Israel.

Thus *pace* Davies and Burge, Matt 5:5 serves as a compelling piece of evidence that Jesus envisioned the kingdom's full eschatological

---

43. Ibid., 136.
44. Ibid.
45. See Horsley, *Bandits, Prophets and Messiahs*.
46. Fuller, *Restoration of Israel*, 247.
47. Ibid.
48. Ibid., 248.

manifestation as concomitant with a territorially restored Israel. And while Stassen and Gushee are certainly correct that the ethical thrust of the teaching and commandments Jesus offers in conjunction with Matt 5:5 is focused on the practices of peacemaking, it is also true that their meaning is not exhausted in peacemaking *in se*. Rather, they forward an ethic and practice of peacemaking as they related to acquiring and governing over Israel's restored land.

5.3 The Lord's Prayer in Matt 6:9–13 ‖ Luke 11:1–4 and Jesus' Appropriation of Isaiah's Jubilee in Luke 4:16–20

Another set of texts that has been used to support an a-territorial reading of Jesus' kingdom proclamation and his ethic are the Lord's Prayer found in Matt 6:9–13 and Luke 11:1–4, and Jesus appropriation of Isaiah in Luke 4:16–20. In keeping with the same pattern I used above, I will first present the arguments of those who claim these texts reject a territorial restoration of Israel, and then often a series of ripostes as to why I think they do.

As several scholars have previously noted, one of the common threads that ties these passages together and one that further suggests that Jesus is operating within a restorative eschatological paradigm are the references to the Jubilee. In particular, as Sharon Ringe observes, while the appearance of the Greek word ἄφεσις ("deliverance, pardon, forgiveness") in Matt 6:12, Luke 11:4, and Luke 4:18 is not dispositive of an explicit link to the Jubilee in and of itself, they, along with numerous other references to the Jubilee in the Synoptics, "suppor[t] the conclusion that it appears quite likely that Jubilee images figured in the teachings and ministry of Jesus himself."[49] This especially seems the case when one considers that the LXX consistently uses ἄφεσις for the Hebrew words דְּרוֹר and יוֹבֵל, both of which mean "liberty" or "release," and both of which are used to describe the Jubilee in Lev 25.[50]

Nevertheless, despite the strong probability of Jesus intentionally invoking the Jubilee tradition within his kingdom proclamation and despite the latter's obvious references to a just distribution and governance of Israel's land, arguments have been put forward that suppress and even deny the

---

49. Ringe, *Jesus, Liberation, and the Biblical Jubilee*, 88.

50. Leviticus 25:10 reads, "And you shall hallow the fiftieth year and you shall proclaim liberty (דְּרוֹר) throughout the land to all its inhabitants. It shall be a jubilee (יוֹבֵל) for you: you shall return every one of you, to your property and every one of you to your family." The LXX renders this verse as "καὶ ἁγιάσετε τὸ ἔτος τὸν πεντηκοστὸν ἐνιαυτὸν καὶ διαβοήσετε ἄφεσιν ἐπὶ τῆς γῆς πᾶσι τοῖς κατοικοῦσιν αὐτήν· ἐνιαυτὸς ἀφέσεως σημασία αὕτη ἔσται ὑμῖν, καὶ ἀπελεύσεται εἰς ἕκαστος εἰς τὴν κτῆσιν αὐτοῦ, καὶ ἕκαστος εἰς τὴν πατριὰν αὐτοῦ ἀπελεύσεσθε" (emphasis mine).

possibility that Jesus' appropriation of the Jubilee had a territorial resonance. One is offered by Sean Freyne. Upon examining Jesus' "radical abandoning of the values of home, family and possessions and his expectation that his followers would do likewise," Freyne notes a strong ethical resonance with the Jubilee tradition of Lev 25 and with its strong emphasis on "total trust in Yahweh's gifts of food, shelter and necessities of life."[51] What such devotion speaks of, says Freyne, is a "recognition of total dependence on God and a confidence to trust in God's benevolent care for all his creation."[52] Thus just as the prophet Isaiah "drew on aspects of the Jubilee in order to point up the social inequalities of the time, which were clearly being ignored in the euphoria of the triumphant return from exile," so also, says Freyne, did Jesus employ "it on his return to lower Galilee, faced with the situation of real human need in the midst of plenty that had resulted from Herodian policies in the region."[53]

Yet in Freyne's judgment, despite drawing clear theological and ethical linkages between Jesus' proclamation of the kingdom, Isaiah's prophetic vision, and the legislation of the Jubilee, Jesus nevertheless chooses to not extend that shared import to the actual physical land. For while Jesus' selection and appointment of twelve disciples certainly could have "[t]heoretically" suggested "that Jesus was espousing a territorial restoration [of Israel]," within the "Jesus tradition," according to Freyne, "the Twelve have a symbolic role to play in the present" and ultimately "the tribes are consigned to a future eschatological setting (Mt. 19:28; Luke 22:30)."[54] Thus the "clear implication" of these passages is not that Jesus is appointing the twelve to rule over and govern a sovereign territorially restored Israel, but rather that "[w]isdom is available to all and repentance is a possibility of non-Jews."[55] More specifically, "[i]nsiders who espouse an ethno-phobic point of view involving total separation clearly cannot share in the eschatological banquet which Jesus envisages."[56] That Jesus therefore lays hold of and claims the theological and ethical frameworks of Isaiah and Jubilee while simultaneously rejecting a restoration of Israel's land shows that his "attitude towards the earth and towards the land" lay closer to "the creator God rather than in the God of Sinai and the Exodus, and that his lifestyle was based more

---

51. Freyne, *Jesus, a Jewish Galilean*, 118.
52. Ibid.
53. Ibid., 118–19.
54. Ibid., 119. See further discussion of Matt 19:28 and Luke 22:30 below.
55. Ibid., 120.
56. Ibid.

on the story of Abraham than on that of Moses."⁵⁷ Jesus, in other words, extracts the ethical universalism of the Jubilee by shucking the husk of landed provincialism.

A similar kind of argument is also articulated by John Howard Yoder in *The Politics of Jesus*. Writing under the subheading "The Platform: Luke 4:14ff.," Yoder notes that it is instructive that Jesus begins his public ministry in Luke by both taking up and reiterating John the Baptist's announcement of the imminent arrival of the kingdom of God, and by publicly reading and messianically applying Isa 61:1–2 to himself. According to Yoder, the implications of reading this particular scriptural citation would have been clear for Jesus' first-century Jewish audience, namely that he was instituting a Jubilee year and thus "the time when the inequities accumulated through the years are to be crossed off and all God's people will begin again at the same point."⁵⁸ Thus in light of this explicit connection between the kingdom's impending inauguration and the institution of the Jubilee "[w]e must conclude," states Yoder, "that in the ordinary sense of his words Jesus, like Mary and like John, was announcing the implementation of a new regime whose marks would be that the rich would give to the poor, the captives would be freed, and the hearers would have a new mentality (μετάνοια) if they believed this news."⁵⁹ And while Yoder acknowledges that the exact timing of how this announcement will come to pass is a bit inscrutable, its content is unambiguously clear: "it is a visible socio-political, economic restructuring of relations among the people of God achieved by divine intervention in the person of Jesus as the one Anointed and endued with the Spirit."⁶⁰ Thus like Freyne, Yoder is confident that Jesus intentionally links his announcement of the kingdom with the Jubilee tradition and furthermore he is equally confident that Jesus did so in order to affirm that the kingdom's manifestation would have concrete ramifications for how a restored Israel would construct and administer its restored socio-political and economic life. Yet like Freyne, Yoder thinks the renewed socio-political and economic reality that Jesus augurs for a restored Israel via the manifestation of the kingdom has little bearing on the composition and governance of its physical land. This is apparent when Yoder begins to further explicate the implications of the Jubilee in fuller detail in chapter three of *The Politics of Jesus*.

In reviewing the Jubilee and Sabbatical traditions, Yoder notes that they contain four specific prescriptions: "(1) leaving the soil fallow, (2) the

---

57. Ibid., 117.
58. Yoder, *Politics of Jesus*, 29.
59. Ibid., 32.
60. Ibid.

remission of debts, (3) the liberation of slaves, (4) the return to each individual of his family's property."⁶¹ He then wants to re-read the Gospels with these prescriptions in mind in order to discern how they are alluded to and applied by Jesus. For our purposes we will focus our attention on Yoder's examination of prescription 2, 3 and 4 since they are the instructions tied most directly to the (re)disposition of Israel's land and also because they consume the bulk of Yoder's focus.

Regarding prescriptions 2 and 3—i.e., the remission of debts and the manumission of slaves—Yoder notes that these provisions "are not marginal but central in the teaching of Jesus." Indeed, they "are even at the center of his theology."⁶² That this is so, argues Yoder, is clearly evidenced in the Lord's Prayer and its request to "remit us our debts as we ourselves have also remitted them to our debtors[.]" As Yoder rightfully states, far too many versions of this prayer have either blunted or occluded the socio-economic thrust and thus the ethical import of the word ὀφείλημα by translating it as a personal offense such that Jesus is enjoining his disciples to forgive the personal annoyances caused by the foibles of others. However, in a first-century Jewish context, and especially one that was riven with growing socio-economic fissures between a shrinking pool of land-holding elites and a burgeoning swell of landless peasant farmers, Jesus' audience would have understood the imperative to "forgive" (ἄφες) "debts" (ὀφείλημα) not as the sloughing off of breaches of personal decorum or the foregoing of social etiquette improprieties, but rather as the liquidation and absolving of real monetary debts.⁶³ Hence as Yoder states, "[i]n the 'Our Father,' then, Jesus is not simply recommending vaguely that we might pardon those who have bothered us or made us trouble, but tells us purely and simply to erase the debts of those who owe us money; that is to say practice the jubilee."⁶⁴

Lest one is prone to think that the language of "forgiving debts" in the Lord's Prayer supplies merely a coincidental connection to the Jubilee, Yoder sees two other parables told by Jesus as offering further proof of

---

61. Ibid., 60.

62. Ibid., 61.

63. To wit in Deut 24, a text that among other things spells out the legislation of the Sabbatical Year, verses 10-13 state, "When you make your neighbor a loan of any kind, you shall not go into the house to take the pledge. You shall wait outside, while the person to whom you are making the loan brings the pledge out to you. If the person is poor, you shall not sleep in the garment given you as the pledge. You shall give the pledge back by sunset, so that your neighbor may sleep in the cloak and bless you; and it will be to your credit before the Lord your God." The word "loan" is the Hebrew word עֲבֹטוֹ and refers to something of worth that is owed. In the LXX, עֲבֹטוֹ is translated into the Greek word ὀφείλημα.

64. Yoder, *Politics of Jesus*, 62.

an explicit link. The first is the parable of the "merciless servant" in Matt 18:23–25. Once again Yoder contends that interpretation of this parable has been distorted on account of its being wrenched from the particularities of its socio-economic and historic context. The point of this parable, he argues, is not to offer "a rather pale picture of the forgiveness of sins which is granted by God to those who forgive their brethren or sisters," but rather is that "[t]here is no divine jubilee for those who refuse to apply it on earth."[65] That this is so is plainly understood once on recognizes that "sad hero of the parable is a real person, a Galilean peasant whose name the disciples of Jesus probably knew."[66] Furthermore this was a Galilean peasant who "had previously been a free property owner" but "had been reduced to the practical equivalent of slavery by way of progressive indebtedness."[67] This then, per Yoder, is "exactly the situation into which the 'unmerciful servant' of the parable had come" and thus Jesus should be understood as describing "the relationship between the rising indebtedness of the poor peasant, the loss of his properties, and the loss of liberty which followed directly."[68]

Accordingly when Jesus tells the story of how this indebted and property-less Galilean peasant has his debts "forgiven" him by the king, it is in the context, posits Yoder, of the "jubilee year having been proclaimed."[69] Yet the parable does not conclude here, but continues, rather disappointingly, with the story of how this "slave who has been freed by the jubilee" nevertheless "meets one of his fellow slaves who owes him a modest sum of seventy francs [sic], and refuses him the benefit of the same jubilee forgiveness from which he himself had profited."[70]

The second parable is that of the "dishonest manager" in Luke 16:1–9. As was the case of the parable of the "unmerciful servant" so too, says Yoder, does this parable "take its point of departure from the peasant at the time of Jesus," that is a situation in which "[a]s a result of the demand of King Herod and his sons and the Roman occupants, most of the former rural property owners had lost their independence."[71] However, Yoder notes that this situation of financial distress and landlessness was exacerbated by another phenomenon, namely "the absenteeism of the [land] owners." As a result of this absenteeism, "a hierarchy of intermediate functionaries" was established for

65. Ibid., 63, 64.
66. Ibid., 63.
67. Ibid.
68. Ibid., 64.
69. Ibid.
70. Ibid.
71. Ibid., 67.

the "collecting of debts."[72] In practice, however, these debt collectors only further compounded the level of indebtedness since they "extorted from the sharecroppers arbitrary sums which widely exceeded the rent and debt and taxes which were really due."[73]

It was precisely such a corrupt debt collector who is the protagonist of this parable and who is confronted with a stark set of choices once his malfeasance is discovered by his employer. Either he could continue to further extort the peasant farmers and accumulate a sufficient amount of money that could repay the amount he had deceitfully embezzled, thereby further alienating himself from his community, or he could choose to forego and cancel these debts, thereby inflaming the anger and wrath of the landowner. Jesus describes him choosing the latter option by "convening his debtors and with a stroke of the pen lowering their debts to the right amount: fifty measures of oil instead of a hundred, eighty measures of wheat instead of a hundred, etc."[74]

Of course such a course of action is fraught with inherent risks since it "would only aggravate the insolvency of the steward" and "reduce him to poverty."[75] "But in acting this way," states Yoder, "he acquired genuine wealth, namely the gratitude and the friendship of his former victims."[76] Furthermore, this "dishonest manager" is also commended by his employer, who, as Yoder notes, is "the representative of God."[77] Whereas in "the parable of the merciless servant it was God who had taken the initiative," in this parable "it is the man who takes the initiative" insofar as "[i]t is he who first, obeying the messianic appeal, practices the jubilee by remitting the debts of those who are at the same time debtors to God and him."[78] "Consequently," Yoder continues, "God praises the intelligent man who before he was even touched by grace practices the redistribution of wealth. The man was able to read the signs of the Kingdom of God and to understand that the reign of unrighteous mammon is of the past."[79] Thus what these two parables and the Lord's Prayer confirm, contends Yoder, is that what Jesus has in mind when connecting the impending arrival of the kingdom with the forgiveness of debts is an authentic Jubilee "conformed to the sabbatical instruc-

---

72. Ibid.
73. Ibid.
74. Ibid., 68.
75. Ibid.
76. Ibid.
77. Ibid.
78. Ibid.
79. Ibid.

tions of Moses" and that was "able to resolve the social problem in Israel by abolishing debts and liberating debtors whose insolvency had reduced them to slavery."[80] Moreover, the "practice of such a jubilee was not optional." Instead, it "belonged to the precursors of the kingdom. Those who would refuse to enter this path could not enter into the Kingdom of God."[81]

From what we have encountered in Yoder's examination thus far, it would seem that he is not only confident that Jesus had the actual re-allocation of Israel's real actual land in mind when emphasizing the importance of the Jubilee practice of debt forgiveness as they are referenced in the Lord's Prayers and the parables of the merciless servant and dishonest manager, but furthermore that such a reallocation of real property as prescribed by the Jubilee is normative for the kingdom. It is therefore quite perplexing that when Yoder turns his attention to examining the ways in which the fourth Jubilee prescription—the return to each individual of his family's property (i.e., land)—appears in Jesus' teachings, he suddenly and inexplicably replaces "property" with the word "capital" as in "Fourth Jubilee Prescription: The Redistribution of Capital."[82] To be sure, both "capital" and "property" are anachronistic economic terms with respect to Jesus and his application of the Jubilee since both are the parlance of the modern free-market economy. Even so, the word "property" still preserves and maintains at some linkage to the actual physical land. "Capital," by contrast, is a much more ambiguous term and while certainly not devoid of some conception of land ownership, in most instances is understood to refer to the production of monetary wealth apart from landed modalities.

Thus by substituting the word "capital" for "property," Yoder uses a hermeneutical principle that stands the previous mode of interpretation he employed on its head. For instead of asking his readers to situate themselves in Jesus' own socio-economic and historical context and to intuit and think about how his invocations of Jubilee would resonate amongst a group of first-century Jewish Galilean peasant farmers who were impoverished, not because of a lack of capital, but because they had been disposed of their actual physical land, Yoder now asks his readers to read Jesus' appeal to the Jubilee in light of the redistribution of monetary wealth. To wit he writes, "So when Jesus formulated the celebrated commandment, 'Sell what you possess and give it as alms' (a better translation would be, 'sell what you possess and put in practice compassion'), this was not a 'counsel of perfection,' but neither was it a constitutional law to found a utopian state of Israel.

80. Ibid.
81. Ibid., 68–69.
82. Ibid., 69.

It was a jubilee ordinance which was to be put into practice here and now, once, in A.D. 26, as a 'refreshment,' prefiguring 'the reestablishment of all things.'"[83]

Thus what we observe in this passage is something akin to what we observed in Freyne's discussion above. For like Freyne, Yoder is certain that Jesus appropriated and worked with the tradition of Jubilee and saw its concrete implementation within first-century Palestine as intimately connected to the establishment of the kingdom of God and thus the restoration of Israel. Furthermore like Freyne, Yoder is also confident that Jesus understood the Jubilee as having real socio-economic and thus ethical impact for the restoration of Israel's national life and its governance. Nevertheless like Freyne, Yoder also concludes that Jesus' invocation of the Jubilee ultimately omits both the reallocation and governance of Israel's actual physical land. I would now like to show why these interpretations need not and most likely are not the case.

Let us begin with a deeper analysis of the Jubilee references that appear in the Lord's Prayer in Matt 6:9-13 and Luke 11:1-4. In terms of composition there are minor variations between the prayers Jesus instructs his disciples to pray in Matt 6:9-13 and the version offered in Luke 11:1-4. More specifically, the Lukan version excludes both the reference to the carrying out of the divine will on earth and the petition to be delivered from the "evil one"[84]—both of which are included in the Matthean version. Despite these minor differences, however, Brant Pitre has noted that the two versions contain a remarkable correspondence insofar as both (1) address the "Father" in the opening petition; (2) call for God's "name" to be "hallowed" and his "kingdom" to "come"; (3) petition for "daily bread"; (4) petition for the "forgiveness" of "debts" or "sins"; and (5) conclude with a request to be spared from "tribulation."[85] Moreover, while the Matthean version is "part of the Sermon on the Mount" and thus "embedded in the center of a series of texts topically joined by the theme of prayer" and the Lukan version "belongs to a tight series of texts thematically focused on prayer," the "basic meaning of the Lord's prayer as a textual unit is quite similar in both Gospels: Jesus'

---

83. Ibid., 70.

84. As has been voluminously noted and debated amongst exegetes, the phrase used for "evil one" in Matt 6:13 is τοῦ πονηροῦ, which is the genitive singular masculine form of the noun πονηρός. However, it is also possible that τοῦ πονηροῦ can be declined as genitive singular neutral. This means then that "evil one" or "evil" are both plausible translations.

85. Pitre, *Jesus, the Tribulation, and the End*, 136-37.

instructs his disciples by giving them a paradigmatic prayer about the coming of God's kingdom."[86]

As already convincingly demonstrated by Ringe, Freyne, and Yoder above, Jesus' instructions of "forgiving debts" (ἄφες ... ὀφείλημα) in Matt 6:12 and "forgiving sins" (ἄφες ... ἁμαρτίαις) in Luke 11:4 provide one of the strongest indications that he is working within the Jubilee tradition. However, there are other elements of both the prayer itself and its parallel structure with the Kaddish that further strengthen this connection and thus support the view that Jesus has Israel's real physical land in mind. Let us first address the other individual elements of the prayer. As Pitre comments, not only would the address "Father" conjure up memories of the original Exodus tradition, but it would also bring to mind "a *New* Exodus in which the scattered tribes of Israel will return to the promise land[.]"[87] This is certainly true of texts like Hos 1:10–11, Isa 63:10–17, and Jer 31:7–9, all of which identify God as a paternal figure and all of which "envisions the eschatological restoration of *all the tribes of Israel* scattered among the Gentiles, not merely the Judean exiles in Babylon."[88] "Hence," as Pitre concludes, "in the Old Testament prophets, the remarkably infrequent imagery of the *fatherhood of God* appears to be distinctly tied to the end of the Assyrian Exile and the restoration of all the tribes of Israel in a New Exodus."[89]

The theme of a New Exodus is also present in the hallowing of God's name and the petition for the kingdom to come (Matt 6:9–10 ‖ Luke 11:2). Here, Pitre points to Ezek 36:22–28 and Mic 4:5–8 as being instructive. Ezekiel 36:22–28 states,

> Therefore say to the house of Israel, Thus says the Lord God: It is not for your sake, O house of Israel, that I am about to act, but for the sake of *my holy name*, which you have profaned among the nations to which you came. *I will sanctify my great name*, which has been profaned among the nations, and which you have profaned among them; *and the nations shall know that I am the Lord*, says the Lord God, when through you I *display my holiness before their eyes. I will take you from the nations, and gather you from all the countries, and bring you into your own land.* I will sprinkle clean water upon you, and you shall be clean from all your uncleannesses, and from all your idols I will cleanse you. A new heart I will give you, and a new spirit I will put within you; and I will remove from your body the heart

---

86. Ibid., 134.
87. Ibid., 138.
88. Ibid., 139.
89. Ibid.

of stone and give you a heart of flesh. I will put my spirit within you, and make you follow my statutes and be careful to observe my ordinances. *Then you shall live in the land that I gave to your ancestors*; and you shall be my people, and I will be your God.[90]

And Mic 4:5–8 reads:

> For all the peoples walk,
> each in the name of its god,
> but *we will walk in the name of the Lord our God
> forever and ever.
> On that day, says the Lord,
> I will assemble the lame
> and gather those who have been driven away,
> and those whom I have afflicted.
> The lame I will make the remnant,
> and those who were cast off, a strong nation;
> and the Lord will reign over them in Mount Zion
> now and for evermore.*
> And you, O tower of the flock,
> hill of daughter Zion,
> to you *it shall come,
> the former dominion shall come,
> the sovereignty of daughter Jerusalem*.[91]

In comparing these two texts, especially the emphasized verses, there are a number of striking parallels. In particular, as Pitre notes, "In Ezekiel, God declares both that we will 'make holy' or 'hallow' his name precisely by bringing scattered Israel back to the land (Ezek 36:23). In Micah, when the people walk 'in the name of the Lord,' he will not only 'reign' as king, but it is explicitly said that 'the dominion' and 'the kingdom' 'shall come' to Jerusalem (Mic 4:7–8). In other words, the exiled remnant shall return to the land."[92]

Thus when Jesus calls for his disciples to prayerfully hallow God's name and petition for the coming of his kingdom, he is, as Pitre states, "speaking of nothing less than the final ingathering of [the] scattered tribes of Israel in accordance of the prophets."[93] The only addendum I would add to Pitre's

---

90. Emphasis Pitre's.
91. Emphasis Pitre's.
92. Pitre, *Jesus, the Tribulation, and the End*, 141–42.
93. Ibid., 143.

statement is that it is not only the re-gathering of Israel's exiled tribes that Jesus is pointing towards in hallowing God's name and soliciting the coming of the kingdom, but the re-gathering of these tribes within a restored land—a territorial connection that is especially emphasized the Matthean "your will be done, on earth [γῆς] as it is in heaven [οὐρανῷ]" (6:10).[94]

For as Dale Allison has persuasively argued, there are a number of striking parallels between the meaning of the "kingdom of God" (βασιλεία τοῦ θεοῦ) in the Synoptics and the "world to come" (עוֹלָם הַבָּא) in rabbinic texts. In particular both imply that to "have life in the world to come is to have life in the kingdom; not to have life in the kingdom is not to have life in the world to come."[95] Thus if "one can pass from speaking about 'the kingdom of God' to 'the world to come' without changing the subject, then the two terms must overlap significantly."[96] What this overlap means with respect to Jesus and his petition that the kingdom "come" (ἐλθέτω) then is that the "[the kingdom of God], in the Synoptics, [is] *a realm* as well as a reign; *it is a place* and a time yet to come in which God will reign supreme."[97]

Third, there is the petition for the provision of daily bread in Matt 6:11 and Luke 11:3. Once again, as with the references to God as "Father" and the hallowing of God's name, so too is this petition suffused with a palpable concretized notion of the kingdom. As Victor Hamilton has noted, there are differences in how this petition is phrased in Matthew and its articulation in Luke. With regard to the former, the language of "give us" (δὸς ἡμῖν) is in the aorist imperative while in the latter "give us" (δίδου ἡμῖν) is the present indicative.[98] Hence the Matthean phrasing has a more punctilious and decisive sense as in "give us this bread now and once and for all" while the Lukan phrasing denotes a more continuous and ongoing activity as in "continually give us this bread." Both forms of this petition, however, contain the phrase "our daily bread" (τὸν ἄρτον ἡμῶν τὸν ἐπιούσιον).

---

94. Despite the yeoman work Pitre performs in drawing the substantive connections between the coming of the kingdom in the Hebrew Bible and Jesus' petition in the Lord's Prayer and how both presuppose a restoration of Israel's land, he nevertheless makes this puzzling comment: "How can a 'kingdom' be said to 'come'? The answer: quite easily, if 'the kingdom' in question does not refer to a 'place,' much less to an abstract 'reign of God,' but rather to *a people* . . . In this context, the 'coming' of God's 'kingdom' is a vivid image for the ingathering of the LORD's scattered people to Zion in the restoration of the twelve tribes" (ibid., 143). Hence, although he recognizes the critical importance of the land, Pitre nevertheless seems to want to draw a distinction between Israel as an ἔθνη and Israel as an אֶרֶץ.

95. Allison, *Constructing Jesus*, 201.

96. Ibid.

97. Ibid.

98. Hamilton, *Exodus*, 260.

The adjective "daily" (ἐπιούσιον) is of special note since scholars have yet to find an occurrence of it outside of the Gospels.[99] Moreover, its meaning is not clear. It could be interpreted as (1) "the bread necessary for subsistence," (2) "bread for the current day, today," or (3) "bread for the coming day, future."[100] Hamilton prefers the third option, although he does not think the "coming day" refers to tomorrow, but rather to a later part of "today." Thus "Jesus may be teaching [his disciples] not only *how* to pray but also *when* to pray, to start one's day with prayer. One does not pray ten minutes before going to bed, 'Give us today our daily bread,' nor does one pray just before falling asleep for the night, 'and lead us not into temptation.' The Lord's Prayer is a morning prayer, and like the manna, which was provided every morning, this petition is for God to provide bread for the day to come, meaning today, this unfolding day."[101]

As Hamilton's observation confirms, the timing of petitioning for bread would not only have evoked memories of *Yahweh*'s provision of the מָן (*manna*) for Israel in the midst of its wilderness wanderings (Exod 16), but so too of course would the petitioning of bread (ἄρτος) itself. And memories of the provision of daily sustenance in the midst of being landless would also bring to mind the provision of a promised land. However, as Brueggemann argues, both the provision and receipt of this promised land is to stand in stark contrast with not only the landlessness of the wilderness but also the previous landedness of Egypt. For as he writes regarding the מָן,

> That is very strange bread, certainly not the kind gathered in the land, in the place of planning and calculation and control. That is bread such as they had not known in Egypt. Egypt was the land and the land is always organized and administered, and the purpose of administration is that some shall always have too much and some shall always have too little. [Thus a] double contrast is established: (a) a contrast between expected hunger and unexpected satiation and (b) a contrast between Egyptian bread and wilderness bread. This second contrast Israel had to learn so many times. What does it mean to receive bread in the wilderness, in a land, without life supports? It surely means to receive bread (sustenance) that refuses to be administered and managed and therefore is not perverted by the destructive inequalities of land-bread. In the wilderness before the surprising eyes of his people, Yahweh makes a protest against managed land-bread.[102]

---

99. Ibid.,
100. Ibid.
101. Ibid.
102. Brueggemann, *Land*, 31–32.

Thus by imploring his disciples to petition God for the provision of their "daily bread," Jesus would not only have been reminding them of how that promised provision was intimately tied to the adjoining promised provision land, but would also be reminding them of what was expected of them once that promise had been fulfilled: namely, that this land was not to be allocated and governed in a manner consistent with the *ethos* of Egypt with its marks of oppression and socio-economic inequality; but instead in a manner that acknowledged that the land itself was a gratuitous provision of God and therefore should be administered and governed in such a way that the basic needs of all were to be met.

Finally, there are the formal and material similarities between the Lord's Prayer and the Kaddish—a daily prayer that was recited by Jews in synagogues during the Second Temple period. As George Wesley Buchanan notes, the Kaddish was most likely composed sometime between the construction of the new temple by King Herod (ca. 20 BCE) and its destruction by Rome (70 CE).[103] It therefore contains several sentiments that "expressed Jewish longings for the restoration of the nation under Jewish control[.]"[104] This is readily apparent in the text of the prayer, which reads, in part, as follows:

> May his great name be exalted and sanctified in the world which he created according to his will ... May his kingdom reign in your lifetimes and in your days and in the days of all the house of Israel, quickly and soon. Amen ... May the prayers and petitions of all Israel be accepted before their Father who is in heaven ... May the One who make peace In his high places make peace over all Israel ... May his great name be magnified and sanctified in the age which he is destined to renew, raise the dead, rebuild the city of Jerusalem, complete the temple, uproot foreign worship from the land and restore the holy worship of Heaven in its place. May his Kingdom rule. May he cause his redemption to spring forth, and may he hasten the consummation of the Kingdom of his Messiah, in your lifetimes and in your days and in the lifetimes of the house of Israel, quickly and soon. Amen.[105]

In terms of structure, there are a number of elements that overlap and echo the Lord's Prayer in Matt 6:9–13 and Luke 11:1–4. There is the invocation of God's name, the reverent hallowing of that name, the petitioning that

---

103. Buchanan, *Jesus, the King*, 36.
104. Ibid.
105. Ibid.

God hasten to quickly establish his kingdom, and a parallel between peaceful rule of heaven and the peaceful rule of Israel on earth. Hence as Buchanan notes, the Jews who prayed this prayer were not simply petitioning that God come near. Rather, "they were asking for something less abstract," namely, "for a kingdom they could see in their lifetimes—a kingdom that would be theirs," a kingdom in which "foreign worship would be uprooted," the "Messiah would rule" and peace "would come to Israel, secure within its borders."[106] In short, this was a prayer for nothing less than a territorial restoration of Israel.

Accordingly, it would be highly peculiar, Buchanan argues, for Jesus to have taught his disciples to pray something tantamount to the Kaddish both in structure and content "and not to have meant anything like that which other Jews meant when they offered the same prayer."[107] For had he done so, "he surely would have confused his disciples, who he was trying to lead."[108] Yet in neither Matthew nor Luke does Jesus offer "one word of explanation indicating that, although he was striving for something that other Jews held uppermost in their minds, he had goals completely different from theirs."[109] On the contrary, "it is reasonable to think that [both Jesus] and they had the same goals. They wanted the kingdom of Heaven to come."[110]

5.4 Jesus' Proclamation of the Jubilee in Luke 4:16–21

Having illuminated the ways in which the Lord's Prayer contains allusions to the Jubilee and a longing for the territorial restoration of Israel that emphasizes a just ethic for how that land is to be governed, I would now like to do the same for Jesus' appropriation of Isaiah's own proclamation of the Jubilee in Luke 4:16–21. Before engaging in a deeper exegesis and analysis of this text, it is first important to remember what precedes it. In particular, it is important to recall that this pericope immediately follows the Lukan narrative of how Jesus, "full of the Holy Spirit" (πλήρης πνεύματος ‘αγίου), is cast out into the "wilderness" (ἐρήμῳ) for forty days and tempted by Satan (Luke 4:1–13).

There are two reasons why this is so. The first is how this account conforms to the larger narrative archetype of a New Exodus. There is, of course, the more obvious parallel between Jesus' time in the wilderness and the

---

106. Ibid., 37.
107. Ibid.
108. Ibid.
109. Ibid.
110. Ibid.

analogous forty-year period of Israel wandering in the wilderness prior to entering into the promised land of Canaan. However, there is also an exilic and cosmic dimension to this episode as well. For as Michael E. Fuller states, "as the point of entry for Jesus' encounter with the Devil, the wilderness is probably understood more comprehensively by Luke to envelope both the nations and Israel," meaning that "Israel's [present] exile is demonic in origin and character."[111] Thus, "Israel will require her own divine agent to [lead] her from captivity to restoration."[112] The second is the overt political nature of the temptations themselves. As Yoder incisively observes, the first part of the Satanic "syllogism" of Luke 4:3—i.e., "If you are the Son of God, then . . ." (Εἰ υἱὸς εἶ τοῦ θεοῦ)—speaks not of "a concept of metaphysical sonship but from kingship."[113] Hence, "all the options laid before Jesus by the tempter are ways of being king."[114]

When viewed from this vantage point, Jesus' subsequent rejection of turning stone into bread (ἄρτος), worshiping Satan, and throwing himself off the pinnacle of the temple in order to put God to the test all speak to the mode of kingship he sought to inhabit. For as Fuller argues, Luke "represents and intimates association between Rome/the nations and the Devil."[115] Accordingly the Satanic temptations are temptations that invite Jesus to rule over Israel's land in a manner that is politically and ethically consistent with how Rome rules over its empire. Thus while Jesus' renunciations of Satan could be read as him rejecting "the idea of world domination as belonging to Israel's restoration," it could also be seen as him "rejecting the means (i.e., worshipping the Devil) to that end."[116] In other words, for Jesus there was to be no ethical and political incommensurability between restoring Israel's territorial sovereignty and the means through which that desired restoration was to occur. A fidelity to both Yahweh and Yahweh's justice was integral to both just as it had been for Israel's original exodus out of the oppressive land of Egypt into the land of blessing.

It is against this narrative background with memories of Israel's first exodus hanging thickly in the air that Jesus, infused with the Spirit's power, departs from the wilderness and returns to Galilee (Luke 4:14). The spatial and narrative movements from wilderness to Galilee would not be without significant import since it would mimic ancient Israel's emergence from its

111. Fuller, *Restoration of Israel*, 233.
112. Ibid.
113. Yoder, *Politics of Jesus*, 24.
114. Ibid., 25.
115. Fuller, *Restoration of Israel*, 234.
116. Ibid.

own wilderness wanderings into its promise land. Furthermore it would also have restorative significance as well. For as Pitre notes, "while the Babylonian Exile of the Judeans had come to an end in 539 B.C., *the Assyrian exile of the northern tribes had not.*"[117] Thus the first-century Jews of Jesus' day "were certainly waiting for 'the End of the Exile'—but not the Babylonian Exile." Instead, "they were waiting for the end of the Assyrian Exile," and more specifically the return of the exiled northern tribes to their land.[118] Thus Jesus' return to Galilee from the wilderness would have suggested that the exile of the northern tribes was coming to a close.

And this thematic emphasis on the end of exile is only reinforced further when Jesus enters the synagogue in Nazareth and publicly quotes Isa 61:1-2: "The Spirit of the Lord is upon me, because he has anointed me to bring good news to the poor. He has sent me to proclaim release to the captives and recovery of sight the blind, to let the oppressed go free, to proclaim the year of the Lord's favor" (Luke 4:18-19).

As already discussed in our examination of Isa 61:1-2 in chapter 4, the reference to the "year of the Lord's favor" (ἐνιαυτὸν Κυρίου δεκτόν) is a clear, albeit messianic, reference to the Jubilee of Lev 25. Thus by appropriating this verse to himself Jesus issues three distinct yet interrelated proclamations. First, by taking up the mantle of being the Lord's "anointed" (ἔχρισέν), Jesus identifies himself as God's appointed messiah. Second, by virtue of being God's messianic agent, Jesus—like the messianic figures of Jeremiah, Isaiah, and *Psalms of Solomon*—announces the end of Israel's exile and thus "proclaims the good news" (εὐαγγελίσασθαι) of the restoration of Israel's land. Third, not only does Jesus announce the "good news" of Israel's landed restoration, but so too does he announce the institution of a Jubilee ethic for the governance of that land. More specifically, and as is consistent with the stipulations of the Jubilee, Jesus proclaims "release" (ἄφεσιν) and "deliverance" (ἀφέσει) for the "poor" (πτωχοῖς), the "captives" (αἰχμαλώτοις), and the "oppressed" (τεθραυσμένους). Once again it is important to bear in mind that these constituencies, which invariably overlapped, are describing not just the socio-economic and political condition of impoverished first-century Jewish peasant farmers but also the root cause of their material and political deprivation, namely landlessness. Correlatively to have Jesus announce their "release" and "deliverance" in conjunction with the provisions of the Jubilee year and while acting under the aegis of being God's "anointed" would necessarily entail addressing and rectifying the root causes of that deprivation. Hence when one juxtaposes the Jubilee announcement with the

---

117. Pitre, *Jesus, the Tribulation and the End*, 34.
118. Ibid., 35.

socio-economic and political nature of the proceeding temptation narrative the territorial content of Jesus' proclamation of the Jubilee in Luke 4:18–19 cannot be avoided.

But what is one to make of the elision of the phrase "and the day of vengeance of our God" in Jesus' quotation of Isa 61:1–2? Might this omission disqualify or at the very least obviate a territorial reading of this passage and thus Jesus' pronouncement of a territorially restored Israel? A reading of Luke 4:24–27 could certainly suggest as much since Jesus recalls Elijah's encounter with the window at Zeraphath (1 Kgs 17:7–24) and Elisha's healing of Naaman the Syrian (2 Kgs 5:1–27) much to the consternation and outrage of his audience. Why would these particular narratives provoke such antipathy? As Ringe astutely argues part of the reason certainly stems from them coming in such close proximity to Jesus' earlier invocation of the Jubilee. For "the Jubilee images in the text from Isaiah were understood by Jesus' contemporaries as referring to blessings promised particularly to Israel at the time of God's eschatological reign."[119] However, by complementing that understanding of the Jubilee and its connection to the kingdom with two narratives in which Gentiles and not Jews are the recipients of God's healing and blessings, Jesus directly "challenged that assumption of privilege, but left the socially revolutionary implications of the Jubilee imagery intact."[120] Thus "the text of promise was turned to a threat: the poor whom the good news would come and the captives who would be set free might be any of God's children" and not Jews alone.[121] In this regard, then, Jesus, argues Freyne,

> was no slavish follower of his tradition, not even Isaiah, with whom he had a special affinity. He was a critical reader, not critical, however, in the sense of modern reading, but in relation to the social situation of his own time and place and the manner in which the inherited religious traditions might be brought to bear on those conditions. Joining a long line of critical prophetic voices from the past in situations that were not dissimilar to the ones he was experiencing, he too felt called to address his own contemporaries with a prophetic challenge to a world of imperial domination and the threat of religious collaboration with the forces that had continued to keep Israel in bondage.[122]

---

119. Ringe, *Jesus, Liberation and the Biblical Jubilee*, 44.
120. Ibid.
121. Ibid.
122. Freyne, *Jesus, a Jewish Galilean*, 121.

This is certainly true and fitting with the idea that even if Jesus was not directly concerned or involved with an explicit mission to Gentiles, the logic of his kingdom proclamation and teachings certainly redounded to their blessing and indeed their salvation.[123] Nevertheless one need not see Jesus' omission of divine vengeance in his Jubilee proclamation nor his favorable depiction of Gentiles immediately following as *ipso facto* a renunciation of Israel restored territoriality. For whether the omission was intentional or not, or a product of later Lukan redaction, there was certainly precedent within Isaiah, Jeremiah, and the *Psalms of Solomon* for linking Israel's restored territoriality with the blessing of Gentiles. Indeed as I argued in our deeper analysis of Isa 56–61 above, Israel's restoration is universal in character but always rooted in its territorial particularity. Thus, as Fuller states, by neglecting to include the reference to the divine vengeance that accompanies the Jubilee, Jesus "indicate[s] that God (and his prophets) have never been absolutely restricted to the Land and Jewish people."[124] Even so, this "does not mean that God's promises of restoration have shifted to the Gentiles; instead Luke [and Jesus] seems to indicate that Israel's restoration does not by definition entail the destruction of the nations. On the contrary, they may be shown favor as well."[125]

I have thus shown why it is plausible and indeed essential to read Jesus' references to the Jubilee in both the Lord's Prayer and his public reading of Isa 61:1–2 in Nazareth as containing direct ties both to the restoration of Israel's land as well as to a socio-political ethic for how that restored land is to be governed. I would now like to address the last of our four test cases, the *Palingenesia* in Matt 8:11–12 || Luke 13:28–29.

5.5 The *Palingenesia*/Kingdom in Matt 19:27–30 || Luke 22:24–30

Let us once again begin with the arguments that favor an a-territorial reading of these passages. One is offered by Davies. In looking at Luke 22:24–30, Davies notes that Jesus' comments in verses 28–30 stand as a "corrective" to the dispute the disciples had previously been engaged in regarding who would attain the status of being the greatest in the kingdom. For instead of emulating the mode of leadership displayed by Rome and other Gentile powers that "lord over" (κυριεύουσιν) their subjects, Jesus instead tells his

---

123. See Sanders *Jesus and Judaism*, esp. 218–21; and Bird, *Jesus and the Origins of the Gentile Mission*.

124. Fuller, *Restoration of Israel*, 237.

125. Ibid., 237–38.

disciples that "the one criterion for greatness is service" and that as servants they "are set over against the world's rulers."¹²⁶ Nevertheless, Jesus still does assure the disciples that they will be given a prominent role in the kingdom, namely sitting on twelve thrones and judging the twelve tribes of a restored Israel. Be that as it may, Davies argues that the "context makes it clear that the kingdom in which they are to do so cannot be compared with the kingdoms of the world."¹²⁷ Instead Jesus makes it clear that they "are to rule in a new kind of kingdom-in another dimension of existence."¹²⁸ Thus since Davies judges the mode of political leadership the twelve disciples are to exercise in the new kingdom to be qualitatively different from that performed in the kingdoms of this "world," so too does he think the nature of this kingdom to be qualitatively different as well, which in this case means landless.

Matthew 19:27-30, by contrast, offers an entirely different context inasmuch as Jesus assures his disciples that as a result of their loyalty and fidelity to him, they will sit on twelve thrones and judge the tribes of Israel upon the παλιγγενεσία or the "renewal of all things." Thus whereas in Luke Jesus describes the kingdom and the disciples' role of judging the twelve tribes as being otherworldly, in Matthew Davies believes Jesus' "*palingenesia* ushers in this world a renewed form, in which "eternal life" is to be enjoyed."¹²⁹ Thus he argues that these verses "point to a perspective which looked forward to a temporal restoration in which the Messiah or Son of Man should govern his people after the manner portrayed in the *Psalms of Solomon*, for example in 17:28 'And he shall gather together a holy people, whom he shall lead in righteousness, and he shall judge the tribes of the people that has been sanctified by the Lord his God.'"¹³⁰

Thus Jesus' use of παλιγγενεσία in Matt 19:28 to describe the restoration of the kingdom and the disciples' role within it certainly seem to have Israel's land in view. And this territorial reading of παλιγγενεσία is further confirmed by the fact that "Josephus uses *palingenesia* of the restoration of the land of Israel[.]"¹³¹ Nevertheless, despite this evidence, Davies concludes that "what it asserts of the future is bare."¹³² This is because "[t]here is no specific reference to the land on which the restored Israel is to dwell,

---

126. Davies, *Gospel and the Land*, 363.
127. Ibid.
128. Ibid.
129. Ibid.
130. Ibid.
131. Ibid., 365.
132. Ibid.

although such is assumed."[133] Furthermore, Davies argues, although Josephus understood παλιγγενεσία to refer to the restoration of Israel's land, it "most frequently . . . evokes a cosmic renewal, so that in [Matt] 19:28 also probably the restoration of the twelve tribes is understood not so much in terms of a restored land of Israel as a renewal of the cosmos."[134] Hence, notwithstanding the plausible and compelling rationale for seeing Jesus speaking of a territorially restored Israel within which the twelve disciples would judge the twelve tribes, Davies once again concludes that Jesus is speaking of a transcendent restoration.

Steven M. Bryan offers another. Like Davies, Bryan thinks there is good reason to believe that Israel's land promises stand behind Jesus' assurances to his disciples in Matt 19:28. Unlike, Davies, however, Bryan does not think Jesus understood παλιγγενεσία to have a cosmic and otherworldly connotation. However, he also thinks it "possible to read this saying not so much as an anticipation of the re-establishment of the tribes in the Land," but instead "as a pointed *rejection* of that expectation!"[135]

That this passage shows Jesus rejecting rather than affirming and anticipating the restoration of Israel's land is evident, argues Bryan, when one compares it with texts like Dan 7 and *1 Enoch*. Daniel 7:9-14 depicts a scene where a Son of Man figure is invested with a kingdom from which he will judge the nations of the world. In Dan 7:22-27 it is now the "holy ones of the Most High" who assume the role of judging the nation. Similarly *1 En.* 90:9 and 91:12 both describe how the righteous of God judge and punish the nations. "There is, then," states Bryan "ample evidence of the belief that the righteous would be the agents of God's judgment of the nations."[136]

In light of this evidence Bryan thinks it likely that Jesus thought in similar terms and suggests Matt 12:4 and Luke 11:32 convey as much insofar as "he involves the penitent of a past generation in the judgment of 'this generation', a designation which we have seen to be decidedly national in scope."[137] "Moreover," he continues, "in their mission to Israel, the twelve exercise a punitive function as witnesses who symbolically consign unbelieving towns to judgment (Matt. 10.14/Mark 6.11/Luke 9.5; cf. Luke 10.11)."[138] Thus Bryan concludes that it is not surprising "that Jesus should

---

133. Ibid.; emphasis mine.
134. Ibid.
135. Bryan, *Jesus and Israel's Traditions*, 169; Bryan's emphasis.
136. Ibid., 170.
137. Ibid.
138. Ibid., 170-71.

assign his followers a role in the judgment."[139] What is surprising, however, "is that for Jesus the objects of judgment are not the enemies of Israel but the tribes of Israel."[140] Thus Bryan does believe that Jesus announced the restoration of the exiled tribes. However, this restoration was not to rule over and govern the land but rather to have their attachment to the land judged and repudiated.

Nevertheless, despite Davies's and Bryan's confidence to the contrary, there are a number of reasons why these passages should not only be read as Jesus affirming a territorial restoration of Israel, but also as him calling his disciples to not just govern Israel's land, but to govern it in a very specific manner that is consistent with the ethical precepts of the messianic Jubilee.

To see how this is so, let us first address the symbolic significance of the twelve disciples and its connection to (the restoration of) Israel's land. As Karen Wenell has shown, the number twelve holds a special theo-political significance within Judaism. Jacob (and later Israel) has twelve sons (Gen 35:22; 42:13, 32), who eventually become the eponymous twelve tribes of Israel (Gen 49:28). Upon entering Canaan, Joshua apportions the land to the twelve tribes so that each has its own נַחֲלָה (Josh 13:7—19:48). Thus as Wenell states, "[g]eneaology and geography are two major lines along which descriptions of the twelve tribes 'work' in various texts where they are mentioned."[141] As such "'Twelve' becomes part of the terminology that might be used when speaking about Israel or some aspect of national life (e.g., leaders and their roles, offerings)."[142] This is especially true with respect to the land since "[w]hen used to depict unity for the people, [the twelve] relates particularly to Israel located within the land, with the twelve tribes together."[143]

In addition to serving as an important symbol of Israel's nationality, including its territoriality, the twelve also signified a specific form of governance. In Numbers 1 Yahweh commands Moses to take a census of Israel in order to select twelve men—one from each of the tribes—to help him lead. Joshua is commanded to do the same immediately prior to crossing the Jordan and entering into the land of Canaan (3:12). Thus the twelve were recognized as possessing direct power and authority from Yahweh over the tribes of Israel. What kind of power and authority were they to exercise? One important responsibility was to determine the size of each tribe's נַחֲלָה,

---

139. Ibid., 172.
140. Ibid.
141. Wenell, *Jesus and Land*, 107.
142. Ibid., 105.
143. Ibid., 111.

or the parcel of land each tribe received to settle and live on (Num 34:26). Yet in addition to apportioning the land, the twelve also played an instrumental role in governing it. This is apparent from the title these leaders receive, namely "judges" or שֹׁפְטִים.

The noun שֹׁפְטִים derives from the Hebrew verb שָׁפַט (Greek κρίνω), which is typically rendered as "judge." However, "judge" fails to adequately encompass the full richness and complexity of this word. For while *shaphat* can indeed have a more juridical and punitive connotation (i.e., condemnation) that Bryan speaks to above (e.g., Deut 25:1), it can also, depending on its context, take on other important meanings as well. For instance, שָׁפַט can also mean to rule or govern and more specifically to rule or govern in a just manner. This is reflected in the fact that שָׁפַט comes from the same word group as מִשְׁפָּט.[144] Thus in Deut 1:16–17, for instance, Yahweh calls upon the appointed "judges" (שֹׁפְטִים) of Israel to "give the member of your community a fair hearing, and judge [וּשְׁפַטְתֶּם] rightly [צֶדֶק] between one person and another, whether citizen or resident alien. You must not be partial in judging [בַּמִּשְׁפָּט]: hear out the small and great alike; you shall not be intimidated by anyone for the judgment [הַמִּשְׁפָּט] is God's."

שָׁפַט can also be closely associated with the Hebrew word הוֹשִׁיעַ, which means "save." So in Judg 3:9, for instance, Othniel is described as a "deliverer"(מוֹשִׁיעַ) of Israel from the oppression of Cushan-Rishathaim, and then in 3:10 is said to have "judged" (וַיִּשְׁפֹּט) Israel. As McConville argues, in this instance "the 'judging'" is "closely analogous to the 'delivering,'" and more specifically, it is "preceded in v. 10 by the statement that 'the spirit of the Lord came upon [Othniel]', which typically announces an empowering to do battle or other acts of great strength, as in the cases of Gideon, Jephthah and Samson (6.34; 11.29; 14.19; 15.14)."[145] Thus when it comes to interpreting the meaning of שָׁפַט the "convergence of 'judging' and 'delivering' is best explained not by trying to distinguish between the terms, nor by appeal to underlying traditions, but by reference to the theme of the narrative from Genesis, that Israel should be freed from tyranny in order to become a people that exhibits justice and righteousness."[146] And as we saw in our examination of Jeremiah, Isaiah, and *Psalms of Solomon* above, both meanings of the twelve—that is Israel's land and a just form of governance—are reiterated in their respective eschatological visions of Israel's restoration.

In light of this, it is now necessary to re-read Matt 19:27–30 || Luke 22:24–30 to determine whether they do in fact de-territorialize Jesus'

---

144. McConville, *God and Earthly Power*, 121.

145. Ibid., 122.

146. Ibid.

kingdom vision and ethic. That they do not is indicated in a variety of ways. Let us follow the order above and first re-engage Matt 19:27–30. Recall from above that Davies acknowledged that Jesus' description of the twelve disciples sitting on twelve thrones and judging the twelve tribes of Israel could, at least on its face, very well "point to a perspective which looked forward to a temporal restoration in which the Messiah or Son of Man should govern his people after the manner portrayed in the *Psalms of Solomon*[.]"[147] In other words, Davies concedes that Jesus' appointment of the twelve to judge the twelve tribes of Israel is consistent with the notions of a territorial restoration of Israel and the reinstitution of a tribal form of government.

What convinces him, however, that this is not the case is the appearance of the phrase "at the renewal of all things" (ἐν τῇ παλινγενεσίᾳ), which he thinks has a cosmic and thus landless meaning. However, as Wenell notes, the "future setting of the renewal envisioned need not exclude the possibility that the setting is (or is modeled on) the land of Israel."[148] On the contrary, it is quite likely that Jesus had Israel's land in mind. To see why this is so, Wenell compares Jesus' description with Dan 7:9–14 and *1 En.* 90:20–25. As discussed by Bryan above, the former passage describes a scene where the Son of Man establishes thrones for the "holy ones" who then receive and possess the kingdom. Similarly, in *1 En.* 90:20 the author envisions an eschatological scene where "a throne was erected in the pleasant land, and the Lord of the sheep sat Himself thereon" and then in 90:24 describes the Lord's judgment (κρίσις).

Thus in view of the parallels between these particular passages and Jesus' own eschatological description of the παλινγενεσίᾳ, "we need not," states Wenell, assume that the latter "is a landless portrait."[149] For while Davies is certainly "not unjustified in pointing out the lack of an explicit reference to the land," there nevertheless "does seem to be a sense in Mt. 19:28 . . . that the eschaton has a spatial aspect to it and that spatial conception seem to most naturally entail the envisioning of a restored Israel in twelve tribes in the land."[150]

That this is the case is even further confirmed by Jesus' assurance in Matt 19:29 that those who have left family members and "fields" (ἀγροὺς) will receive these one "hundredfold" (ἑκατονταπλασίονα), and also will "inherit" (κληρονομήσει) "eternal life" (ζωὴν αἰώνιον). As explained by Allison above, the phrase "eternal life" was understood by first-century Jews

---

147. Davies, *Gospel and the Land*, 363.
148. Wenell, *Jesus and Land*, 125.
149. Ibid., 126.
150. Ibid.

to be synonymous with the "world to come" and thus with Israel's restoration. To be assured then that they would "inherit"—κληρονομήσει, which is the Greek cognate for נָחַל—eternal life along with "fields" (ἀγροὺς) in the παλινγενεσίᾳ would only further confirm to Jesus' twelve apostles that their respective thrones of judgment would have a territorial locale within the land of Israel.

Even so, another reason Davies thinks the *palingenesia* of Matt 19:28 is evocative of a landless kingdom is that he believes it contradicts what Jesus tells his disciples in Mark 10:35–45:[151]

> James and John, the sons of Zebedee, came forward to him and said to him, "Teacher, we want you to do for us whatever we ask of you." And he said to them, "What is it you want me to do for you?" And they said to him, "Grant us to sit, one at your right hand and one at your left, in your glory." But Jesus said to them, "You do not know what you are asking. Are you able to drink the cup that I drink, or be baptized with the baptism that I am baptized with?" They replied, "We are able." Then Jesus said to them, "The cup that I drink you will drink; and with the baptism with which I am baptized, you will be baptized; but to sit at my right hand or at my left is not mine to grant, but it is for those for whom it has been prepared." When the ten heard this, they began to be angry with James and John. So Jesus called them and said to them, "You know that among the Gentiles those whom they recognize as their rulers lord it over them, and their great ones are tyrants over them. But it is not so among you; but whoever wishes to become great among you must be your servant, and whoever wishes to be first among you must be slave of all. For the Son of Man came not to be served but to serve, and to give his life a ransom for many."

Upon reading this passage it is difficult to understand why Davies would see it as contradicting a landed reading of Matt 19:28, especially since it parallels it at significant points.[152] For as Wenell observes, both passage imply "that Jesus has the authority to assign places in the eschatological kingdom" and both also "assume 'that his followers will be next to him'."[153] Furthermore, I would add that both assume that the disciples will occupy thrones since James and John specifically request that they "sit" next to Je-

---

151. Davies, *Gospel and the Land*, 365.

152. To his credit, as Wenell notes, Davies later rescinded this position in the volume he coauthored with Allison, *A Critical and Exegetical Commentary on the Gospel According to Saint Matthew*.

153. Wenell, *Jesus and the Land*, 127.

Jesus and the Kingdom

sus. Thus, as Wenell claims, "there is nothing in this context which necessitates a landless scenario."[154] Moreover, there is nothing in this passage that subverts or contradicts the idea that the reason the twelve are appointed to thrones is to rule over and govern a reconstituted Israel.

What is significantly discontinuous, however, is the manner in which Jesus calls his disciples to rule. For as opposed to the Gentile rulers who "lord over" (κατακυριεύουσιν) their subjects and are "tyrants" (κατεξουσιάζουσιν) to them, Jesus tells his disciples that they are to emulate his own example of just leadership by being a "servant" (διάκονος) and a "slave" (δοῦλος) to all. In other words, they are to pattern themselves after Israel's former שֹׁפְטִים. As such "the text in Mark does not give the impression that for Jesus and the Twelve, 'what is governed' is of a completely different nature from the domains of Gentile rulers, only that their behavior is to be radically different from those leaders."[155]

Of course the same could be said for Jesus' words in Luke 22:24–30. Once again, as with Mark 10:35ff, the catalyst for Jesus' discussion of appointing the twelve disciples to twelve thrones to "judge" (κρίναντες) the twelve tribes is a dispute amongst the over who will be the greatest. And once again Jesus in no way disputes the notion that the twelve will occupy thrones and exercise judgment over a reconstituted Israel. Instead he chastises the disciples for wanting to mimic the oppressive patterns of Gentile leadership and reiterates his call for them to be "serving" (διακονῶν) just as he is serving them. But does this pattern of leadership necessarily entail the rejection of Israel's land as Bryan argues?

That it does not is indicated by two things. First, Jesus tells his disciples that he is presently "conferring" (διατίθεμαι) upon them a "kingdom" (βασιλείαν). As Fuller argues, in "this instance, the kingdom is clearly bound up with Israel," meaning that the kingdom clearly includes Israel's land. It would thus be quite a *non sequitur* not to mention utterly confusing for Jesus to first definitively assure the twelve disciples that he is appointing them to positions of authority it a territorially restored Israel only to then immediately pivot *volte face* and reject the kingdom's very territoriality. Second, as was apparent in our discussion of שָׁפַט above, while "judging" (κρίνοντες) can certainly denote a sense of punitive sanction and condemnation, it also can convey a sense of ruling and deliverance. In fact in several instances elements of all three meanings can co-exist simultaneously. To argue then, as Bryan does, that κρίνοντες exclusively means "judging" in a punitive sense overlooks the fact that Jesus—as is consistent with Isaiah, Jeremiah, and

---

154. Ibid., 128.
155 Ibid.

the *Psalms of Solomon*—is envisioning an eschatological scenario in which the twelve disciples will rule over and govern the twelve tribes of Israel in a manner that is consistent with the dictates of justice (מִשְׁפָּט) and deliverance (הוֹשִׁיעַ). Indeed as Craig Evans notes, "[i]n this case, the saying not only does not threaten punishment, but anticipates Israel's restoration."[156] As such, it is therefore once again incredibly difficult to imagine Jesus telling his disciples that they are to reject Israel's land when every indication seems to be that he is telling them that they are to rule over it in a specific way.

Thus in re-reading Matt 19:27–30 and Luke 22:24–30, we are able to find several points at which Jesus' understanding of the twelve coincides both with a restoration of Israel's land and with the restoration of a specific form of land governance. Richard Horsley sums up the matter well when he writes,

> The principal point to be derived from Matthew 19:28 and Luke 22:30, of course, is that, whether in the already-present reality of the kingdom or in the imminent future of the kingdom's realization, Jesus is concerned with the restoration or renewal of the people of Israel, as symbolized during his ministry in the constitution of the twelve disciples. Just as they were sent out to heal and preach to the lost sheep of the house of Israel, so in the final restoration of the people in the land, they would still carry out functions of redemption and the establishment of justice for the twelve tribes of Israel.[157]

I have now demonstrated how three Gospel pericopes that have been said to be dispositive in proving that Jesus' deterritorialized the kingdom and its ethic are actually quite hospitable to a territorial reading. In fact, I believe I have shown that absent a restoration of Israel's land and a restoration of a just ethic for governing that land, these kingdom teachings become virtually unintelligible. I should now like to conclude this chapter and by extension this project by offering some brief reflections on what implications Jesus' vision for a territorially restored kingdom and its ethic of territorial governance has for Christian ethics.

---

156. Evans, "Sitting on the Twelve Thrones of Israel: Scripture and Politics in Luke 22:24–30," in Chilton and Evans, *Jesus in Context*, 472.

157. *Jesus and the Spiral of Violence*, 206. And yet on the very next page Horsley inexplicably states that "when Jesus preached that the kingdom of God was at hand, he *was not referring to a place* [emphasis added] or to some particular cataclysmic final eschatological act of God that would bring an end to history. The 'kingdom of God' in Jesus' preaching refers to God's saving action, and the people who receive benefit from God's gracious action are expected to glorify God in gratitude" (207).

5.6 Toward Articulating a Christian Ethic of Territorial Governance: A Proposed Normative Framework

Having produced a compelling body of evidence that I believe shows that Jesus' proclamation of the kingdom envisioned both a territorial restoration of Israel as well as the restoration of a prophetic ethic for how that land was to be governed, I would now like to turn my attention to the constructive question of what significance and import does Jesus' landed kingdom ethic how for Christian ethical discourse today.

Ultimately providing an adequate answer to this question is worthy of an extended examination beyond the scope of this project and therefore one I hope to purse in the near future. Nevertheless our preceding discussion provides a substantive basis from which it possible to, if not develop a fully formulated set of normative practices, then at least distill the contours of a normative framework from which such practices should derive. This then is what I should like to do in brief as a way of concluding.

However, even while the articulation of a normative framework for a Christian ethic of territorial governance is possible and indeed necessary, it is, at last, a pursuit fraught with complexity and even more importantly, danger. For as I alluded to in the introduction, to have such a conversation is to be painfully reminded of how it has both played out in the past and even now in the present often with disastrous results. Indeed as I write this, there a number of armed conflicts taking place throughout the world in which competing claims to divinely sanctioned land are at the fore, with the Israeli-Palestinian conflict being one of the more prominent and divisive.

The latter conflict in particular has come to assume a totemic status among Christians in the United States and with few exceptions has devolved into an internecine exchange of maximalist positions, with voices like Stephen Sizer and Gary Burge arguing that Israel's land no longer has any theological relevance for Christians and Christian Zionists like John Hagee implying that criticism of Israel's settlement policies is tantamount to anti-Semitism and apostasy.

As such not only is it impossible to think about a Christian ethic of territorial governance apart from this contentious theo-political context, but so too is it theologically and ethically irresponsible. For to assert that Jesus does proclaim and embody an ethic of territorial governance within the kingdom but then abscond when it comes to thinking about how such an ethic would apply both to current territorial conflicts and territorial governance in general for fear of getting ensnarled in the to and fro of protracted arguments is to commit an iteration of the heresy of *docetism* and to ask, as

Yoder rightfully does, if Jesus is not the norm for Christian ethics then what other norm is there?[158]

And yet as I demonstrated in chapter three above, the problem with Yoder's argument vis-à-vis Jesus and Israel's land is not that he takes Jesus' kingdom proclamation seriously enough, but rather that he thinks that it ultimately detaches the kingdom from Israel's land. Conversely what makes Christian Zionists arguments problematic is not that they take Israel's connection to the land seriously, but rather that they tend to detach that connection from Jesus' proclamation of the kingdom. In either case then, neither Jesus' proclamation of the kingdom nor Israel's connection to the land are taken seriously enough. Or perhaps they are taken too seriously—Jesus to the exclusion of Israel's land and Israel's land to the exclusion of Jesus.

And yet this makes both Jesus' and Israel's prophetic relationship to the land significant and therefore different from the current diaspora versus Zionist paradigm is that neither seeks to collapse or harmonize the tensions of this relationship. Or as Peter Ochs argues,

> The stark separation that both Yoder *and* conservative Zionists assert between exile and land is a lingering mark of this immediately past and present period of transformation. It is, however, not a mark of the near future, and it is, in that sense, not prophetic. The voice of prophecy begins by observing the separation that Israel is about to suffer between its body and spirit, but it ends, each time, with the vision of that historically specific new heaven/new earth that will be realized in the religion that is immediately to come. This is a religion in which Israel's body and spirit will be reintegrated once again.[159]

Indeed, as David Frankel argues, what makes Israel's prophetic witness about the land distinctive is that

> in this conception [Israel's law] is not meant to keep Israel isolated from the nations but to as a spiritual pull, attracting the nations! The borders, in this conception, no longer serve a double function. They are meant to keep the Israelites in but not to keep outsiders out. It is in basic accordance with this approach that the prophet envisions a multitude of peoples' making pilgrimage to Zion to learn the ways of the Lord so that peace may be established among the nations (Isa 2:1–5; Mic 4:1–5). Israel does not expand outward toward the nations and harbors no

---

158. Yoder, *Politics of Jesus*, 8–10.

159. Ochs, "See How They Go with Their Faces to the Sun," in Yoder, *Jewish-Christian Schism Revisited*, 204.

visions of political imperialism. Rather, nations whose complete independence is fully respected come of their own free will to Zion to learn the ways of God. Subsequent to this, they return to their national territories, and international peace is established, with no nation ruling over another nation. Israel, following this model is implicitly called upon to represent and reflect the universal divine attributes of wisdom and justice and thereby serve as a source of peace and spiritual inspiration for mankind.[160]

Thus what both Ochs's and Frankel's comments speak to is that there is no biblical ethic of territoriality to be had apart from the dynamic that underpins the particularity of Israel and the universality of its witness. Or as Kendall Soulen argues in *The God of Israel and Christian Theology*, the divine economy the biblical canon presents is not ultimately one of redemption, but instead of consummation wherein "God's work as Consummator engages the human family in a historically decisive way in God's election of Israel as a blessing to the nations. The resulting distinction and mutual independence of Israel and the nations is the fundamental form of the economy of consummation through which God initiates, sustains, and ultimately fulfills the one human family's destiny for life with God. So conceived, God's economy of consummation is essentially constituted as *an economy of mutual blessing* between those who are and who remain different."[161]

In light of this "economy of mutual blessing" Soulen thus argues that the hermeneutical grid through which the Christian canon should be read and performed is a "double focus" wherein the "eschatological reign of the God of Israel provides the indispensable hermeneutical context for the center of Christian faith, namely the gospel about God's kingdom and the name of Jesus Christ."[162]

Thus when it comes to examining the relationship between Jesus' proclamation of the kingdom of God and the restoration of Israel's land John Nugent has acknowledged that there must be not so much a rejection but a re-narration of Yoder's diasporatic reading. More specifically, in keeping with Soulen's notions of mutual blessing and maintaining a double hermeneutical foci, such "a revision might suggest that God had two purposes that would be carried out by two distinct equally Jewish groups following the monarch's collapse."[163]

---

160. Frankel, *Land of Canaan*, 398–99.
161. Soulen, *God of Israel*, 111.
162. Ibid., 113.
163. Nugent, *Politics of Yahweh*, 160.

"One purpose," he continues, "embodied in Jeremiah's commission, required God's people to begin spreading throughout out the earth in ways that prepare for the future messianic mission."[164] God's other purpose," on the other hand, "required maintaining a clear sense of Jewish identity back in Jerusalem in preparation for Jesus who would launch the global mission from there. Far from abandoning Jerusalem because of the people's unfaithfulness, God fulfills his purpose for Jerusalem and honors his chosen people by launching his salvific mission from there and not some other diasporic locale."[165]

While I would still object to Nugent's suggestion that Jeremiah's commission was entirely diasporic (see above) I think his proposed re-narration provides a means through which to read Jesus' proclamation of the kingdom of God as equally committed to the restoration of Israel's land as well as to the restoration of an ethic of justice for how that and all other lands should be ruled. It therefore provides an entry point into the articulation of a normative framework for a Christian ethic of territorial governance that I would now like to exposit further by way of Michael Walzer's conception of reiteration.

5.6.1 Walzer's Reiteration—a Normative Model for a Christian Ethic of Territorial Governance

As Moshe Weinfeld has noted,

> What is unique about Israel's relationship to the land is neither the divine promise nor the permanence of the patrimony, but rather the religious and moral ramifications of the promise: the belief that, in order to dwell safely in the land, it was necessary to fulfill the will of the God who gave the land. The land was thus transformed into a kind of mirror, reflecting the religious and ethical behavior of the people; if the people were in possession of the land it was a sign that they were fulfilling God's will and observing his commandments; if they lost the land, it was an indication that they had violated God's covenant and neglected his commandments. All of biblical historiography is based upon this criterion: the right to possess land.[166]

---

164. Ibid.
165. Ibid.
166. Weinfeld, *Social Justice in Ancient Israel*, 184.

And as Weinfeld explains further, part of what it meant to obey Yahweh's commandments was for Israel to do justice especially as stated in Jer 22:3–5 to the robbed, the *stranger*, the fatherless and the widow.[167] Thus we could say that an integral part of why Jesus would envision a territorial restoration of Israel was so that it live justly with those both inside and outside its geographic borders. This emphasis on sharing the land also provides both the canonical and normative basis for why Gerald Schlabach wants to pry Yoder's Constantinianism out of its primacy in Christian ethical reflection and instead pay more attention to what he calls the "Deuteronomic Juncture." Says Schlabach,

> We would do better, then, to understand Constantinianism as only the most prominent instantiation of an even more basic problem, which bears with it an even more subtle temptation. This is the temptation of which Deuteronomy 6–9 warned God's people, and which arose precisely because they *were* God's people . . . For the day in which they seemed most fully to have entered the land and appropriated God's gift was actually the moment when they had proven most likely to forget the Lord, to trust and credit their own power, or to use selective memory of God's gracious deliverance as irrevocable validation for them to possess the land in any way they chose.[168]

It follows then, Schlabach maintains, that the real ethical conundrum for Christian ethics is not one of whether "our ethical reflection" should be solely focused "on the effort to avoid evil and unfaithfulness" as it is in Constantinianism, but instead on the "challenge of embracing the good in a faithful manner," which the "Deuteronomic Juncture" helps to do by asking "how to receive and celebrate the blessing, the *shalom*, the good, or 'the land' that God desires to give, yet to do so without defensively and violently hoarding God's blessing."[169]

And lest one read Schlabach's "Deuteronomic Juncture" as just a figurative heuristic, he makes it perfectly clear that literal territoriality is one of the greatest gifts and temptations that ethical reflection has to adjudicate. "Those of us who are theological intellectuals," he writes, "may be able to read the Exodus abstractly as a journey into 'freedom' or 'history' rather than into actual land, but human rights are more basic, less abstract and most earthy for those who need them most. If Constantinian *ways* of living in the land are what have left us uneasy about speaking to this question,

167. Ibid., 198.
168. Schlabach, "Deuteronomic or Constantinian," 450–51.
169. Ibid., 451.

then we should *both* renounce Constantine *and* demonstrate positive models for dwelling in the land without ejecting other inhabitants."[170]

A description of such a model is, in one sense, what Michael Walzer does in his essay "Nation and Universe."[171] In the essay's introduction Walzer draws a distinction between what he calls a "covering-law universalism," which stipulates that "there is one God, so there is one law, one justice, one correct understanding of the good life or the good society or the good regime, one salvation, one messiah, one millennium for all humanity," and "reiterative universalism" whose difference with "covering-law universalism" is "its particularist focus and its pluralizing tendency."[172] Interestingly enough, to more vividly illustrate the difference between these two types of universalism, Walzer quotes Amos 9:7, which reads,

> Are ye not as children of the Ethiopians unto me, O children of Israel . . .
>
> Have I not brought Israel out of the land of Egypt,
> and the Philistines from Caphtor, and the Syrians from Kir?

What this string of queries suggest, says Walzer, is "that there is not one exodus, one divine redemption, one moment of liberation, for all mankind, the way there is, according to Christian doctrine, one redeeming sacrifice." Rather, "liberation is a particular experience, repeated for each oppressed people."[173] Reading these two kinds of universalism into the political concept of communal self-determination, Walzer concludes that reiterative universalism provides a more instructive way of examining the issue since "if we value autonomy, we will want individual men and women to have their own lives."[174] This is because the variety of national experience and nations themselves shows that there "is no single mode of 'having' a life of one's own."[175]

Walzer makes a similar claim with respect to the nature of nationalism itself. "A nation," he states, "is a historic community, connected to a meaningful place, enacting and revising a way of life, aiming at political and cultural self-determination."[176] Thus Walzer believes that the "critical test" of nationalism "comes when it has to cope with the surprise of a new

170. Ibid., 463–64.
171. "Nation and Universe," in Walzer, *Thinking Politically*, 184.
172. Ibid., 184–86.
173. Ibid., 186.
174. Ibid., 190.
175. Ibid.
176. Ibid., 214.

nation, or more accurately, of a new liberation movement laying claim to nationhood."[177] Reiterative universalism is more conceptually and morally equipped to handle this test than is covering-law universalism, since its pluralistic understanding "provides the best account of nationalism in general and the most adequate constraint on its various immoralities."[178] More specifically Walzer notes that while there "is no universal model for national culture, no covering law or set of laws that controls the development of the nation," there is, nevertheless, a "universal model for the behavior of the nation toward others," which Walzer thinks is characterized by Isaiah Berlin's point that "one community, absorbed in the development of its own native talent should not respect a similar activity on the part of others."[179]

But how does reiterative universalism ensure that this sense of mutual respect, which is another way of sharing the land, is kept amongst and between nations? Constructing a supra national moral arbiter to enforce this universal norm of respect is not really a practical feasibility. But even if it were, Walzer would be highly suspicious of such a body since it would undoubtedly squelch the pluriformity of nations that could show that respect. Nevertheless, Walzer recognizes that politics "aims at unity: from many one." So there are better ways at getting toward this unity than others. As Walzer explains, "this unity can be achieved in very different ways: by accommodating difference (as in the case of religious toleration) as well as repressing it, by inclusion as well as forced assimilation, negotiation as well as coercion, federal or corporate arrangements as well as centralized states."[180] Accordingly, the value of reiterative universalism is that it "favors the first alternative in each of these pairs."[181]

Walzer admits that his discussion of reiterative and covering-law universalism and its meaning for politics and international relations is "conceptual and not practical" in orientation.[182] Be that as it may, it is not that far a leap from the conceptual boat of reiterative universalism to the practical dock of just peacemaking. The reiterative unity of accommodation corresponds to advancing democracy and human rights; inclusion to cooperative conflict resolution; negotiation to taking independent initiatives; and federal arrangements to strengthening the UN and other international bodies—just to name a few of the more obvious.

177. Ibid., 211.
178. Ibid., 209.
179. Ibid., 212.
180. Ibid., 215.
181. Ibid.
182. Ibid., 209.

Let us now step back once again to view this theology of territoriality and ethics of just peacemaking, as articulated by Schlabach and Walzer. Schlabach's thoughts on the 'Deuteronomic Juncture' pay close attention to Jesus' view that the land was to be shared with others and especially with those who were enemies. Walzer's notion of reiterative universalism presents a compelling moral vision for how and why states can use the practices of just peacemaking in order to respect the cultivation of native talent. Furthermore Schlabach's caution that Christian ethics needs to pay attention to how territoriality is both a gift and moral obligation, which in turn is fleshed out further by Walzer's description of how nations can respect each other's right to self-determination within and without their borders. Thus here are the normative contours of a Christian ethic of territorial governance. In light of them we can agree with Yoder that Jesus was indeed for the nations. However, we can also say that the reason he was so was because both he and Yahweh were first for the nation.

Bibliography

Allison, Dale C. *Constructing Jesus: Memory, Imagination, and History*. Grand Rapids: Baker Academic, 2010.

———. *The Sermon on the Mount: Inspiring the Moral Imagination*. New York: Crossroad, 1999.

Bader-Saye, Scott. *Church and Israel after Christendom: The Politics of Election*. Boulder, CO: Westview, 1999.

Bammel, Ernst, and C. F. D. Moule, eds. *Jesus and the Politics of His Day*. Cambridge: Cambridge University Press, 1984.

Barclay, John M. G. *Jews in the Mediterranean Diaspora: From Alexander to Trajan (323 BCE–117 CE)*. Edinburgh: T. & T. Clark, 1996.

Bauckham, Richard. *Jesus and the Eyewitnesses: The Gospels as Eyewitness Testimony*. Grand Rapids: Eerdmans, 2006.

Bergsma, John Sietze. *The Jubilee from Leviticus to Qumran: A History of Interpretation*. Leiden: Brill, 2007.

Beutler, J. "Two Ways of Gathering: The Plot to Kill Jesus in John 11.47–53." *New Testament Studies* 40 (1994) 399–406.

Bird, Michael F. *Jesus and the Origins of the Gentile Mission*. London: T. & T. Clark, 2006.

Birnbaum, Ellen. *The Place of Judaism in Philo's Thought: Israel, Jews, and Proselytes*. Atlanta: Scholars, 1996.

Bock, Darrell L. "The Parable of the Rich Man and Lazarus and the Ethics of Jesus." *Southwestern Journal of Theology* 40 (1997) 63–72.

Borg, Marcus J. *Conflict, Holiness, and Politics in the Teachings of Jesus*. Harrisburg, PA: Trinity, 1998.

———. *The Heart of Christianity: Rediscovering a Life of Faith*. San Francisco: HarperSanFrancisco, 2003.

———. "Me & Jesus—the Journey Home: An Odyssey." *Fourth R* 6, no. 4 (1993). http://www.westarinstitute.org/resources/the-fourth-r/me-jesus-the-journey-home/. Accessed July 27, 2016.

Boyarin, Daniel. *A Radical Jew: Paul and the Politics of Identity*. Berkeley: University of California Press, 1997.

Boyd, Gregory A. "The Kingdom as a Political-Spiritual Revolution." *Criswell Theological Review* 6 (2008) 23–41.

Brueggemann, Walter. *A Commentary on Jeremiah: Exile and Homecoming*. Grand Rapids: Eerdmans, 1998.
———. *The Land: Place as Gift, Promise, and Challenge in Biblical Faith*. Minneapolis: Fortress, 2002.
Bryan, Steven M. *Jesus and Israel's Traditions of Judgment and Restoration*. Cambridge: Cambridge University Press, 2002.
Buchanan, George Wesley. *Jesus, the King and His Kingdom*. Macon, GA: Mercer University Press, 1984.
Burge, Gary M. *Jesus and the Land: The New Testament Challenge to "Holy Land" Theology*. Grand Rapids: Baker Academic, 2010.
Cahill, Lisa Sowle. "The Ethical Implications of the Sermon." *Interpretation* 41 (1987) 144–56.
———. "Nonresistance, Defense, Violence and the Kingdom." *Interpretation* 38 (1984) 380–97.
Caird, G. B. *Jesus and the Jewish Nation*. London: Athlone, 1965.
Carter, Craig A. *The Politics of the Cross: The Theology and Social Ethics of John Howard Yoder*. Grand Rapids: Brazos, 2001.
Carter, J. Kameron. *Race: A Theological Account*. Oxford: Oxford University Press, 2008.
Cavanaugh, William T. *Migrations of the Holy: God, State, and the Political Meaning of Church*. Grand Rapids: Eerdmans, 2011.
———. *Theopolitical Imagination*. New York: T. & T. Clark, 2002.
Charlesworth, James Hamilton, ed. *The Messiah: Developments in Earliest Judaism and Christianity*. First Princeton Symposium on Judaism and Christian Origins. Minneapolis: Fortress, 1992.
Chilton, Bruce. *Pure Kingdom: Jesus' Vision of God*. Grand Rapids: Eerdmans, 1996.
Chilton, Bruce, and Craig A. Evans. *Jesus in Context: Temple, Purity, and Restoration*. Leiden: Brill, 1997.
Chilton, Bruce, and James I. H. McDonald. *Jesus and the Ethics of the Kingdom*. Grand Rapids: Eerdmans, 1988.
Crossan, John Dominic. *God and Empire: Jesus against Rome, Then and Now*. San Francisco: HarperSanFrancisco, 2007.
———. "The Parables of Jesus." *Interpretation* 56 (2002) 247–59.
Curry, Michael R. "'Hereness' and the Normativity of Place." In *Geography and Ethics: Journeys in a Moral Terrain*, edited by James D. Proctor and David M. Smith, 95–105. London: Routledge, 1999.
Davies, W. D. *The Gospel and the Land: Early Christianity and Jewish Territorial Doctrine*. Berkeley: University of California Press, 1974.
———. *Paul and Rabbinic Judaism: Some Rabbinic Elements in Pauline Theology*. London: SPCK, 1955.
———. *The Territorial Dimension of Judaism*. Minneapolis: Fortress, 1991.
Davies, W. D., and Dale C. Allison. *A Critical and Exegetical Commentary on the Gospel according to Saint Matthew*. Vol. 3, *Commentary on Matthew XIX–XXVIII*. Edinburgh: T. & T. Clark, 1997.
DeBorst, Ruth Padilla. "'Unexpected' Guests at God's Banquet Table: Gospel in Mission and Culture." *Evangelical Review of Theology* 33 (2009) 63–79.
Dennis, John A. *Jesus' Death and the Gathering of True Israel: The Johannine Appropriation of Restoration Theology in the Light of John 11:47–52*. Tübingen: Mohr/Siebeck, 2006.

Donahue, John R. "The 'Parable' of the Sheep and the Goats: A Challenge to Christian Ethics." *Theological Studies* 47 (1986) 3–31.
Dunn, James D. G. *Jesus Remembered*. Christianity in the Making 1. Grand Rapids: Eerdmans, 2003.
Evans, Craig A. "Assessing Progress in the Third Quest of the Historical Jesus." *Journal for the Study of the Historical Jesus* 4 (2006) 35–54.
———. *Jesus and His Contemporaries: Comparative Studies*. Leiden: Brill, 1995.
———. "Jesus and the 'Cave of Robbers': Toward a Jewish Context for the Temple Action." *Bulletin for Biblical Research* 3 (1993) 93–110.
———. "Jesus' Parable of the Tenant Farmers in Light of Lease Agreements in Antiquity." *Journal for the Study of the Pseudepigrahpa* 7 (1996) 65–83.
Fager, Jeffrey A. *Land Tenure and the Biblical Jubilee: Uncovering Hebrew Ethics through the Sociology of Knowledge*. Sheffield: JSOT, 1993.
Frankel, David. *The Land of Canaan and the Destiny of Israel: Theologies of Territory in the Hebrew Bible*. Winona Lake, IN: Eisenbrauns, 2011.
Fredriksen, Paula. *Jesus of Nazareth, King of the Jews: A Jewish Life and the Emergence of Christianity*. New York: Knopf, 1999.
Freyne, Sean. *Galilee, Jesus, and the Gospels: Literary Approaches and Historical Investigations*. Philadelphia: Fortress, 1988.
———. *Jesus, a Jewish Galilean: A New Reading of the Jesus Story*. London: T. & T. Clark, 2004.
Fuller, Michael E. *The Restoration of Israel: Israel's Re-gathering and the Fate of the Nations in Early Jewish Literature and Luke-Acts*. Berlin: de Gruyter, 2006.
Gafni, Isaiah M. *Land, Center and Diaspora: Jewish Constructs in Late Antiquity*. Sheffield: Sheffield Academic, 1997.
Garroway, Joshua. "The Invasion of a Mustard Seed: A Reading of Mark 5.1–20." *Journal for the Study of the New Testament* 32 (2009) 57–75.
Givens, Tommy. "The Election of Israel and the Politics of Jesus: Revisiting John Howard Yoder's *The Jewish-Christian Schism Revisited*." *Journal of the Society of Christian Ethics* 31 (2011) 75–92.
Gottwald, Norman K. *The Politics of Ancient Israel*. Louisville: Westminster John Knox, 2001.
———. *The Tribes of Yahweh: A Sociology of the Religion of Liberated Israel, 1250–1050 B.C.E.* Maryknoll, NY: Orbis, 1979.
Greenfield, G. "The Ethics of the Sermon on the Mount." *Southwestern Journal of Theology* 35 (1992) 13–19.
Grosby, Steven Elliott. *Biblical Ideas of Nationality: Ancient and Modern*. Winona Lake, IN: Eisenbrauns, 2002.
Guevin, Benedict. "The Moral Imagination and the Shaping Power of the Parables." *Journal of Religious Ethics* 17 (1989) 63–79.
Habel, Norman C. *The Land Is Mine: Six Biblical Land Ideologies*. Minneapolis: Fortress, 1995.
Hagner, Donald A. "Ethics and the Sermon on the Mount." *Studia Theologica* 51 (1997) 44–59.
Hamilton, Victor P. *Exodus: An Exegetical Commentary*. Grand Rapids: Baker, 2011.
Harrington, Hannah K. *Holiness: Rabbinic Judaism and the Graeco-Roman World*. London: Routledge, 2001.

Hauerwas, Stanley. *After Christendom? How the Church Is to Behave if Freedom, Justice, and a Christian Nation Are Bad Ideas.* Nashville: Abingdon, 1991.

———. *Against the Nations: War and Survival in a Liberal Society.* Minneapolis: Winston, 1985.

———. *A Better Hope: Resources for a Church Confronting Capitalism, Democracy, and Postmodernity.* Grand Rapids: Brazos, 2000.

———. "The Sermon on the Mount, Just War, and the Quest for Peace." *Concilium* 195 (1988) 36–43.

Hauerwas, Stanley, and James Fodor. "Remaining in Babylon: Oliver O'Donovan's Defense of Christendom." *Studies in Christian Ethics* 11 (1998) 30–55.

Hauerwas, Stanley, and William H. Willimon. *Resident Aliens: Life in the Christian Colony.* Nashville: Abingdon, 1989.

Hauerwas, Stanley, et al., eds. *Theology Without Foundations: Religious Practice and the Future of Theological Truth.* Nashville: Abingdon, 1994.

———. *The Wisdom of the Cross: Essays in Honor of John Howard Yoder.* Grand Rapids: Eerdmans, 1999.

Hays, Richard B. *The Moral Vision of the New Testament: Community, Cross, New Creation; A Contemporary Introduction to New Testament Ethics.* San Francisco: HarperSanFrancisco, 1996.

Herzog, William R., III. *Jesus, Justice, and the Kingdom of God: A Ministry of Liberation.* Louisville: John Knox, 1994.

———. *Parables as Subversive Speech: Jesus as Pedagogue of the Oppressed.* Louisville: Westminster John Knox, 1994.

———. *Prophet and Teacher: An Introduction to the Historical Jesus.* Louisville: Westminster John Knox, 2005.

Hoffman, Lawrence A., ed. *The Land of Israel: Jewish Perspectives.* Notre Dame: University of Notre Dame Press, 1986.

Holmén, Tom, and Stanley E. Porter, eds. *Handbook for the Study of the Historical Jesus.* Vol. 3, *The Historical Jesus.* Leiden: Brill, 2011.

Horsley, Richard A., ed. *In the Shadow of Empire: Reclaiming the Bible as a History of Faithful Resistance.* Louisville: Westminster John Knox, 2008.

———. *Jesus and Empire: The Kingdom of God and the New World Disorder.* Minneapolis: Fortress, 2003.

———. *Jesus and the Spiral of Violence: Popular Jewish Resistance in Roman Palestine.* San Francisco: Harper & Row, 1987.

———. *Jesus in Context: Power, People, & Performance.* Minneapolis: Fortress, 2008.

———. *Sociology and the Jesus Movement.* New York: Crossroad, 1989.

Horsley, Richard A., with John S. Hanson. *Bandits, Prophets, and Messiahs: Popular Movements in the Time of Jesus.* San Francisco: Harper & Row, 1988.

Horsley, Richard A., and Neil Asher Silberman. *The Message and the Kingdom: How Jesus and Paul Ignited a Revolution and Transformed the Ancient World.* New York: Grossett/Putnam, 1997.

House, H. Wayne, ed. *Israel, the Land and the People: An Evangelical Affirmation of God's Promises.* Grand Rapids: Kregel, 1998.

Irenaeus, St. *Against the Heresies.* Translated by Dominic J. Unger. Mahwah, NJ: Newman, 1992.

Johnston, Philip, and Peter Walker, eds. *The Land of Promise: Biblical, Theological, and Contemporary Perspectives.* Downers Grove, IL: InterVarsity, 2000.

Johnston, Robert K., ed. *The Use of the Bible in Theology: Evangelical Options*. Atlanta: Knox, 1985.

Jones, Ivor H. *The Matthean Parables: A Literary and Historical Commentary*. Leiden: Brill, 1995.

Justin Martyr. St. *Dialogue with Trypho*. Translated by Thomas B. Falls. Washington, DC: Catholic University of America Press, 1965.

Kim, Joon-Sik. "'Your Kingdom Come on Earth': The Promise of the Land and the Kingdom of Heaven in the Gospel of Matthew." PhD diss., Princeton Theological Seminary, 2001.

Kvalbein, Hans. "The Kingdom of God in the Ethics of Jesus." *Studia Theologica—Nordic Journal of Theology* 51 (1997) 60–84.

Laaksonen, Jari. *Jesus und das Land: das Gelobte Land in der Verkündigung Jesu*. Åbo, Finland: Åbo Akademis, 2002.

Levenson, Jon Douglas. *Resurrection and the Restoration of Israel: The Ultimate Victory of the God of Life*. New Haven: Yale University Press, 2006.

Lindblom, Johannes. *The Servant Songs in Deutero-Isaiah: A New Attempt to Solve an Old Problem*. Lund, Sweden: Gleerup, 1951.

Longenecker, Richard N., ed. *The Challenge of Jesus' Parables*. Grand Rapids: Eerdmans, 2000.

Low, Setha M., and Denise Lawrence-Zuniga, eds. *The Anthropology of Space and Place: Locating Culture*. Oxford: Blackwell, 2003.

Malina, Bruce J. *The Social Gospel of Jesus: The Kingdom of God in Mediterranean Perspective*. Minneapolis: Fortress, 2001.

———. *The Social World of Jesus and the Gospels*. London: Routledge, 1996.

March, W. Eugene. *Israel and the Politics of Land: A Theological Case Study*. Louisville: Westminster John Knox Press, 1994.

Marchadour, Alain, and David Neuhaus. *The Land, the Bible, and History: Toward the Land That I Will Show You*. New York: Fordham University Press, 2007.

Marshall, Christopher D. *Beyond Retribution: A New Testament Vision for Justice, Crime, and Punishment*. Grand Rapids: Eerdmans, 2001.

McCartney, Dan G. "Ecce Homo: The Coming of the Kingdom as the Restoration of Human Viceregency." *Westminster Theological Journal* 56 (1994) 1–21.

McClendon, James William. *Systematic Theology*. Vol. 1, *Ethics*. 2nd ed. Nashville: Abingdon, 2002.

McConville, J. G. *God and Earthly Power: An Old Testament Political Theology, Genesis–Kings*. London: T. & T. Clark, 2006.

McKnight, Scot. *A Light among the Gentiles*. Minneapolis: Fortress, 1991.

———. *A New Vision for Israel: The Teachings of Jesus in National Context*. Grand Rapids: Eerdmans, 1999.

Meier, John P. *A Marginal Jew: Rethinking the Historical Jesus*. Vol. 2, *Mentor, Message, and Miracles*. New York: Doubleday, 1994.

Mendels, Doron. *The Land of Israel as a Political Concept in Hasmonean Literature: Recourse to History in Second Century B.C. Claims to the Holy Land*. Tübingen: Mohr, 1987.

———. *The Rise and Fall of Jewish Nationalism*. New York: Doubleday, 1992.

Meyer, Ben F. *The Aims of Jesus*. London: SCM, 1979.

Moltmann, Jürgen. *God in Creation: A New Theology of Creation and the Spirit of God*. Translated by Margaret Kohl. San Francisco: Harper & Row, 1985.

Moore, Anne. *Moving beyond Symbol and Myth: Understanding the Kingship of God of the Hebrew Bible through Metaphor.* New York: Lang, 2009.
Moxnes, Halvor. *Putting Jesus in His Place: A Radical Vision of Household and Kingdom.* Louisville: Westminster John Knox Press, 2003.
Murphy, Nancey C. *Bodies and Souls, or Spirited Bodies?* Cambridge: Cambridge University Press, 2006.
Myers, Ched. *Binding the Strong Man: A Political Reading of Mark's Story of Jesus.* Maryknoll, NY: Orbis, 1988.
Neusner, Jacob, et al., eds. *Judaisms and Their Messiahs at the Turn of the Christian Era.* Cambridge: Cambridge University Press, 1987.
Newman, Carey C., ed. *Jesus & the Restoration of Israel: A Critical Assessment of N. T. Wright's* Jesus and the Victory of God. Downers Grove, IL: InterVarsity, 1999.
Nugent, John C. *The Politics of Yahweh: John Howard Yoder, the Old Testament, and the People of God.* Eugene, OR: Cascade, 2011.
Oakman, Douglas E. *Jesus and the Economic Questions of His Day.* Lewiston, PA: Mellen, 1986.
Ochs, Peter. *The Free Church and Israel's Covenant.* Winnipeg: Canadian Mennonite University Press, 2010.
O'Donovan, Oliver. *The Desire of the Nations: Rediscovering the Roots of Political Theology.* Cambridge: Cambridge University Press, 1996.
Ollenburger, Ben C., and Gayle Gerber Koontz, eds. *A Mind Patient and Untamed: Assessing John Howard Yoder's Contributions to Theology, Ethics, and Peacemaking.* Telford, PA: Cascadia, 2004.
Pao, David W. *Acts and the Isaianic New Exodus.* Grand Rapids: Baker Academic, 2002.
Parrent, A. M. "The Sermon on the Mount, International Politics, and a Theology of Reconciliation." *Sewanee Theological Review* 42 (1999) 176–90.
Pathrapankal, J. "The Ethics of the Sermon on the Mount: Its Relevance and Challenge to Our Times." *Jeevadhara* 27 (1997) 389–407.
Pennington, Jonathan T. *Heaven and Earth in the Gospel of Matthew.* Leiden: Brill, 2007.
Perrin, Norman. *Jesus and the Language of the Kingdom: Symbol and Metaphor in New Testament Interpretation.* Philadelphia: Fortress, 1976.
Pitre, Brant James. *Jesus, the Tribulation, and the End of the Exile: Restoration Eschatology and the Origin of the Atonement.* Tübingen: Mohr/Siebeck, 2005.
Proctor, James D., and David M. Smith. *Geography and Ethics: Journeys in a Moral Terrain.* London: Routledge, 1999.
Ravens, David. *Luke and the Restoration of Israel.* Sheffield: Sheffield Academic, 1995.
Reed, Esther D. "Refugee Rights and State Sovereignty: Theological Perspectives on the Ethics of Territorial Borders." *Journal for the Society of Christian Ethics* 30 (2010) 59–78.
Reimarus, Hermann Samuel, and Gotthold Ephraim Lessing. *Von dem Zwecke Jesu und seiner Jünger: noch ein Fragment des Wolfenbüttelschen Ungenannten.* Translated by George Wesley Buchanan. Leiden: Brill, 1970.
Rensberger, David K. *Johannine Faith and Liberating Community.* Philadelphia: Westminster, 1988.
Ringe, Sharon H. *Jesus, Liberation, and the Biblical Jubilee: Images for Ethics and Christology.* Philadelphia: Fortress, 1985.
Rohrbaugh, Richard L. "A Peasant Reading of the Parable of the Talents/Pounds." *Biblical Theology Bulletin* 23 (1993) 32–39.

Sanders, E. P. *Jesus and Judaism*. Philadelphia: Fortress, 1985.
Schlabach, Gerald. "Deuteronomic or Constantinian: What Is the Most Basic Problem for Christian Social Ethics?" In *The Wisdom of the Cross: Essays in Honor of John Howard Yoder*, edited by Stanley Hauerwas et al., 449–71. Grand Rapids: Eerdmans, 1999.
Schüssler Fiorenza, Elisabeth. *In Memory of Her: A Feminist Theological Reconstruction of Christian Origins*. New York: Crossroad, 1983.
Scott, Bernard B. *Hear Then the Parable: A Commentary on the Parables of Jesus*. Minneapolis: Fortress, 1989.
Scott, James M. "Philo and the Restoration of Israel." In *SBL 1995 Seminar Papers*, edited by E. H. Lovering Jr., 553–75. Atlanta: Scholars, 1995.
Scott, James M., ed. *Restoration: Old Testament, Jewish, and Christian Perspectives*. Leiden: Brill, 2001.
Sechrest, Love L. *"A Former Jew": Paul and the Dialectics of Race*. London: T. & T. Clark, 2009.
Smith-Christopher, Daniel L. *A Biblical Theology of Exile*. Minneapolis: Fortress, 2002.
Sobrino, Jon. *Jesus the Liberator: A Historical-Theological Reading of Jesus of Nazareth*. Translated by Paul Burns and Frances McDonagh. Maryknoll, NY: Orbis, 1993.
Soulen, R. Kendall. *The God of Israel and Christian Theology*. Minneapolis: Fortress, 1996.
Stassen, Glen Harold. "The Fourteen Triads of the Sermon on the Mount (Matthew 5:21—7:12)." *Journal of Biblical Literature* 122 (2003) 267–308.
———. *Just Peacemaking: Transforming Initiatives for Justice and Peace*. Louisville: Westminster John Knox, 1992.
———. *Living the Sermon on the Mount: A Practical Hope for Grace and Deliverance*. San Francisco: Jossey-Bass, 2006.
Stassen, Glen Harold, and David P. Gushee. *Kingdom Ethics: Following Jesus in Contemporary Context*. Downers Grove, IL: InterVarsity, 2003.
Stassen, Glen Harold, et al. *Authentic Transformation: A New Vision of Christ and Culture*. Nashville: Abingdon, 1996.
Stegemann, Wolfgang, et al., eds. *The Social Setting of Jesus and the Gospels*. Minneapolis: Fortress, 2002.
Strecker, Georg, ed. *Das Land Israel in biblischer Zeit: Jerusalem-Symposium 1981 Der Hebraischen Universitat und der Georg-August-Universitat*. Göttingen: Vandenhoeck & Ruprecht, 1983.
Talbott, Rick F. "Nazareth's Rebellious Son: Deviance and Downward Mobility in the Galilean Jesus Movement." *Biblical Theology Bulletin* 38 (2008) 99–113.
Theissen, Gerd, and Dagmar Winter. *The Quest for the Plausible Jesus: The Question of Criteria*. Translated by M. Eugene Boring. Louisville: Westminster John Knox, 2002.
Turner, Max. *Power from on High: The Spirit in Israel's Restoration and Witness in Luke-Acts*. Sheffield: Sheffield Academic, 1996.
Vander Hart, Mark D. "Possessing the Land as Command and Promise." *Mid-America Journal of Theology* 4 (1988) 139–55.
Verhey, Allen. *Remembering Jesus: Christian Community, Scripture, and the Moral Life*. Grand Rapids: Eerdmans, 2002.
Vos, C. J. A. "A Hermeneutical-Homiletic Reading of Psalm 37 with Reference to H J C Pieterse's Homiletics." *Verbum et Ecclesia* 23 (2002) 575–85.

Walzer, Michael. *Thinking Politically: Essays in Political Theory.* Edited by David Miller. New Haven: Yale University Press, 2007.

Warshal, Bruce S. "Israel's Stake in the Land." *Theology Today* 35 (1979) 413–20.

Weinfeld, Moshe. *The Promise of the Land: The Inheritance of the Land of Canaan by the Israelites.* Berkeley: University of California Press, 1993.

———. *Social Justice in Ancient Israel and in the Ancient Near East.* Minneapolis: Fortress, 1995.

Wenell, Karen J. *Jesus and Land: Sacred and Social Space in Second Temple Judaism.* London: T. & T. Clark, 2007.

Wenham, David. *Paul: Follower of Jesus or Founder of Christianity?* Grand Rapids: Eerdmans, 1995.

Wilken, Robert Louis. *The Land Called Holy: Palestine in Christian History and Thought.* New Haven: Yale University Press, 1992.

Willitts, Joel. *Matthew's Messianic Shepherd-King: In Search of "the Lost Sheep of the House of Israel."* Berlin: de Gruyter, 2007.

Wright, Christopher J. H. *God's People in God's Land: Family, Land, and Property in the Old Testament.* Grand Rapids: Eerdmans, 1990.

———. *Old Testament Ethics for the People of God.* Downers Grove, IL: InterVarsity, 2004.

———. "Theology and Ethics of the Land." *Transformation: An International Journal of Holistic Mission Studies* 16 (1999) 81–86.

Wright, N. T. *Jesus and the Victory of God.* Christian Origins and the Question of God 2. Minneapolis: Fortress, 1996.

———. "The New Testament and the 'State.'" *Themelios* 16 (1990) 11–17. http://www.theologicalstudies.org.uk/article_state_wright.html. Accessed July 27, 2016.

Wyschogrod, Michael. *The Body of Faith: God and the People of Israel.* Northvale, NJ: Aronson, 1989.

Yoder, John Howard. *Body Politics: Five Practices of the Christian Community before the Watching World.* Scottdale, PA: Herald, 2001.

———. *The Christian Witness to the State.* Scottdale, PA: Herald, 2002.

———. *For the Nations: Essays Evangelical and Public.* Grand Rapids: Eerdmans, 1997.

———. *The Jewish-Christian Schism Revisited.* Edited by Michael G. Cartwright and Peter Ochs. Grand Rapids: Eerdmans, 2003.

———. *Nevertheless: The Varieties and Shortcomings of Religious Pacifism.* Rev. and exp. ed. Scottdale, PA: Herald, 1992.

———. *The Original Revolution: Essays on Christian Pacifism.* Scottdale, PA: Herald, 1977.

———. *The Politics of Jesus; Vicit Agnus Noster.* 2nd ed. Grand Rapids: Eerdmans, 1994.

———. *The Priestly Kingdom: Social Ethics as Gospel.* Notre Dame: University of Notre Dame Press, 1984.

———. *The Royal Priesthood: Essays Ecclesiological and Ecumenical.* Edited by Michael G. Cartwright. Scottdale, PA: Herald, 1998.

Yoder, John Howard, et al., eds. *The War of the Lamb: The Ethics of Nonviolence and Peacemaking.* Grand Rapids: Brazos, 2009.

Subject Index

Abraham, 126n6
Abrahamic covenant
   covenantal implications of de-territorialization, 109–11
   covenant community, Israel as, 17
   Kingdom of God and, 17, 102–4, 106, 110
Adam, 112
Against Heresies (Irenaeus), 98–99
Against the Nations: War and Survival in a Liberal Society (Hauerwas), 69
Allison, Dale, 160, 175, 187–88
Alt, Albrecht, 57–58n12
Amos, repentance in, 48
apostles
   appointment of, 29–30
   number of tribes of Israel compared, 185–87, 189–90
   Palingenesia and, 182–90
Assyrian exile, 18, 58n14, 88, 152, 173, 180

Baal, 123–24
Babylonian exile
   generally, 37, 58n14, 152, 180
   de-territorialization, effect on, 18–19, 88
   restoration and, 125–28, 132
Bader-Saye, Scott, 74, 76, 91
Bar Kokhba rebellion, 58
Barth, Markus, 83n105
Beatitudes
   generally, 160–61n38

contemporary Christianity, relevance to, 66
   Kingdom of God and, 27–29, 63, 67
   restoration and, 154–65
Bergsma, John Sietze, 131, 135–37, 140–42
Biblical Ideas of Nationality (Grosby), 57–58n12
biblical realism, 83n105
Blessing of meek
   generally, 160–61n38
   Davies on, 154–56, 164–65
   Kingdom of God and, 27–29
   restoration and, 154–65
Bodies and Souls, or Spirited Bodies (Murphy), 114
Borg, Marcus J.
   generally, 2, 14, 84, 91
   Davies and, 31, 33–34, 46
   on de-territorialization, 31–46, 52–53, 55
   on Kingdom of God, 31–46, 41n134, 42n138, 45n151, 64
   on restoration, 121–22
   Wright and, 47–48
Brandon, S.G.F., 24
Brueggemann, Walter, 9, 124, 126–32
Bryan, Steven M., 9–10n5, 56–57, 61–63, 67, 86, 184–87
Buchanan, George Wesley, 177–78
Bultmann, Rudolf, 33
Burge, Gary M., 155–57, 164–65, 191

207

Subject Index

Caird, G.B., 14–15n14
Caligula, 35
Carter, J. Kameron, 96–98
Cerbonnier, Edmund, 83n105
Cerfaux, Lucien, 22
Chiliasm, de-territorialization and, 94–96
Chilton, Bruce, 65–66, 65n35
Christianity
    Judaism and, 103–7
    Sermon on the Mount, relevance of, 66
    territorial governance, ethic of, 194–98
church, restoration and, 104–5
"Churchified" spatial reality, 69–71
cleansing of Temple, 36–38
Conflict, Holiness and Politics in the Teachings of Jesus (Borg), 14, 31–46
Constantinianism, 93, 118–19, 195
covenant
    covenantal implications of de-territorialization, 109–11
    covenant community, Israel as, 17
    Kingdom of God and, 17, 102–4, 106, 110
Curry, Michael R., 7, 117–18
Cushan-Rishathaim, 186

daily bread in Lord's Prayer, 175–77
Daniel, restoration and, 18–19
David, 88–89, 130, 148–49
Davies, W.D.
    generally, 2, 8, 52–53, 55, 91
    on blessing of meek, 154–56, 164–65
    Borg and, 31, 33–34, 46
    on Gospels, 23n52, 25n60, 27–28nn71–72, 30n80
    on Kingdom of God, 14–30
    on *Palingenesia*, 182–85, 187–88, 188n152
    on restoration, 121–22
    Wright and, 47, 50
debt forgiveness
    Jubilee and, 167–69
    in Lord's Prayer, 173

depoliticization of Jesus, 23–24, 31–34
De Praemis et Poenis (Philo), 12–13n11
The Desire of the Nations: Rediscovering the Roots of Political Theology (O'Donovan), 73–74
de-territorialization
    overview, 53–57, 90–91
    Borg on, 31–46, 52–53, 55
    chiliasm and, 94–96
    "churchified" spatial reality and, 69–71
    covenantal implications of, 109–11
    Diaspora and, 61, 89
    ecclesiofication and, 69–71
    eschatological analysis, 76–77, 80–81
    ethical implications of, 114–19
    Gnosticism and, 96–99
    historical etiology, 57–64
    implications of, 92–94, 120
    Kingdom of God and (*See* Kingdom of God)
    Late Second Temple Judaism and, 58
    nonviolent enemy love and, 83–90
    paradigmatic analysis, 72–76, 80
    peaceable non-territorial reign and, 87–90
    place-less ethical performance and, 65–68
    praxification and, 65–68
    provisional paradigm for holy space and, 72–83
    supersessionist implications of, 111–13
    theological etiology, 57–64
    theological implications of, 109–19
    typofication and, 72–83
    typological analysis, 76–79, 82
"Deuteronomic Juncture," 195–96, 198
Dialogue with Trypho (Justin Martyr), 100–102, 105
Diaspora
    de-territorialization and, 61, 89
    Irenaeus on, 102
    restoration and, 9, 12, 51, 149–50
"Dishonest manager" parable, 169–71
Docetism, 191–92
Dodd, C.H., 22

Subject Index

Ecclesiastes, 18
Ecclesiofication, 69–71
economics
    economic supersessionism, 111
    restoration and, 158–59, 164
Edomites, 147
Elijah, 181
Elisha, 181
Epistles, Kingdom of God in, 20–21n39, 20–23, 79
Esau, 147
eschatological analysis, 76–77, 80–81
Essenes, 34–36, 84
Esther, 18
ethical implications of de-territorialization, 114–19
ethical symbiosis, 122–24
ethnicity, Jewish territorialism and, 60–61
Eusebius, 118
Evans, Craig A., 54–55n2
Eve, 112
exile
    in Assyria, 18, 58n14, 88, 152, 173, 180
    in Babylon (*See* Babylonian exile)
    Jesus in wilderness compared, 178–82
Ezekiel, 43–44

fasting, restoration and, 135–36
"Fig tree" parable, 26–27
forgiveness of debt
    Jubilee and, 167–69
    in Lord's Prayer, 173
A Former Jew: Paul and the Dialectics of Race (Sechrest), 60
Frankel, David, 124n5, 192–93
Fredriksen, Paula, 107
The Free Church and Israel's Covenant (Ochs), 127n10
Freyne, Sean, 132, 157, 159, 166–67, 172–73, 181
Fuller, Michael E., 149–50, 164, 179, 189

Gentiles
    governance by, 182–83, 189
    Jesus and, 38–39, 51, 55–56, 182
    Jewish territorialism and, 59
    Kingdom of God and, 25n60, 81, 102–4
    restoration and, 132–33, 132n35, 135, 137, 147
Georgi, D., 23
Gideon, 186
Givens, Tommy, 109
Gnosticism
    criticism of, 113–14
    de-territorialization and, 96–99
    implications of de-territorialization and, 96–99
    Irenaeus and, 96–99, 107–8
    Justin Martyr and, 96–101, 107–8
    Paul and, 97
    pneumatics and, 96–97, 103
The God of Israel and Christian Theology (Soulen), 111, 193
The Gospel and the Land: Early Christianity and Jewish Territorial Doctrine (Davies), 14–30
Gospels. *See also specific book*
    Davies on, 23n52, 25n60, 27–28nn71–72, 30n80
    Kingdom of God in, 23–30, 79
    lack of territorialization in, 55
    restoration in, 152–90
Gottwald, Norman K., 17–18n25
governance
    by Gentiles, 182–83, 189
    by Romans, 182–83
    territorial governance (*See* Territorial governance)
Grosby, Steven Elliott, 57–58n12
Gushee, David, 65–70, 65n35, 154, 156–57, 163, 165

Habel, Norman, 122–23, 130
Hagee, John, 191
hallowing of God's name in Lord's Prayer, 173–75
Hamilton, Victor, 175–76
Hanamel, 128–29
Hauerwas, Stanley, 69–70

Heaven and Earth in the Gospel of Matthew (Pennington), 159–60
Herod, 169, 177
Hexateuch, 16
"Hidden talent" parable, 27
holiness
    Jesus on, 35–40
    Kingdom of God and, 35–40
Horsley, Richard, 38, 158–59, 190, 190n157

implications of de-territorialization
    generally, 92–94, 120
    covenantal implications, 109–11
    ethical implications, 114–19
    supersessionist implications, 111–13
    theological implications, 109–19
Irenaeus
    generally, 113–14, 118, 160–61n38
    chiliasm and, 94–96
    on Diaspora, 102
    Gnosticism and, 96–99, 107–8
    on Kingdom of God, 100–109
Isaiah
    generally, 152–53
    Jeremiah compared, 133–36, 140
    Jubilees compared, 145–46
    justice in, 132–43
    Kingdom of God in, 65–66, 160
    Psalms of Solomon compared, 147–48
    restoration in, 18–19, 132–43, 163–64, 182, 186, 189–90
Israel, territorial governance in, 191–92

Jacob, 146–47, 185
James (Apostle), 188
Jephthah, 186
Jeremiah
    generally, 48, 152–53
    Isaiah compared, 133–36, 140
    Jubilees compared, 145–46
    justice in, 125–32
    Kingdom of God in, 160
    Psalms of Solomon compared, 147–48
    restoration in, 122–32, 163–64, 182, 186, 189–90

    theological and ethical symbiosis in, 122–24
Jerusalem, etymology of, 125–26, 126n6
Jesus. *See specific topic*
Jesus and the Jewish Nation (Caird), 14–15n14
Jesus and the Land (Burge), 155
Jesus and the Language of the Kingdom (Perrin), 42n138
Jesus and the Victory of God (Wright), 1, 14, 46–50
Job, 18
Johannine Faith and Liberating Community (Rensenberger), 11–12n10
John (Apostle), 189
John the Baptist, 48, 167
Jonah, 18
Joseph (Patriarch), 146–47
Josephus, 184
Joshua, 185
Jubilee
    generally, 165n50
    debt forgiveness and, 167–69
    "dishonest manager" parable and, 169–71
    Jesus and, 84–85n110, 178–82
    Kingdom of God and, 77–78
    Lord's Prayer compared, 172–78
    in *Luke*, 178–82
    "merciless servant" parable and, 169, 171
    mitzvot and, 59
    property and, 170–72
    restoration and, 130–31, 136, 140–43, 145, 150, 178–82
    slavery and, 168–69
    Yoder on, 84–85n110, 167–73, 179
Jubilees
    generally, 152–53
    Isaiah compared, 145–46
    Jeremiah compared, 145–46
    justice in, 143–47
    Kingdom of God in, 160
    Psalms of Solomon compared, 147–48
    restoration in, 143–47, 163–64
Judah, restoration of, 123–30

Judaism, Christianity and, 103–7
judges of Israel, 186
justice
   in *Isaiah*, 132–43
   in *Jeremiah*, 125–32
   in *Jubilees*, 143–47
   Kingdom of God and, 69–71
   restoration and, 125–32, 162–64
   territorial governance and, 194–96
Justin Martyr
   generally, 113–14, 118, 160–61n38
   chiliasm and, 94–96
   Gnosticism and, 96–101, 107–8
   on Kingdom of God, 100–109
just peacemaking, 198

Kaddish, 173, 177–78
Kingdom Ethics: Following Jesus in Contemporary Context (Stassen and Gushee), 65
kingdom of God. *See also* Restoration
   overview, 8, 50–52
   Abrahamic covenant and, 17, 102–4, 106, 110
   appointment of apostles and, 29–30
   Beatitudes and, 27–29, 63, 67
   Borg on, 31–46, 41n134, 42n138, 45 151, 64
   as "churchified" spatial reality, 69–71
   contemporary Christianity, relevance to, 63–64
   conundrums regarding, 9–14
   covenant community, Israel as, 17
   Davies on, 14–30
   depoliticization of Jesus and, 23–24, 31–34
   "fig tree" parable and, 26–27
   Gentiles and, 25n60, 81, 102–4
   in Gospels, 23–30, 79
   "hidden talent" parable and, 27
   holiness and, 35–40
   implications of de-territorialization and, 100–109
   internalization and individuation of religion and, 18–19
   Irenaeus on, 100–109
   in *Isaiah*, 65–66, 160
   in *Jeremiah*, 160
   Jesus on, 40–46, 51
   Jubilee and, 77–78
   in *Jubilees*, 160
   justice and, 69–71
   Justin Martyr on, 100–109
   in Lord's Prayer, 173–75
   Maccabeans and, 16–17, 20–21n39
   "meek inheriting the earth" and, 27–29
   nomadic ideal, rejection of, 16
   Palingenesia and, 182–90
   Paul and, 81–83
   in Pauline epistles, 20–21n39, 20–23, 79
   as place-less ethical performance, 65–68
   "Prodigal Son" parable and, 48
   as provisional paradigm, 72–83
   in *Psalms of Solomon*, 160
   repentance and, 48–49
   scholarly incongruities regarding, 9–14
   Sermon on the Mount and, 27–29, 63, 67
   synagogue versus Temple and, 19
   Targum and, 65, 68
   texts examined, 14
   "Third Quest" and, 53, 56–57, 63, 83–84, 90
   transcendentalization of land and, 19
   universal concerns versus land concerns and, 18
   Wright on, 46–50, 62–64
   Zealots and, 16–17, 20–21n39, 24
Knox, W.L., 22
Kvalbein, Hans, 10

The Land Called Holy: Palestine in Christian Thought and History (Wilken), 95
The Land of Canaan and the Destiny of Israel (Frankel), 124n5
Late Second Temple Judaism
   generally, 3, 6, 9, 13, 16, 53
   de-territorialization and, 58
   restoration and, 122, 143–50, 152
Light metaphor, 138–40

Lord's Prayer
    daily bread in, 175–77
    debt forgiveness in, 173
    hallowing of God's name in, 173–75
    Jubilee compared, 172–78
    Kaddish and, 173, 177–78
    Kingdom of God in, 173–75
    restoration and, 165–78
    Sermon on the Mount, as part of, 172
Luke
    Jubilee in, 178–82
    restoration in, 178–90

Maccabeans, 16–17, 20–21n39
Matthew
    Lord's Prayer, 165–78 (*See also* Lord's Prayer)
    "meek inheriting the earth," 154–65 (*See also* "Meek inheriting the earth")
    Palingenesia, 182–90 (*See also* *Palingenesia*)
    restoration in, 154–78
McClendon, James, 114, 116–17
McDonald, J.I.H., 66
"meek inheriting the earth"
    generally, 160–61n38
    Davies on, 154–56, 164–65
    Kingdom of God and, 27–29
    restoration and, 154–65
Mendels, Doron, 58–61, 60n21, 143, 146–47
"Merciless servant" parable, 169, 171
Messiah, restoration and, 140–42, 148–50
Meyer, Ben, 53
Mitzvot, 58–59
morality
    de-territorialization and, 114–18
    Paul on, 117
Moses, 185
Murphy, Nancy, 114–17

Naaman, 181
Naḥalah, 122–24
nationalism, 196–97
nomadic ideal, rejection of, 16

non-reductive physicalism, 114
nonviolent enemy love, 83–90
normativity of place, 117–19
Nugent, John, 193–94

Ochs, Peter, 110, 127n10, 192–93
O'Donovan, Oliver, 73–76, 80
Old Testament Ethics for the People of God (Wright), 72
Ollenburger, Ben, 84–85n110
Origen, 118
The Original Revolution (Yoder), 1
Othniel, 186
overview, 1–3

Palingenesia
    Davies on, 182–85, 187–88, 188n152
    restoration and, 182–90
paradigmatic analysis, 72–76, 80
Paul
    generally, 11, 29n76, 30
    epistles, Kingdom of God in, 20–21n39, 20–23, 79
    Gnosticism and, 97
    Jewishness of, 20n37
    Kingdom of God and, 81–83
    on morality, 117
Pennington, Jonathan, 159–60
Perrin, Norman, 42, 42n138
Pharisees, 34–36, 38, 56, 84–86
Philo, 12–13n11
Pitre, Brant, 143–44, 172–75, 175n94, 180
place-less ethical performance, 65–68
pneumatics, 96–97, 103
politics, restoration and, 158–59, 164
The Politics of Jesus (Yoder), 54–55n2, 84–85n110, 167
Pompey, 58, 147
Pontius Pilate, 11, 54–55n2
possession, 74–76
praxification, 65–68
"Prodigal Son" parable, 48
prolegomena, 3–5
property, Jubilee and, 170–72
prophets
    generally, 16

restoration in, 122–43
Proverbs, 18
provisional paradigm for holy space, 72–83
Psalms, restoration in, 161–64
Psalms of Solomon
  generally, 152–53, 183
  Isaiah compared, 147–48
  Jeremiah compared, 147–48
  Jubilees compared, 147–48
  Kingdom of God in, 160
  restoration in, 147–50, 163–64, 182, 186, 189–90
punishment, restoration and, 144–46, 150, 161–62
punitive supersessionism, 111

Race: A Theological Account (Carter), 96
Rauschenbusch, Walter, 69–70
reiteration, 194–98
reiterative universalism, 196–98
Rensenberger, David K., 11–12n10
repentance, Kingdom of God and, 48–49
restoration. *See also* Kingdom of God
  overview, 121–22, 150–51
  Babylonian exile and, 125–28, 132
  Beatitudes and, 154–65
  Borg on, 121–22
  Church and, 104–5
  Daniel and, 18–19
  Davies on, 121–22
  Diaspora and, 9, 12, 51, 149–50
  economics and, 158–59, 164
  fasting and, 135–36
  Gentiles and, 132–33, 132n35, 135, 137, 147
  in Gospels, 152–90
  in *Isaiah,* 18–19, 132–43, 163–64, 182, 186, 189–90
  in *Jeremiah,* 122–32, 163–64, 182, 186, 189–90
  Jubilee and, 130–31, 136, 140–43, 145, 150, 178–82 (*See also* Jubilee)
  in *Jubilees,* 143–47, 163–64
  of Judah, 123–30
  justice and, 125–32, 162–64
  Late Second Temple Judaism and, 122, 143–50, 152
  light metaphor and, 138–40
  Lord's Prayer and, 165–78 (*See also* Lord's Prayer)
  in *Luke,* 178–90
  in *Matthew,* 154–78, 182–90
  "meek inheriting the earth" and, 154–65
  Messiah and, 140–42, 148–50
  Palingenesia and, 182–90
  politics and, 158–59, 164
  in Prophets, 122–43
  in *Psalms,* 161–64
  in *Psalms of Solomon,* 147–50, 163–64, 182, 186, 189–90
  punishment and, 144–46, 150, 161–62
  resurrection and, 100–101
  Sabbath and, 133–34, 136–37, 145, 150
  Sermon on the Mount and, 154–65
  socioeconomics and, 158–59, 164
  territorialization and, 136–38
  theological and ethical symbiosis, 122–24
  "Third Quest" and, 122
  universalism, 132–43
  Wright on, 121–22
  Yoder on, 127n10
resurrection, restoration and, 100–101
Ringe, Sharon, 165, 173, 181
The Rise and Fall of Jewish Nationalism (Mendels), 58
Romans
  governance by, 182–83
  Jesus and, 38–39, 51, 84
  Jewish territorialism and, 59–60

Sabbath
  generally, 168n63
  mitzvot and, 59
  restoration and, 133–34, 136–37, 145, 150
Sabbatical Year, 59
Samson, 186
Sanders, E.P., 3n2, 36, 48, 91
Satan, 179

Saturninus, 99
Schlabach, Gerald, 119, 194, 198
Schweitzer, Albert, 32
Sechrest, Love, 60–61
Sermon on the Mount
   generally, 160–61n38
   contemporary Christianity, relevance to, 66
   Kingdom of God and, 27–29, 63, 67
   Lord's Prayer as part of, 172
   restoration and, 154–65
Sherwindt, Mark, 69–70
Sizer, Stephen, 191
slavery, Jubilee and, 168–69
Smith-Christopher, Daniel, 92
Social Gospel, 69
socioeconomics, restoration and, 158–59, 164
Solomon, 89, 147
Song of Songs, 18
Soulen, Kendall, 111–13, 193
Stassen, Glen, 65–70, 65n35, 154, 156–57, 163, 165
structural supersessionism, 112
supersessionist implications of de-territorialization, 111–13
Swartley, Willard M., 84–85n110
symbiosis, 122–24
Synagogue versus Temple, 19

Targum, 65, 68
Temple
   cleansing of, 36–38
   as dwelling place of God, 126
   synagogue versus, 19
   territorial governance
      Christian ethic of, 194–98
      "Deuteronomic Juncture," 195–96, 198
      in Israel, 191–92
      justice and, 194–96
      Kingdom of God, relevance of, 63–64
      nationalism, 196–97
      proposed normative framework, 191–98
      reiteration, 194–98
      reiterative universalism, 196–98

Sermon on the Mount, relevance of, 66
   Walzer on, 194–98
   Yoder on, 191–93, 195, 198
   theological implications of de-territorialization, 109–19
   theological symbiosis, 122–24
   thesis, 5–7
"Third Quest"
   generally, 3, 15
   Kingdom of God and, 53, 56–57, 63, 83–84, 90
   restoration and, 122
transcendentalization of land, 19
Tresmontant, Claude, 83n105
tribes of Israel, number of apostles compared, 185–87, 189–90
The Tribes of Yahweh and the Politics of Ancient Israel (Gottwald), 17–18n25
typofication, 72–83
typological analysis, 76–79, 82

universal concerns versus land concerns, 18
universalism, 132–43

Vander Hart, Mark, 162
Vos, C.J.A., 161

Walker, Peter W.L., 94
Walzer, Michael, 194–98
Weder, Hans, 157
Weinfeld, Moshe, 141, 194
Weiss, Johannes, 32
Wenell, Karen, 185, 187, 188n152
Wenham, David, 20–21n39
wilderness, Jesus in, 178–82
Wilken, Robert L., 95–96
Wright, Christopher J.H., 9–10, 72, 76–83, 91
Wright, N.T.
   generally, 1–2, 14, 52–53, 55
   Borg and, 45–48
   Davies and, 47, 50
   on Kingdom of God, 46–50, 62–64
   on restoration, 121–22
Wyschogrod, Michael, 110–11

Yoder, John Howard
  generally, 1–2
  on Jubilee, 84–85n110, 167–73, 179
  on nonviolent enemy love, 83–91
  on restoration, 127n10
  on territorial governance, 191–93, 195, 198

zealots
  Jesus and, 31–32, 34, 36, 56, 84–86, 157
  Jewish territorialism and, 59
  Kingdom of God and, 16–17, 20–21n39, 24
Zedekiah, 130–31
Zionists, 191–92

Scripture Index

Old Testament

Genesis

1	143
1–3	112
15:18–21	17
48:22	146

Exodus

4:22	80
12	143
21	131
21:1–12	131
23:30	123
28:41	140
29:7	140
32:13	123
40:13–15	140

Leviticus

23:26–32	136
25	84–85n110, 129, 131, 142, 165–66, 180
25:8–55	129
25:9–10	142
25:10	131, 165n50
25:11–13	84–85n110
25:25–28	128
26:27–39	26
27	84–85n110

Numbers

32:25	140
35:8	123
35:9–34	142

Deuteronomy

6–9	195
12:1	57–58n12
15	84–85n110, 131
15:2–3	84–85n110
15:9	84–85n110
19:14	123
24	168n63
24:10–13	168n63

1 Samuel

9:16	140n47
10:1	140n47
16:3	140n47

2 Samuel

2:7	140n47
5:17	140n47
19:10	140n47

Subject Index

1 Kings

1:34	140n47
5:1	140n47
17:7–24	181
19:15	140n47
19:16	140

2 Kings

5:1–27	181
9:3	140n47
9:6	140n47
9:12	140n47

Psalms

37	154, 161–64
37:1–11	161
37:3	155, 162–63
37:4–8	163
37:5–8	162–63
37:9	155, 162
37:10–11	155
37:11	28–29, 154, 155–56, 160, 162
37:12	162
37:12–26	161
37:13	155
37:14	162
37:18	155
37:19	162
37:21	162
37:22	155, 162
37:27–40	161
37:29	155, 162
37:32	162
37:34	162

Isaiah

2:1–4	138
2:1–5	192
11	149
11:1–4	149
11:2	149
11:4	149
24:23	68
31:4	68
42	140
42:1	140
42:1–7	141
49:6, 132	134
49:7–13	142
52:7–10	142
55	150
56	137
56–61	132–43, 182
56:1–2	133
56:3–7	134
56:3–8	133
56:4	134
56:6	134
56:6–7	137
56:7	37, 134
56:9–12	133
57:1–13	135
57:13b	18
57:14–19	135
58	136
58:1–5	135
58:3–6	136
58:5	136
58:6	84–85n110
58:6–7	136
58:9–10	136
58:12	136
58:13	136
58:14	136
60–61	137–38, 140
60:3	137–38
60:4	137
60:4–10	137
60:14	137–38
60:16	142
60:19–20	138
60:21	137
61	84–85n110, 142, 154
61:1	131, 140, 155–56
61:1–2	84–85n110, 153, 167, 180–82
61:1–3	140, 141–42
61:2	142

Subject Index

61:3	138–39
61:4–11	139
61:5	137
61:7	139
61:8–9	139
62:12	142
63:10–17	173
65:13–16	18

Jeremiah

2:7	123
2:23	123
3:1–10	123
5:20–31	124
5:26–29	124
7:11	37
7:15	124
10:16	123
16:13	123
17:4	123
22:3–5	195
22:13–14	130
22:24–30	130
29	126
29–33	122, 125, 133, 135, 140
29–34	125–32, 142
29:5–6	125, 128
29:5–7	135
29:7	88, 125, 127n10
30–31	127
30:3	127
31:4–6	128
31:7–9	173
31:8	128
32	128–29
32–33	136
32:15	128
33:12–13	130
33:12–15	130
33:15	130
34:8	131
34:8–22	130
34:10	131
34:15	131
34:17	131

Ezekiel

36:22–28	173–74
36:23	174

Hosea

1:10–11	173

Amos

9:7	196

Micah

4:1–5	192
4:5–8	173–74
4:7–8	174

Zechariah

9:9	37, 156

New Testament

Matthew

2:6	155
5	164
5–7	163
5:3	28, 157, 160
5:5	10, 25, 27–28nn71–72, 27–29, 55, 67, 153, 154–65
5:7–10	28n72
5:8	156
5:9	39

Subject Index

Matthew (continued)

5:10	156
5:12	156
5:18	155
5:21–48	163
5:25–34	159
5:30	156
5:35	155
5:43–44	38
5:45	39
6:9–10	173
6:9–13	44, 153, 165–78
6:10	175
6:11	175
6:12	165, 173
6:13	172n84
6:19ff	159
6:25–34	164
7:29	62
8:11	25n60
8:11–12	45, 153, 182
10:6	38
11:8	159
12:28	43
13:5	155
18:23–25	169
19:28	25, 29–30, 44, 55, 166, 166n54
21:18–19	26n63
22:1–14	132
25:14–30	25, 27, 55
25:25	27
28:16–20	55

Mark

9:12–13	62
10:35ff.	30, 30n80
11:12–14	26n63
11:15–19	36
11:20–21	26n63

Luke

4:1–13	178
4:3	179
4:14	179
4:14ff	167
4:16–20	165–78
4:16–21	178–82
4:18	165
4:18–19	84–85n110, 153, 180–81
4:24–27	181
4:25	155
6:17–49	154
6:20	10
6:27	38
11:1–4	44, 153, 165–78
11:2	173
11:3	175
11:4	165, 173
11:20	43
13:6–9	25, 26–27, 55
13:28–29	45, 153, 182
14:16–24	132
15:11–32	48
16:1–9	169
19:11–27	27
21:25	155
22:24–27	29
22:28–30	29
22:29–30	44
22:30	25, 29–30, 55, 166, 166n54

John

18:28–19:25	11n10
18:33	11
19:13–16	11n10

Acts

1:6	12

Romans

11	97

Ephesians

2:11–3:6	81

Philippians

3:20–21	22

Revelation

20:1–6	95

Pseudepigrapha

Jubilees

23:18–23	144–45
23:26–31	145–46
34	146
34:1–9	146
34:5	146
34:9	147
37–38	146–47
38:11	147
38:12	147

Psalms of Solomon

2:1	148
2:3	148
2:12	148
2:29	148
4:9–13	148
8:22–26	148
17	148
17–18	148
17:1–4	148
17:5–6	148
17:11	148
17:12	150
17:21	148
17:22–23	149
17:24	149
17:26–29	149
17:26–32	149
17:31	149

Apocrypha

Sirach

48:10	62

www.ingramcontent.com/pod-product-compliance
Lightning Source LLC
Chambersburg PA
CBHW051642230426
43669CB00013B/2404